Robert S. Devine

BUSH VERSUS THE ENVIRONMENT

Robert S. Devine has been a freelance journalist since 1982, writing mostly about the environment, natural history, and outdoor travel for a number of publications including *The Atlantic Monthly, Audubon, National Geographic Traveler*, and *Travel & Leisure*. He has written four books and coauthored four books published by the National Geographic Society. Devine lives in Corvallis, Oregon, with his wife and daughter.

ALSO BY Robert S. Devine

Alien Invasion:
    America's Battle with Non-native Animals and Plants

National Geographic Guide to America's Outdoors:
    Western Canada

National Geographic Guide to America's Outdoors:
    Pacific Northwest

National Geographic's Driving Guides to America:
    Pacific Northwest

BUSH VERSUS THE ENVIRONMENT

BUSH VERSUS
THE ENVIRONMENT

Robert S. Devine

ANCHOR BOOKS

A DIVISION OF RANDOM HOUSE, INC.   NEW YORK

AN ANCHOR BOOKS ORIGINAL, JUNE 2004

Copyright © 2004 by Robert S. Devine

All rights reserved under International and Pan-American Copyright Conventions. Published in the United States by Anchor Books, a division of Random House, Inc., New York, and simultaneously in Canada by Random House of Canada Limited, Toronto.

Anchor Books and colophon are registered trademarks of Random House, Inc.

Library of Congress Cataloging-in-Publication Data
Devine, Robert S., 1951–
   Bush versus the environment / Robert S. Devine.—1st Anchor Books ed.
     p. cm.
   Includes bibliographical references and index.
   ISBN 1-4000-7521-1
    1. Environmental policy—United States.
   2. United States—Politics and government—1993–
   I. Title.
   GE180.D48 2004
   333.72'0973'090511—dc22

                      2003063832

Book design by Mia Risberg

www.anchorbooks.com

Printed in the United States of America
10 9 8 7 6 5 4 3 2 1

To my wife, Mary, for understanding the importance of this book's message and forgiving me for disappearing so often into my office on evenings and weekends during its writing. And to my daughter, Sarah, and the rest of her generation, who deserve to inherit a healthy planet from their elders.

CONTENTS

Foreword		xi
Author's Note		xvii
Introduction:	Let's Roll(back)	3
Chapter 1:	The Fox Is Guarding the Henhouse	21
Chapter 2:	Playing with Fire	39
Chapter 3:	The Best Offense Is a Bad Defense	84
Chapter 4:	There Ought to Be a Law Enforcer	110
Chapter 5:	Inexact Science	160
Chapter 6:	Bean Counters Rule	190
Chapter 7:	What's Next?	231
	Notes	239
	Bibliography	249
	Acknowledgments	255
	Index	259

by Robert F. Kennedy, Jr.

George W. Bush is the worst environmental president in American history. The Bush Administration has undermined or is trying to gut hundreds of laws and regulations that protect our health, our wildlife, our public lands, our air, and our water. At every turn the President's actions favor corporate interests over the public interest. If the White House is allowed to carry out a significant portion of its agenda, America will effectively have little environmental law left. We may still have statutes on the books, but they will be unenforceable and America will be like Mexico, which has wonderful, even poetic environmental laws, but they're toothless. Few people know of them and almost nobody complies.

Consider New York City's reservoir system. As the chief prosecuting attorney for Riverkeeper I've worked for almost 20 years to protect that 2,000-square-mile watershed, reaching far upstate into the Catskill Mountains. This area is largely undeveloped and has been protected from pollution for more than 100 years. Last year we were shocked to learn that the fish in these reservoirs are unsafe to eat due to mercury contamination from the air. Most species of fish in New York are now unsafe to eat regularly because of mercury, as are the fish in more than 40 other states. The principal source of airborne mercury in America is 1,100 dinosaur coal-fired power plants. A plan developed by the Clinton administration would have required these power plants to eliminate their mercury emissions within three and a half years, but the Bush administration scuttled that plan for a proposal that will allow the mercury discharges to continue for decades.

This angers me both as a citizen and as a father. My kids are among the millions who can no longer enjoy the seminal American experience of fishing locally with their dads and eating their catch. But other children suffer far greater problems from mercury. Society has long known that mercury in the environment can severely harm people, a fact confirmed and elaborated on in recent reports from the National Academy of Sciences, the Centers for Disease Control and Prevention, and even Bush's own Environmental Protection Agency. Even small doses of mercury, particularly when ingested by pregnant women, can cause deficits in attention, fine-motor function, language, visual-spatial abilities, and memory. Exposed children often struggle in school and require remedial classes or special education. Studies show that nearly 8 percent of American women of childbearing age have unsafe levels of mercury in their bodies, and 600,000 American children born each year are at risk. And it's only going to get worse under Bush's plan.

The power plants that emit so much mercury also belch pollutants that have sterilized half the lakes in the once pristine Adirondacks with acid rain and that trigger the asthma attacks that afflict millions of America's children, including three of my own kids. The costs of this pollution to our country are enormous, not just in health care and lost school days and workdays from pulmonary illness, but the loss to the next generation of Americans of the opportunity to live in communities that provide them with the same potential and enrichment as the communities that our parents gave us.

The coal industry and the utilities that own those polluting coal-fired power plants donated millions of dollars to the President's election campaigns, and they are now reaping billions of dollars in regulatory favors. King Coal and the utilities are representative of many other industries that likewise are supporting Bush and getting favorable treatment as a payback. But those corporate profits come from transferring billions of dollars in costs onto the American people in lost lives, illness, and a degraded natural environment. In making themselves rich these industries are making the rest of us poor, raising standards of living for their executives and owners by lowering the quality of life for everyone else.

There's no stronger advocate for free-market capitalism than myself, but in a true free-market economy you can't make yourself rich without also enriching your neighbors and your community. Show me a polluter and I'll show you a subsidy—a fat cat who is using political clout to escape the discipline of the free market and forcing the public to pay his costs of production. When the utilities burn dirty coal without removing the pollutants, they're imposing costs on the rest of us through dirty air, sick children, acidified lakes, depleted fisheries, and damaged building facades that, in a true free-market economy, would be reflected in the price of their products in the marketplace. Polluters externalize their costs—imposing them on the rest of us—by stealing the commons, the public trust assets like air, water, wandering animals, wetlands, and fisheries. Since ancient times the public's interest in those communal assets has been protected by laws that ensure that everyone has a right to use them but never in a way that will diminish their use and enjoyment by other members of the community. Pollution is theft, and the thieves, through the legalized bribery of campaign contributions, have been permitted to privatize the commons. Those coal plants have stolen the fish in 45 states—fish that belong to the people of those states. They've also stolen the air from my children's lungs.

The federal environmental laws passed after Earth Day 1970 were meant to restore the ancient legal protections to the commons and also restore the free-market economy by forcing polluters to internalize their costs the same way they internalize their profits. I don't even consider myself an environmentalist anymore. I think of myself as a free marketeer who goes out into the marketplace and catches the cheaters and forces them to begin paying the true costs of bringing their product to market. Because when someone cheats the free market, it distorts the entire marketplace and none of us gets the advantage of the efficiencies and democracy that true free-market capitalism promises our people.

But the Bush Administration despises the free market that requires strong regulations to maintain. They favor instead corporate crony capitalism, which is as antithetical to democracy in America as it is in Nigeria. The Bush Administration tries to portray sound environmental protections as antibusiness, but this is misleading. Good environmental policy is always identical to good economic policy, if we measure our economy—and this is how we ought to measure it—based on how it produces jobs and how it preserves the value of our nation's assets over the long term. The current Washington regime wants us to treat America as if it's a business in liquidation and convert our national resources to cash as quickly as possible. This may produce profits for a few corporations and fuel a few years of pollution-based prosperity, but our children are going to pay for that joyride with poor health, denuded landscapes, vanishing wildlife, and huge cleanup costs that they will never be able to pay. Environmental injury is deficit spending. It's a way of loading the costs of profits onto the backs of other people and future generations.

During the 1970s Congress passed dozens of major environmental statutes, including such landmark laws as the Clean Air Act, the Clean Water Act, and the Endangered Species Act, and it created the Environmental Protection Agency to apply and enforce these new laws. Polluters would be held accountable; those planning to use the commons would have to compile Environmental Impact Statements and hold public hearings, and citizens were given the power to prosecute environmental crimes. Right-to-know and toxic-inventory laws made government and industry more transparent. American citizens could participate in the dialogue and decisions that determined the destinies of their communities.

However, between the 1970s and the present, the government/ business complex has not been idle. With lavish funding from corporate coffers, it made strong bids to undo environmental progress during the 1980s and the mid-1990s, but with little success. The new generation of would-be robber barons kept running into the broad, bipartisan support for robust protections. Polls show that about 75 percent of the public favors strong environmental laws, and there's little difference between registered Democrats and Republicans. My own experience confirms those polls. I speak all around the country, often to politically conservative organizations, and invariably I receive strong positive responses even from people and organizations considered right-wing and business-oriented. Most Americans care about this country and the outdoors, and they understand that we have to practice some self-restraint. They also know that over the long term what is good for the environment is good for the economy.

The Bush Administration's rollbacks are the latest manifestation in a relentless campaign by big polluters and the political toadies to weaken America's environmental safeguards. Aware of past failures to overrun environmental safeguards, the Bush Administration and its cronies in industry are using stealth and outright deceit to mask their agenda. Robert Devine's *Bush Versus the Environment* exposes the slippery tactics and underhanded methods employed by the White House. The book's detailed exploration of *how* the Bush Administration operates is as important as the book's revelations about *what* the Administration is doing. Whether they're Democrats or Republicans, the more that citizens learn about Bush's environmental agenda, the less likely it is to succeed. If they learn the truth, most Americans would share my fury that this president is allowing his corporate pals to steal America. If we get the message out, we win.

AUTHOR'S NOTE

While reading this book you may at times come across information or comments critical of the Bush Administration's environmental policies and wish there were a response from the Administration. I, too, wish there were more such responses. Though a few of the President's appointees either granted me an interview or answered my e-mailed questions, nearly all of them remained out of reach, surrounded by a wall of staffers. Given the importance of the book's subject, I had hoped to speak with more of the people who help develop the Administration's environmental agenda, but these secretaries, assistant secretaries, and other high-level officials are powerful and busy people, and perhaps they simply couldn't spare the time. Fair enough. I would have been content to speak to members of their staffs. But for the most part they, too, remained behind a wall, an outer bulwark of media relations people. As it turned out, the media relations people often didn't provide any information, either; sometimes they didn't even return calls or answer e-mails. This was especially surprising when

I simply was trying to double-check my facts. I had heard about the secretive nature of the Bush Administration, but I hadn't expected it to be so extreme in shutting out the public.

Perhaps members of the Administration were uncommunicative because they realized that many of their environmental policies would be hard to defend. This makes me think of an internal memo, subsequently leaked, that then–Environmental Protection Agency Administrator Christine Whitman sent to Vice President Dick Cheney on May 4, 2001. Whitman was responding to a draft of the energy plan that Cheney and a group of energy company executives and lobbyists had created in closed-door meetings. Referring to an element of the plan that would undercut enforcement of the Clean Air Act, she wrote, "It will be hard to refute the charge that we are deciding not to enforce the Clean Air Act." Indeed, it would be hard for the President or his officials to refute many such charges of mistreating the environment.

One other quick note: In the book I often refer to "industry" and "business," as in, "Industry pushed for weaker rules regulating discharges into rivers," or "Business supported the Administration's undermining of endangered species protections." Such use of "industry" and "business" is a rhetorical convenience, albeit one based on the reality that in the industrial sectors that inflict the greatest environmental harm most of the players do try to evade regulation and responsibility. Nevertheless, I realize that not all businesses are the same in their attitudes toward the environment and that some members of industry are exemplary environmental citizens.

BUSH VERSUS THE ENVIRONMENT

Let's Roll(back)

Maybe you saw a television news segment that covered the President's push to open the Arctic National Wildlife Refuge (ANWR) for oil and gas development. Or perhaps you read a story in your local paper about his rebuff of the Kyoto Protocol and its requirements for reducing greenhouse gas emissions, which contribute to global warming. If you were listening to the radio in February 2002, you may have heard about the Administration's plan to clean up the Hudson River. Through such occasional reports you've likely gotten the general idea that George W. Bush and his appointees have been somewhat involved with environmental matters and that they tend to favor development over environmental protection. Unless you've taken a particular interest and have been reading a lot of fine print in obscure documents, you don't know the half of it—probably not even the tenth of it.

This Administration has been profoundly involved with environmental matters and has fervently favored development over environmental protection. Few people realize this because most of the Administration's efforts have not made the news. But make no mistake. The White House quietly has been making fundamental regulatory and procedural changes that could unravel decades of progress in protecting human health, wildlife, and natural places.

It is these quiet changes to which I pay special attention in this book. Each chapter provides a detailed look at one of the strategies that Bush is using to make those changes, such as weakening landmark environmental laws in the name of "streamlining" or twisting scientific information to make it support the Administration's position. As you come to understand the means this White House employs, you'll better understand the ends that it seeks to achieve, and you'll see how the means and the ends fit together to form Bush's broad antiregulatory agenda.

In part, the shallow coverage of the President's environmental policies stems from the media's understandable preoccupation with the wars in Iraq and Afghanistan and the aftermath of the September 11 terrorist attacks. In part, the sketchy coverage stems from the media's inherent shortcomings in handling complex stories. But this Administration also has worked hard to mask many of Bush's environmental actions. The President and his advisors are keenly aware that a whopping majority of Americans favor a strong federal role in environmental protection. Bush seems to realize that many of his initiatives, if presented openly, will be unpopular. He doesn't want a public outcry to interfere with his plans nor does he want to antagonize the swing voters for whom the environment is a key issue. The Administration has learned from the past about the dangers of openly degrading the environment in order to promote development. When President Reagan and his first Interior Secretary, James Watt, who suffered from a severe case of "foot-in-mouth" disease, made their unabashed assault on the environment in the 1980s, they didn't get far and they got hurt politically. Likewise, in the 1990s, when Speaker of the House Newt Gingrich and his fellow Republican Revolutionaries hawked the Contract with America, its antienvironmental provisions proved unpopular and generally failed to make it into law.

For all these reasons, the White House tries to slip through its more dubious proposals with minimal fanfare. For example, when proposing regulatory changes, by law the Administration must make those proposals and the subsequent final rules public. Bush's appointees have complied with the letter of the law, but frequently they have evaded its spirit by releasing information about regulations late on Friday afternoons or just before holidays, when their decisions likely will attract less media attention. They chose New Year's Eve 2002, for instance, to unveil a polluter-friendly rule weakening clean air standards. They have used this ruse so often that critics have begun referring to this ploy as the "Friday-night follies." More substantially, the White House usually has chosen to avoid the bright lights and wide-open debates of Congress. As this book will demonstrate, instead of pushing legislation, the Administration often has pursued its goals through obscure administrative actions and in closed-door legal settlements with industry.

When the White House has operated in full view, it has labored to disguise the nature and impact of its actions, assigning its initiatives appealing names such as "Healthy Forests" and "Clear Skies" and arguing that its elixir of market-based mechanisms, voluntary programs, and supposedly local solutions will heal what ails the environment. In their speeches, Administration officials sometimes sound as if they have just come from an Audubon meeting. Here's a sample from the President, speaking in May 2001: "Our duty is to use the land well, and sometimes, not to use it at all. This is our responsibility as citizens; but, more than that, it is our calling as stewards of the Earth. Good stewardship of the environment is not just a personal responsibility, it is a public value. Americans are united in the belief that we must preserve our natural heritage and safeguard the land around us."

Just how seriously the President and his party take their public relations effort regarding the environment became apparent in 2003 when a 16-page memorandum on the subject surfaced. Referred to as the "Luntz memo," this guide to sounding green came from the Luntz Research Companies, a polling and "message development" firm that devotes its marketing expertise to Fortune 500 companies and to conservative Republicans and their causes. The first sentence in the memo's summary captures the urgency of projecting a more environmentally friendly image: "The environment is probably the single issue on which Republicans in general—and President Bush in particular—are most vulnerable." The bulk of the memo dishes out specific advice, derived from focus groups and extensive testing, such as urging Republicans to use the term "climate change" instead of "global warming" to make the problem sound "less frightening." (Some observers might say that citizens have good reason to be frightened of global warming . . . er, climate change.) The Luntz memo also provides a list of proven warm-and-fuzzy words, such as "common sense" and "balance," which the memo encourages Republicans to use as often as possible when discussing the environment. And they do. Since the Luntz memo was passed around in GOP circles, starting a few months before the 2002 elections, Republican politicians and Administration officials, including Bush, have laden their speeches with these words and phrases. For example, the President said "common sense" repeatedly in his speech launching the Healthy Forests Initiative.

Displaying considerable chutzpah, Karl Rove, the President's most influential political advisor, asserted that Bush is a great Republican environmentalist president, cut from the same cloth as Teddy Roosevelt. This would be the President Teddy Roosevelt who said, "I do not intend that our natural resources shall be exploited by the few against the interests of the many." The Teddy Roosevelt who said, "The rights of the public to the nation's natural resources outweigh private rights." This comparison to TR has been a recurring theme in the White House's portrayal of Bush as a friend of the environment.

Martha Marks has done perhaps the best job of examining the attempt to pass the mantle of Republican environmental champion from Teddy Roosevelt to George W. Bush. Marks is president of REP America (Republicans for Environmental Protection), an organization of GOP members who support environmental protections and whose Web site is festooned with quotes from TR. In an op-ed that appeared in 2002, Marks writes:

Even my Republican eyes can see that President Bush has a long way to go before his conservation record can hold a candle to TR's. Consider the following: Roosevelt established national forests, parks, monuments and wildlife refuges to prevent special interests from squandering the nation's natural bounty. Bush has appointed a stable of industry lobbyists to open up more of those lands to the same kind of special interests Roosevelt fought throughout his presidency. Roosevelt established the first national wildlife refuge to stop poachers from destroying a public resource for private gain. Bush wants to open America's largest national wildlife refuge so oil companies can compromise a public resource for private gain. Roosevelt founded the Boone and Crockett Club, which successfully campaigned to protect Yellowstone from exploitation by railroad and mining interests. Bush wants to roll back protections against snowmobile pollution [in Yellowstone], catering to off-road vehicle interests. I am a lifelong Republican and have served as an elected Republican officeholder in Illinois for 10 years. The GOP's conservation tradition was one

*reason I became a Republican. Over the past 20 years, how-
ever, the Republican Party seems to have lost its way on conservation.*

Marks is not the only Republican to disapprove of the President's performance on the environment. Though the leadership
and a large majority of the party stand stoutly with Bush on this as
they do on almost every issue, a significant number of moderate
senators, representatives, and other GOP luminaries are not lining
up behind him. Those still in office usually temper their criticism—
with some notable exceptions, such as Senator John McCain—but
those out of harm's way sometimes have voiced strong disagreement.
Take Russell Train, Administrator of the Environmental Protection
Agency (EPA) under Republican Presidents Nixon and Ford. Com-
menting on the nomination, in 2003, of Michael Leavitt to head
the EPA, Train wrote, "The real issue facing us today is not the
environmental record of Michael Leavitt. The real issue is whether
Congress and the country will stand idly by to watch the continued
weakening of the EPA by the Bush administration and its steady
unraveling of the environmental protection programs that have been
a crowning achievement of the United States in recent history."
Another voice from another Republican administration delivered
a similar message, as quoted in a September 2003 syndicated
Knight Ridder newspaper story. "There's a lot of dramatic change
going on," said Dan Esty, Deputy Assistant Administrator for Policy at the EPA under the first President Bush and now the head of
the Center for Environmental Law and Policy at Yale University.
"And a good bit of [it] would be thought of by many as not very
environmentally sound." Grassroots Republicans also have
voiced their disapproval of some of Bush's environmental policies.
In January 2004, for example, a group of predominantly Republican hunters, anglers, and businesspeople publicly criticized the

Bush energy plan for weakening protections for wildlife habitat on western public lands in order to speed up energy development.

The remarks of Marks, Train, Esty, and those grassroots westerners join an outpouring of disapproval from the environmental community and Democratic officeholders. As a way of summarizing all that condemnation, let me note that the League of Conservation Voters, which evaluates the environmental records of politicians, gave Bush an F for his first two years in office. "President Bush is well on his way to compiling the worst environmental record of any president in the history of our nation," said the League's president, Deb Callahan.

About the only people who support Bush's overall environmental approach are those who have a financial stake in loosening regulations, political partisans, and those who feel a philosophical antipathy to government oversight of private enterprise. Generally these supporters praise Bush not for doing more to protect the environment but for doing less. The aforementioned Knight Ridder story captures the essence of this support in comments from Bill Kovacs, the vice president for environmental issues at the U.S. Chamber of Commerce, and from lobbyists for major industries. Referring to a flurry of Administration decisions in the summer of 2003 that weakened a variety of environmental regulations, Kovacs pointed out that corporations had come out on top of more environmental disputes during the last week of August than they had during the eight years in which Clinton occupied the Oval Office. The lobbyists said that so far under George W. Bush their industries had gotten every change they wanted. And both Kovacs and the lobbyists reported that the President had given the business community nearly everything it had put on its antiregulatory to-do list in January 2001, at the start of this Administration. The story's headline proclaims, "White House Fulfills Corporate Wish List." Rather than trying to cloak his pro-development policies, perhaps the President should acknowledge them and try to make his case that favoring industry over the environment makes sense for America.

Boosters of the President have two ready replies when confronted with criticism. One applies primarily to environmental groups and Democratic politicians. It accuses environmentalists of raising money by attacking the Administration's policies, and politicians of scoring political points by attacking the Administration. These accusations are true as far as they go, but they also imply that all such attacks have no aim other than raising money or scoring political points, which is too cynical to take seriously, and that the criticisms are unfounded, a more serious charge. Indeed, whether the criticisms are unfounded is a key question, but one you should not try to answer yet. Wait until you've read this book—and a variety of reports and articles, too—and then pass judgment.

The second ready reply goes something like this: "Well, Bill Clinton also did some pretty lousy things to the environment." Again, true as far as it goes. But it would be an unsupportable stretch to claim that Clinton did nearly as many lousy things as Bush has. Furthermore, as our mothers taught us, just because someone else is doing something wrong doesn't make it right. (I also think that conservatives would be reluctant to use Clinton as a role model.)

Inevitably comparisons between this or that environmental program of Clinton's and some program of Bush's crop up in the book, given that Bush is reshaping an environmental system that he inherited from Clinton. Though these comparisons nearly always make Bush look bad, they are not partisan attacks. (Though I expect the Administration and its supporters to characterize them as such.) History also compels me to place Bush's environmental policies in the context of the policies of presidents other than Clinton, including Republicans—and that list features GOP chief executives like Richard Nixon and Gerald Ford, not just Teddy

Roosevelt. These comparisons, too, make Bush look bad, so clearly it's not a partisan matter. Besides, as noted above by Martha Marks, the REP America president, the GOP has a decent tradition of protecting the environment and may one day return to that heritage. Writes Marks, "Conservation is conservative: protecting our nation's natural resources is consistent with true conservative principles of prudence and stewardship." So, this book is not about liberals versus conservatives or Democrats versus Republicans. It's about what the title says: Bush versus the environment.

So, what has Bush done? Having discussed theories, we should talk about actions. The Administration got off to a fast start. On Bush's inauguration day, just hours after he had assumed the presidency, his chief of staff issued a memo directing federal agencies to hold up pending regulations developed by the Clinton administration, including more than a dozen significant environmental rules. Since bursting out of the blocks that day they've proceeded apace, issuing regulations, making personnel changes, altering existing rules, addressing legal challenges, instituting new procedures, and working through their allies in Congress to produce legislation.

Contrary to what some extreme critics of the President's environmental policies say, the Administration has done some good things. If you ask Administration officials to name their environmental accomplishments, the item they nearly always mention first—and with good reason—is the non-road diesel rule, proposed by the EPA in 2003. This measure would greatly reduce air pollution from diesel-powered bulldozers, tractors, boats, and other off-road engines, the source of enormous amounts of harmful emissions. This rule would save thousands of lives and prevent innumerable illnesses. The Administration could have pushed for tighter deadlines on compliance and perhaps closed up some potential loopholes, but its final proposal went far enough to draw some complaints from industry: a rarity for this White House. Democrats and the environmental community tipped their hats to the EPA and Bush on this one, though some are nervous because the details of these standards have yet to be established.

Another accomplishment the Administration is quick to point out also came from the EPA. In 2002, it signed on to a preliminary cleanup plan for the Hudson River, portions of which are badly contaminated by polychlorinated biphenyls (PCBs). PCBs accumulate in fish, posing a cancer risk to anglers who consume fish from the Hudson. Locals and environmental groups, who had been lobbying for years to get the PCBs removed, praised the Administration.

However, I must note that the Hudson River cleanup plan was developed by the EPA during the Clinton years. The Administration deserves credit for furthering this matter, but it's not the same as building a major environmental initiative from scratch. At the time of this writing, to my knowledge the Administration has not developed and carried out any major, clearly beneficial environmental program except the non-road diesel rule.

The Administration would not agree with my assessment, of course. Sitting in front of me as I write this is a White House document entitled "The Bush Administration's Record of Environmental Progress," which lists dozens of supposed achievements. But upon close examination this record of progress turns out to be threadbare. Some of the items fall into the category mentioned above—follow-ups on Clinton initiatives. Others are minor affairs. Many belong in a gray zone; they're better than nothing, maybe even pretty good, but not as good as they could or should be.

One occupant of the gray zone is funding of our national parks. During the 2000 campaign, Bush pledged that within five years he would eliminate the $5 billion backlog of maintenance needs in our national parks. In "The Bush Administration's

Record of Environmental Progress" and in other documents and speeches, White House officials state that the President is fulfilling this pledge. This is not true. The Administration has provided some additional money for the backlog, but not nearly as much as it claims. To make it appear that Bush is sticking to his promise, the Administration has played accounting games, such as using much of the money supposedly going to the backlog to instead pay for new construction and current maintenance. Questioned at a Senate hearing, National Park Service Deputy Director Donald Murphy acknowledged that of the $730 million supposedly dedicated to the backlog in fiscal year 2003, only $200 million to $300 million actually was new money. (More broadly, underfunding is one of the Administration's favorite and most effective tools in weakening environmental programs that inhibit development.)

The White House also parlays its claim to be fully funding the parks into a boast that it is generally taking good care of the national parks. The foremost public interest group that watches over our parks, the National Parks Conservation Association, begs to differ. In its view, Bush is guilty of so many sins of commission and omission in regard to the national parks that the association gave him an overall grade of D- on its report card.

Many of Bush's putative gifts to the environment may be more accurately seen as gifts to industry. Probably the most important example is the FreedomCAR program, which the President announced in his 2003 State of the Union speech. He proposed spending $1.2 billion to develop a pollution-free, hydrogen-powered vehicle that would be commercially available by 2020. He painted a rosy picture of cars "producing only water, not exhaust fumes." Bush scored big points with environmentally minded voters with this initiative; people concerned about clean transportation have long dreamed of hydrogen-powered vehicles. But before they celebrate, they'd better take a closer look at Bush's quest, for in his speech, Bush neglected to mention the sources of the hydrogen that would fuel his FreedomCARs. For years clean transportation advocates have envisioned a decentralized network of wind, solar, and other renewable energy-powered facilities producing hydrogen cleanly from water. This would mean no pollution at any step in the process. The Administration seems to have other ideas. In 2002, the Department of Energy gathered hundreds of experts at the National Hydrogen Energy Roadmap Workshop to lay out the future of hydrogen vehicles and a hydrogen-powered nation in general. Ominously, the sessions on hydrogen production were dominated by fossil fuel and nuclear interests. Their vision, which the Administration apparently shares, is to rely largely on oil, gas, coal, and nuclear energy to produce hydrogen. Experts predict that producing hydrogen from these dirty sources would create so much pollution—including carbon dioxide, the main contributor to global warming—that it would negate most of the gains realized by having hydrogen-powered cars. Hydrogen's future is not yet settled, but the Administration is putting most of its funding muscle into creating a hydrogen system that favors fossil fuels and nuclear power over renewables. Once such a system is in place and the infrastructure built, the United States would be committed for decades to a hydrogen path that may do little to clean up air pollution, to slow global warming, or to decrease America's dependence on imported oil.

Once you start looking for hidden benefits for industry in Bush's environmental programs, it's clear that most of his "achievements" do more for development interests than they do for the environment. Examples crop up on nearly every page of "The Bush Administration's Record of Environmental Progress." On page four, for instance, the document cites the Administration's reforms of New Source Review, a Clean Air Act program designed to reduce air pollution from old, coal-fired power plants and other industrial facilities. But these changes in New Source Review actually will make life much easier for polluters and much harder for the people downwind of them.

On pages 13 and 14 the White House lists several accomplishments regarding the protection of wetlands, but this Administration in fact has proposed or implemented several major rules that will cause widespread damage to wetlands, including some of the "accomplishments" on pages 13 and 14. For example, the White House congratulates itself for "clarifying" a rule about "fill material"—the waste dirt and rock produced by mountaintop removal mining operations. But the real-world result of this clarification is to allow coal mining companies to shear off the tops of mountains and dump that waste into the wetlands and other bodies of water in the valley bottoms. The Administration also proposed redefining "waters of the United States" in a way that excludes millions of acres of wetlands from the protections provided by the Clean Water Act for the last 30 years. The White House also relaxed the requirements for getting a permit to fill or dredge wetlands, making it easier for developers to turn wetlands into malls.

On page 22 the White House notes its recommendation of a new, 1.4-million-acre wilderness area in the Chugach National Forest, in Alaska. This inclusion arguably takes the prize for gall, as there never has been an Administration that has done so much harm to wilderness protection, including a specific assault on the Chugach. The Administration has repeatedly tried to decimate the Roadless Rule, a Clinton initiative intended to protect 58.5 million acres of unspoiled forests. One provision specifically took away safeguards for millions of acres on the Chugach and its fellow national forest in Alaska, the Tongass—the two largest units in the national forest system. In 2003, the Administration used a loophole to resurrect right-of-way claims under a Civil War–era mining law, which Congress had repealed in 1976. The regulations issued by Interior Secretary Gale Norton—if they survive legal challenges—will enable states, counties, and individuals to claim jeep trails, old wagon roads, horse trails, and the like as roads, and to build actual roads along these routes. The presence of these right-of-ways might preclude millions of acres of wilderness-quality public lands from ever being officially designated as wilderness, which means that the Bureau of Land Management (BLM) could open them for development. Some of these right-of-way claims cross national parks, national wildlife refuges, and national monuments.

On page 30, the White House points out that Bush favors an international treaty that bans or restricts 12 hazardous chemicals. He proclaimed his support for the Stockholm Convention on Persistent Organic Pollutants at an Earth Day event in 2001, and received approval from the environmental and health communities. But a year later in the legislation to implement the treaty, Bush backtracked from a full commitment by cutting a key provision that would have enabled the list of banned chemicals to be expanded as necessary. I mention this example in particular to make the point that though this book focuses on national issues, Bush's negative impact on the environment extends to the international level. "The Administration's performance in international environmental matters is simply abysmal," says Glenn Wiser, a senior attorney for the Center for International Environmental Law.

That was the good side of Bush's environmental profile. Now let's consider the downside.

The Administration has directed the BLM to cut back environmental reviews in an effort to boost oil and gas development on the public lands that the agency oversees. The Administration has undercut popular farmland conservation programs by dragging its feet on providing technical assistance funding to farmers and ranchers. Despite the fact that there are hundreds of candidates, the Administration has not yet put a single new species on the endangered species list, except when forced by court order or petition. The Administration has shifted the costs of cleaning up toxic Superfund sites from industry to taxpayers. Pressed by oil companies, utilities, and OPEC countries, the Administration declined to renominate Robert Watson as head of the Intergovernmental Panel on Climate Change; Watson is a widely respected scientist who kept warning the world that global warming is a serious problem caused largely by pollution. Even though a plan to reintroduce grizzly bears to Idaho and Montana had taken years to develop and involved locals, conservationists, and industry, the Administration killed the effort. The Administration weakened the rules governing water pollution from gold, copper, and other hard-rock mines. It has exempted the Department of Defense from compliance with a number of environmental laws, despite comments by agency officials that compliance didn't significantly interfere with any military activities and the fact that the Department of Defense is one of the nation's biggest polluters. The Administration has repeatedly tried to force California to accept offshore oil drilling, even after the state sued the Interior Department over the issue and won in court. It has delayed and weakened efforts to reduce the water and air pollution from the enormous livestock feeding facilities that have cropped up around the country in recent years. The Administration has reduced funding for research on energy efficiency, despite a Department of Energy study that showed $30 billion in avoided energy costs resulting from $712 million the government spent on efficiency. And so on.

If I fleshed out each example with a few paragraphs of detail and attempted to be comprehensive, I could fill the entire book with a list of the environmental misdeeds of George W. Bush and his Administration. And what about the things they're not doing? Many worthy Clinton-era initiatives that had been in the works were left outside to die. Many other vital environmental projects that need doing are not being done or even considered. If Bush were to get reelected and spend the next four years as he has spent his first term, his environmental record would be the worst of any president, ever.

Contemplating this record, it's easy to get the feeling that the President and his people don't like the environment. Indeed, some concerned citizens have accused the Administration of targeting the environment for destruction. I disagree. I'd guess that Bush and his appointees would be perfectly happy to have clean water, clean air, abundant wildlife, lush forests, and plenty of wilderness. I don't think they would mind keeping species from going extinct, stopping harmful chemicals from being used as pesticides, arresting global warming, and preventing pollution from killing people. Yes, they would say, these are nice things. Nice, but not important; a healthy and sustainable environment is a low priority to them. If having these nice things gets in the way of doing business, Bush will go with business nine times out of ten—at least.

It ultimately comes down to values. Despite the Administration's words about respecting and protecting the environment, its actions favor profits over protection, material wealth over natural wealth. The Administration's actions also value the rich over the middle class and the poor. Time and time again the Administration has pursued pollution regulations that protect high profits for corporate shareholders and managers at the expense of the health and welfare of people who don't belong to country clubs or wear Rolexes. Finally, the Administration's actions value the present over the future. It continues to push policies that favor fossil fuel development, that accelerate the already precipitous extinction rate of animals and plants, that encourage sprawl across already crowded landscapes—not the acts of someone concerned about the next generation, let alone the next seven generations. Administration officials for the most part behave as if they harbor the nineteenth-century frontier view that nature is little more than a source of raw materials for industry and a place upon which to build houses and cities, while leaving a few pretty places for some parks. I imagine that no Administration official would publicly admit to embracing such venal, soulless values. I imagine, too, that many truly don't hold such values in their hearts. But if that's the case, their true values are in conflict with their actions, and for all our sakes they had better resolve that conflict soon.

To the extent that Administration officials are ignorant rather than uncaring, they can be forgiven for their damaging behavior—and many do seem profoundly ignorant about the environment and the natural world. Most Bush officials have at least one foot in the Wise Use culture, a culture that knows so little of nature that, for example, its adherents mock efforts to save plants and insects and fungi rather than just game animals and maybe some eagles. The Wise Users don't seem to realize that the web of life that supports them and the rest of creation would fall apart without those "little things that run the world," as E. O. Wilson famously said of ants. Allan Fitzsimmons, chosen to head the Interior Department's wildfire program—a job that requires an appreciation of the complexity of ecosystems—has stated that he doesn't believe there is any such thing as an ecosystem and that "public recreational benefit is the principal reason for conserving natural features." The President's budgets have cut funding for all sorts of environmental research, which will only deepen the Administration's ignorance. The Bush Administration, like the Wise Use crowd, seems to take nature for granted. It acts as if it doesn't realize that excessive development is impairing nature's ability to provide flood control, water purification, a decent climate, pest control, new soil, and all those other essential ecosystem services. Not to mention the intangible but nonetheless very real spiritual need we humans have to sometimes get away from malls, television, traffic, computers, machinery, and walls and spend some time in the natural world.

In the end, balance is the key. You may recall from the early part of this chapter that "balance" is one of those feel-good words that the Luntz memo advises the President and others in his party to use to make their efforts seem more environmentally friendly. But don't let the marketing gurus' cynical deployment of the word spoil the idea. Environmental policy really is all about balance. We do need raw materials. We do need industry. We do need places upon which to build homes and human communities. We do need to live with some pollution. And, as noted, we need nature. So the trick is to find ways to meet the needs on both sides of the equation in a manner that can be sustained indefinitely. No one would advocate clear-cutting every forest in America and no one would advocate never cutting another tree in America. Assuming there is no technological answer (such as a cheap and environmentally benign substitute for wood), the debate is about the balance, about how many trees, what age of trees, how often to cut, how to log less destructively, and so on. I contend that President George W. Bush and his Administration are pushing the fulcrum too far to one side so that the interests of industry far outweigh the interests of the environment and, by extension, the public. Once you've read this book you'll be better able to decide if you agree that this President's view is unbalanced.

CHAPTER 1

The Fox Is Guarding
the Henhouse

During the 2000 presidential campaign, Bush offered clues as to how he would deal with the environment. In his speeches he said nice things about cleaning up pollution and protecting wildlife and supporting parks, even going so far as to make some specific promises (several of which he broke soon after assuming office). But people who looked beneath his words and heeded the old Watergate adage—follow the money—quickly saw where Bush's loyalties lay. The trail of campaign dollars led to big corporations and powerful industries, many of which will lose a lot of money if the federal government does a better job of protecting the environment, and will make a lot of money if the government weakens certain environmental regulations. The Center for Responsive Politics, a nonprofit, nonpartisan research group, took the campaign contribution data compiled by the Federal Election Commission and coded it by industry. Using that coded information, Public Campaign, a progressive public interest group, and Earthjustice, an environmental law firm, figured out how much money the various industries affected by environmental regulation had given to which politicians and political parties. Mining, timber, chemical and other manufacturing, oil and gas, and coal-burning utilities together contributed a staggering $44.1 million to the Bush-Cheney campaign and to the Republican National Committee.

Public Citizen and Earthjustice then did something even more interesting. They took the industry-by-industry breakdown of campaign contributions and compared it with the environmental policies undertaken by the Administration during Bush's first 18 months as president. For example, the timber industry gave $3.4 million and the Administration introduced and pushed an initiative designed in part to open up more federal lands to logging. In another example, the coal-burning utilities gave $2 million and the Administration has made regulatory changes and has not enforced existing laws so that these utilities can avoid the expense of installing the most effective pollution-control technology.

Now, for a moment I'd like to indulge in some educated speculation. From what I've learned about the President and his values, I'd guess that his generous treatment of the industries that filled his war chest is for the most part not a matter of simple corruption. The simple corruption scenario goes like this: a politician needs money for his campaign; he gets money from a corporation, a union, a wealthy individual, or some other contributor who is shopping for access and influence; after the politician gets elected, he gets a visit he can't refuse from lobbyists working for the contributor; some arm-twisting ensues, and then the politician gives the contributor at least some of what he wants, even if it requires doing something that is not in the public interest. However, I think that usually there is an essential difference in the way this Administration interacts with its big campaign contributors.

Rather than getting a visit they can't refuse and having their arms twisted by lobbyists, the Administration invites the lobbyists to the White House and together they map out mutually satisfying plans that require no arm-twisting. Corporate leaders and owners from oil and gas, timber, chemical manufacturing, mining: these are George W. Bush's people. It comes as no surprise that he would cater to them and that they would contribute to his campaigns. Consider the notorious energy task force convened by Vice President Dick Cheney, which brought dozens of energy industry honchos together behind closed doors to help develop the President's energy policy. In addition, much of the time industry doesn't even have to meet with White House officials to make its desires known because the Administration is run largely by people from industry, and they are already on the same wavelength with industry lobbyists.

Nowhere is this close-knit relationship between the White House and industry more apparent than in the people that the President has appointed to offices in the natural resource agencies. The main agencies are the Department of the Interior and the Environmental Protection Agency (EPA). Interior's responsibilities include national parks, national monuments, national wildlife refuges, fish and wildlife, and the vast range and mineral resources of the hundreds of millions of acres managed by the Bureau of Land Management (BLM). EPA addresses a wide variety of issues but is especially concerned with pollution, pesticides, and other environmental influences on human health. Several other agencies, such as the Department of Energy and the Department of Agriculture (which includes the Forest Service), devote a significant minority of their time to environmental matters.

As you read this book, you may get the feeling that these agencies are schizophrenic, one moment acting as champions of the environment, the next moment serving industry at the expense of the environment. Partly, this inconsistency reflects a fundamental tension between the appointees, who occupy the top ranks of the agencies, and the career civil service employees, who hold the rest of the positions. Though the appointees hold the upper hand and can get most of what they want, the career employees enjoy institutional savvy and certain protections, so sometimes they can influence decisions when they disagree with the appointees. In the Bush Administration, struggles occur constantly between appointees and ecologists, land managers, wildlife biologists, and other career civil servants. Often the Administration has retaliated against agency employees whose views and scientific studies impede the President's agenda, but still there remain pockets of resistance to some environmentally harmful White House policies.

Though the Bush White House demands strict adherence to its agenda and dictates in unusual detail what it wants its appointees to do, the nature of the people who occupy the top positions still matters a great deal. Bush may be the commander in chief, but these appointees are the generals and colonels, and they exert enormous influence on America's environment. I've chosen for brief examination three Administration figures. They occupy prominent posts and are representative of the kinds of people Bush has placed in nearly every high-level office and in most of all the appointed positions.

As Chair of the Council on Environmental Quality (CEQ), James Connaughton is the President's senior advisor regarding the environment. He is responsible for developing the broad policies that constitute Bush's environmental agenda. He also serves as one of the head cheerleaders for the President's purported approach to the environment, zealously spreading the gospel of free-market solutions and voluntary compliance with environmental laws. Connaughton previously was a partner in the Environmental Practice Group in the law firm of Sidley & Austin, where he counseled a wide array of corporations and trade associations. For example, he represented companies that were balking at cleaning up sites that were so wretchedly polluted that the EPA had placed them on the Superfund list. Among those clients was General Electric, responsible for more Superfund sites than any other corporation in America, according to one measure used by EPA. Connaughton also lobbied government on Superfund matters on behalf of Atlantic Richfield, the Chemical Manufacturers Association, the Aluminum Company of America, and other corporate interests looking to avoid cleanup bills. In 1993, Connaughton coauthored a law journal article entitled "Defending Charges of Environmental Crime—The Growth Industry of the '90s."

Mark Rey serves in the Department of Agriculture as Undersecretary for Natural Resources and Environment, which means that his main job is to oversee the management of the U.S. Forest Service and our 190 million acres of national forests and grasslands. This makes him Bush's quarterback on the logging of public lands. No doubt Rey appreciates the irony of his position, given that for most of his career he has been one of the most prominent figures on the other side of the desk, lobbying the Forest Service in an effort to increase logging in the national forests. From 1976 to 1994, Rey worked for a variety of major timber entities, such as the American Paper Institute and the National Forest Products Association, including a stint as vice president for forest resources for the American Forest & Paper Association, one of the nation's leading proponents of logging in national forests. After that he worked on the staff of the U.S. Senate Energy and Natural Resources Committee.

Rey often has pushed to reduce public involvement in forest management decisions. While on the Senate committee staff, he authored a version of the National Forest Management Act for Senator Larry Craig (R-ID), a strong advocate for more logging on public lands, which would have done away with citizen oversight committees and other opportunities for the public to protect our national forests. Rey also cowrote the notorious "salvage rider," which suspended environmental laws that controlled the clear-cutting of old-growth forests in the Pacific Northwest. Over the years Rey has maintained ties to the Wise Use movement, a loose coalition of antiregulatory groups quietly backed by resource extraction industries. The extreme attitudes of many in the Wise Use movement are evident in the words of one the movement's founders and leading lights, Ron Arnold, who said, "Our goal is to destroy, to eradicate the environmental movement. We want to be able to exploit the environment for private gain, absolutely."

Secretary of the Interior Gale Norton arguably occupies the most powerful environmental position in America, overseeing some 500 million acres of public lands, including our national parks and our national wildlife refuges. She began her long antiregulatory career in 1979, when she joined the Mountain States Legal Foundation. Mountain States provides the legal muscle for the Wise Use agenda, working to remove environmental safeguards and open more public lands for logging, oil and gas exploration, mining, off-road vehicle use, snowmobiling, and the like. In the mid-1980s she followed James Watt (another Mountain States stalwart) to Reagan's Department of the Interior, where she served as Associate Solicitor. One of her tasks was to help draft a paper supporting oil drilling in the Arctic National Wildlife Refuge. During most of the 1990s, she served as the Attorney General for Colorado, where she is remembered for numerous antienvironmental actions, such as cutting the state's environmental budget and declining to sue polluters even though they repeatedly broke air pollution laws.

Over the years Norton has taken many antiregulatory positions, always pushing her basic theme that government, especially the federal government, should back off and let the market take care of the environment. For example, while working at Mountain States she argued in one case that the court should declare the Surface Mining Act unconstitutional; now, as Interior Secretary, she is supposed to enforce that act. In 1995, she filed a brief in a case before the U.S. Supreme Court in which she argued that killing endangered species by degrading habitat should not be considered illegal under the Endangered Species Act. The Supreme Court didn't see things Norton's way. Her interpretation would have gutted the act, given that habitat modification—clear-cutting, overgrazing, draining wetlands, etc.—is by far the biggest threat to imperiled animals and plants. As head of Interior, Norton is in charge of enforcing the Endangered Species Act.

The question arises: what have these and other Bush appointees done to the environment lately? Their pasts are suggestive, but what really counts is what they're doing now that they're in office. I don't recall any of them leaning into the microphone at a nomination hearing and telling the Senate committee that he or she intended to manipulate the system to benefit industry or to pursue ideology-driven antiregulatory agendas. Far from it. The President's nominees swore to protect America's environment and uphold our environmental laws. So, despite their antienvironmental backgrounds, have Bush's appointees indeed protected the environment?

Not often. Many of his appointees have, in fact, spent most of their time manipulating the system to benefit industry or pursuing ideology-driven antiregulatory agendas.

Connaughton, Rey, Norton, and any of dozens of other appointees could serve to illustrate the ties between their pasts and their presents, but instead let's have a look at J. Steven Griles. As Deputy Secretary of the Department of the Interior, Griles is the number-two person at Interior, right below Norton—and some employees of the department and some Interior watchers say that Griles largely runs the place, at least on a day-to-day basis.

Griles knows his way around the halls of Interior. He worked there for the eight years of the Reagan administration, serving as Deputy Director of the Office of Surface Mining, then Deputy Assistant Secretary for Land and Water, and finally as Assistant Secretary of Lands and Minerals Management. While in these positions he advocated for the expansion of oil and gas development on public lands; he weakened environmental regulations and enforcement pertaining to mining operations; and he pushed for offshore oil drilling in California. Some say he pushed too hard for the offshore drilling; in 1989, he wrote a memo attacking the U.S. Fish and Wildlife Service findings about the harmful environmental effects of such drilling. Just before he left office he gave a parting gift to coal companies by reducing coal royalties, then he took a job in the coal industry as senior vice president for coal giant United Company.

After working for King Coal, in 1995 Griles formed his own lobbying firm, J. Steven Griles & Associates. That same year he also went to work for a high-powered lobbying outfit called National Environmental Strategies (NES), founded by former Republican National Committee Chairman Haley Barbour. Between 1995 and his appointment to Interior in 2001, Griles represented dozens of major corporations and industry associations on environmental matters. A large majority of his clients were coal companies, outfits seeking and extracting coal-bed methane (a form of natural gas), offshore drilling interests, and corporations fighting air pollution regulations. His roster included Shell Oil, Arch Coal, Texaco, the American Petroleum Institute, Chevron, Pittson Coal, the Chemical Manufacturers Association, Unocal, the Coal Bed Methane Ad Hoc Committee, Dominion Resources, and Occidental Petroleum. When Bush nominated Griles, John Grasser, spokesman for the National Mining Association, expressed approval, calling him "an ally of industry."

Following his appointment as Deputy Secretary at Interior, Griles had to abide by ethics rules and cut his ties to his own lobbying shop and to NES. But he left a few connections, which in the summer of 2003 stirred up controversy, a lawsuit, an investigation by Interior's Inspector General, and a call for both a special counsel and a grand jury to investigate various aspects of Griles's dealings. Upon Griles's departure, NES had agreed to pay him $1.1 million for his "client base." Never mind that some observers have challenged the legitimacy of such a sale and the fact that as of this writing the Department of the Interior, despite a Freedom of Information Act request, has refused for more than a year to turn over documents about the sale to environmental and government ethics organizations. What has raised eyebrows is the fact that rather than follow the traditional route of giving Griles a lump sum before he entered government service, NES and Griles instead arranged for him to receive $284,000 a year for four years. Government ethics officials approved this arrangement and the president of NES says his firm couldn't afford to pay Griles in one lump sum, but watchdog groups worry that these payments give Griles an ongoing stake in NES and its clients, creating a conflict of interest. Those clients, such as the companies mentioned in the previous paragraph, stand to make or lose millions, maybe even billions of dollars, depending on decisions made by the Interior Department. Will Griles work for the public interest or his former clients' interests?

Legally and ethically, when Interior decisions directly involve his former clients and NES's clients, Griles should recuse himself. According to the Interior Department spokesman, Griles indeed has stayed away from such cases, just as he promised in front of a Senate committee in 2001. The record indicates otherwise. According to *The Washington Post*, Griles attended a meeting of executives connected to the Edison Electric Institute, a former client of his, that addressed the Administration's proposal to weaken enforcement of air pollution by utilities. In the end, the Administration did indeed weaken those enforcement rules. The *Post* also reports that Griles met several times with the National Mining Association, another former client, during the time that the Association was lobbying the Administration to relax the regulations governing mountaintop mining operations. Through a Freedom of Information Act request, Friends of the Earth, an environmental group, obtained Griles's daily calendars, which revealed that he kept close tabs on the development of a pivotal Environmental Impact Statement (EIS) regarding mountaintop mining and that he urged other agencies to soften the regulations on coal mining companies. Griles denies that he discussed inappropriate matters at the meetings with mining interests, but his recusal agreements make his participation highly problematic. When the mountaintop mining EIS finally came out, it had turned nearly 180 degrees from its original direction of tightening the regulations and instead relaxed them.

Griles also got involved with an EIS that would open the door to the drilling of tens of thousands of coal-bed methane wells and more than 5,000 conventional oil and gas wells on public and private lands in Wyoming and Montana. The drilling could proceed despite resistance from many ranchers and other landowners, and despite a negative evaluation of the projects by EPA. In his lobbying days Griles had worked to advance coal-bed methane drilling in those areas and his former outfit, National Environmental Strategies, continues to represent corporations that are currently pushing coal-bed methane development in Wyoming and Montana.

The furor surrounding Griles touches on many important issues, but its tangle of details may distract us from a simple question about Griles and other pro-industry appointees that may be more important than any of the specifics: If the President really considered protecting the environment to be a priority, would he have appointed Griles to one of the nation's top environmental positions? Or Connaughton or Rey or Norton or the dozens of other like-minded individuals whose histories emphatically demonstrate that they put profit ahead of protection?

———————

The New Environmentalism. This phrase crops up from time to time in speeches by Administration officials. Fairly typical, though a little vague and effusive, is a talk given in 2002 at the National Press Club by Interior Secretary Gale Norton. "The day I leave office I want to know that I helped build an America with a healthier environment and a more secure economy. To achieve this, we need to initiate a new era of conservation—what I call a 'new environmentalism.' In launching this new era, we build upon a rich tradition begun at the turn of the last century with President Teddy Roosevelt." Norton continues: "We need a new environmentalism, based on what I call the Four Cs—Communication, Consultation, and Cooperation, all in the service of Conservation." A little later Norton appropriates the memory of revered conservationist Aldo Leopold: "New Environmentalism captures Aldo Leopold's vision of a nation of citizen-conservationists." This theme gets expanded during much of the remainder of the talk, as Norton speaks glowingly of individuals caring for the environment, of local landowners being the best stewards of the land they love, of government empowering people to "know the land, love the land, and take care of the land in the greatest tradition of our nation."

Frankly, I don't know quite what to make of such sentiments coming from Norton and the Bush Administration. My immediate reaction is to fulminate at their shameless hypocrisy. Aligning themselves not only with TR but with Aldo Leopold! And the Four Cs! This from an Administration that rarely Communicates, Consults, or Cooperates with anyone who disagrees with its positions, and that has not done much to serve Conservation. However, after I settle down, a more complex reaction sets in. I remain convinced that coming from most Administration figures, such words are in fact hypocritical, but I recognize that some Bush officials no doubt do believe some or all of their talk about a New Environmentalism.

Moreover, I feel a tug at my heart, because deep down I love the idea of the citizen-conservationist and the Four Cs; that is exactly how it ought to work. Wouldn't it be great if all citizens, from local farmers to the most extreme environmentalists to CEOs of multinational corporations, cooperated and treated the environment as something precious while understanding the need for resources and for people to make a living? Wouldn't it be a profound relief to junk all those convoluted environmental regulations, knowing that well-informed and well-meaning individuals and companies were doing the right thing on their own? I know that I wouldn't mind never again having to read the fine print of some 400-page document on toxic waste disposal, and I'm sure companies would be even happier to never again have to abide by such regulations. If only individuals and corporations would take responsibility for the welfare and sustainability of our planet. Alas, too many of them neglect the public good in their myopic pursuit of profit, so the rest of us, including the companies that do try to operate in an environmentally responsible manner, are stuck with the burden of regulations until the miscreants clean up their act. At least, I hope that we retain enough of our more reasonable regulations to protect our world until such time as enough people behave responsibly. It would be disastrous if the Bush Administration succeeded in getting rid of too many regulations before our society is ready to handle the freedom.

This overreliance on good behavior by individuals and corporations is a basic flaw of the New Environmentalism. The ideals of "self-motivated citizen-stewards" and various interests finding "consensus and common ground," as Norton puts it, actually can work and have worked in certain cases, particularly when there's a local problem to rally around, like restoring a degraded stretch of river. We as a society should do everything we can to encourage such productive collaborations and I applaud the Administration's genuine efforts along these lines. But when dealing with major industries, powerful corporations, and self-serving and unethical individuals, one would have to be naive to proceed as if New

Environmentalism's idealistic approach can provide sufficient environmental protections. Have we so quickly forgotten about the machinations of managers at Enron, WorldCom, Arthur Andersen, Tyco, and all those other scandal-ridden companies? Some Administration officials give a perfunctory nod to the need to stiffen voluntary programs with federal standards and enforcement, but generally their hearts aren't in it. Industry knows that and can take advantage of it.

Like his Interior Secretary, Bush has a history of advancing voluntary solutions. As governor of Texas, in 1997, he announced with great fanfare the creation of a program that would reduce air pollution from the state's oldest and dirtiest industrial facilities without resorting to government-mandated regulations. The state government would grant these companies immunity for past violations of pollution laws and would set up an easy permitting process that excluded most public participation. To receive these benefits, the companies simply had to voluntarily obtain a permit and abide by the program's modest pollution requirements. Governor Bush assured his fellow Texans, who were breathing some of the most noxious air in the country, that this effort would dramatically reduce air pollution in a business-friendly way.

Dozens of companies representing 73 polluting plants signed on as "early volunteers." In 1998, the governor's office reported that "Governor Bush's early efforts have already resulted in dozens of plants reducing emissions the equivalent to the smog of 500,000 vehicles." Bush also cited these reductions during the 2000 presidential campaign. But the reductions were almost entirely fiction.

Environmental Defense did two studies of Governor Bush's program. (Note that Environmental Defense is a conservation group that avidly promotes appropriate voluntary programs.) They found all sorts of accounting shenanigans used to make the program look successful, such as counting promised future reductions as if they'd already occurred. In reality, almost three years after Governor Bush and some of the early volunteers had stood on a platform and congratulated one another, only 19 of the 73 "early volunteers" had even bothered to officially get with the program by obtaining a permit. Only five of those 19 had taken all the necessary steps to start making significant reductions. In addition to the supposed early volunteers, some 700 facilities were eligible to get permits. Only 10 got them.

Looking at emissions from nonutility sources, such as oil refineries, Environmental Defense found that actual emission reductions amounted to a paltry three-tenths of one percent. The program was a bust and the air in Texas was as foul as ever. The voluntary program had succeeded only in delaying much-needed action for several years. After Bush ascended to the presidency, the Texas legislature nixed the voluntary program and instituted mandatory regulations, and now Texans are breathing a little easier.

New Environmentalism also emphasizes the use of the market instead of so-called "command-and-control" regulation. This approach has been used in and out of government for a number of years with some success. For example, Environmental Defense runs a program that provides incentives for private landowners to protect endangered species. Properly designed and applied to the right situation, market forces can be a powerful tool. Unfortunately, the Bush White House promotes them as the answer to almost every problem and often designs them more to profit industry than to achieve a blend of environmental and economic benefits. This abuse of the concept may give market-based regulation a bad name and end up discouraging people from using the market even in appropriate situations.

Start a conversation about market-based solutions with an Administration official, and within moments you'll be talking about the acid rain program. Acid rain forms when water vapor chemically combines with various airborne pollutants and returns to earth as sulfuric and nitric acid, causing extensive harm to forests and aquatic life. Many of the airborne pollutants come from power plants, especially those that burn coal, so when the problem of acid rain came to light environmentalists pushed for regulations requiring utilities to install effective but expensive pollution-control technologies or to switch fuels, which also can be costly. The utilities pushed back and nothing much happened. To break this impasse, as part of the 1990 Clean Air Act Amendments, Congress set up a market-based trading system. Under this system, each utility was given a "baseline" allowance that permitted each power plant to emit a certain amount of sulfur dioxide annually. Plants that could cheaply clean up did so, thus reducing emissions below the baseline and accumulating pollution credits. They then sold their excess credits to utilities that couldn't clean up cheaply, allowing those power plants to avoid expensive cleanups. The program worked fairly well. Overall emissions in the country diminished and those reductions happened in a cost-effective way, with the market steering the spending on pollution controls to the least expensive places.

The acid rain model is the darling of the White House. They tout it as the answer to all sorts of environmental issues, even though it is suited only to certain circumstances. They also point to it when they're talking about market-based proposals that may differ in essential ways from the acid rain model. For example, the acid rain program had a cap on the total amount of emissions that would be allowed nationwide; the government left it to industry to use the trading system to work out how to achieve those reductions. But not all trading programs use caps, which can make a big difference. In addition, compliance with the acid rain program was easy for government to monitor, given that the pollution was coming out of big smokestacks that easily were fitted with continuous emissions monitors, so there was minimal cheating. In other, less easily monitored programs, studies have shown noncompliance to be widespread.

The Bush EPA urged states to adopt a variation of the acid rain model called "open-market trading" that lacks both a cap and easy monitoring. New Jersey tried it, and then threw it out after an EPA investigation discovered fraud in the program. The EPA's Inspector General also investigated the New Jersey program and found additional reasons to junk it, noting that the open-market approach encouraged dubious trades, led to the trading of invalid credits, and lacked safeguards. Despite this Inspector General's report, and four previous Inspector General reports that reached similar conclusions, the Administration bulled ahead with open-market trading.

Even when there are caps, even when there is easy and rigorous monitoring, even when talking about the vaunted acid rain program itself, serious flaws often emerge. For example, trading programs tend to concentrate pollution around the industrial facilities that would have to spend the most to upgrade, so people living near these sites sometimes suffer from increased pollution and the associated health problems even if emissions in the nation as a whole decline. Often these old, dirty facilities that trading may leave behind are located in poor and minority communities, raising concerns about justice and equity.

More fundamentally, some trading programs implement unstated values that are highly debatable. In essence, these market-based solutions often tilt the balance away from human health and environmental protection and toward the economic concerns of certain industries. Eric Schaeffer has an insider's knowledge of those implicit values. Currently the director of the Environmental Integrity Project, a nonprofit that watchdogs environmental enforcement, Schaeffer formerly served as Director of the Office of Regulatory Enforcement at EPA, until he quit in 2002 in protest over Bush's new air pollution proposals. He points out that the acid rain program has managed to reduce sulfur dioxide emissions by about a third since its inception, in 1990—a significant improvement. But perhaps the Administration and other champions of market-based solutions should pause in giving each other high fives and take a look at the traditional regulatory effort to protect Germany's famed Black Forest from acid rain. The German government saw the problem, mandated that industry quickly clean up, enforced that mandate, and in five or six years emissions had been reduced by 90 percent. Germany's traditional regulatory approach rapidly reduced acid rain, but free-market orthodoxy insists that it must have cost far more than a trading program. Well, not necessarily. Researchers at the University of Karlsruhe, in Germany, tried to answer this complex question by studying facilities in several European countries to determine the potential for savings through pollution trading. They concluded that "a reasonably designed Ordinance is as cheap as [trading] alternatives, but it guarantees emission reduction."

One critic of the acid rain trading system, Curtis Moore, Republican counsel to the U.S. Senate Committee on Environment and Public Works from 1978 to 1989, points out that the German program did indeed cost more than its U.S. counterpart, but he thinks that's because the U.S. program set far more modest goals. "Put simply, it costs less to do less." Moore notes that while Germany was achieving a 90 percent reduction, the U.S. has managed only about a 40 percent reduction. And the U.S. has taken more than twice as long to get less than half as far. Though such information should not promote a blanket reduction of all trading systems, it does suggest the value of healthy skepticism. Perhaps the President's and industry's love of trading programs stems from the programs' potential for masking lower standards.

"Why is the market trading always right?" asks Schaeffer. "It's a religious belief in policy making in the United States. Just say 'market,' 'trading,' 'flexibility,' and it's got to be a better thing. But it's not always analytically sound." Schaeffer thinks the Administration often gets its priorities reversed. He says that it tackles a problem by first deciding that it will use a market-based approach and then trying to make that approach work. Instead, he thinks it should first look at the harm that an environmental problem is causing to people and nature and then decide what approach will work best to alleviate that harm as rapidly as possible at a reasonable cost. "If you are religiously obsessed with market solutions," continues Schaeffer, "then the market decides how much we're going to reduce pollution. We don't decide what we need to do to protect human health, and then consider whether a market-based mechanism is the best way to get there."

As of this writing, Bush is talking up his Clear Skies Initiative, a massive trading program that addresses air pollution issues. But it will achieve poorer results and achieve them more slowly than would rigorous enforcement of the traditional regulations in the Clean Air Act. Studies indicate that if Clear Skies replaces the Clean Air Act, it will lead to tens of thousands of additional deaths, millions of additional illnesses, and lots more environmental damage. By insisting on using this inadequate market-based program while trumpeting the magic of the marketplace, the Administration is obscuring the tradeoffs its plan involves and making an unspoken decision that these deaths and illnesses and damages are justified in order to provide financial benefits to industry and the economy. Such momentous decisions could be made openly, with a full debate of the pros and cons, if the Administration would rein in its ideology and consider all the regulatory tools in its toolbox.

CHAPTER 2

Playing with Fire

President George W. Bush emerged from his entourage and stepped onto the rough wooden platform erected for his visit. Before him, arrayed on a dirt logging road, were several dozen people, including four governors from western states, the secretaries of the Departments of Interior and Agriculture, several members of Congress, the head of the President's Council on Environmental Quality, and—most important for this photo op—the media.

A few yards from the President jutted charred conifer skeletons whose bark and green needles had been burned away. It was this recently incinerated forest, site of the Squires Fire, that had brought Bush to this ridge in southwest Oregon on the morning of August 22, 2002, to announce his new forest fire policy: the Healthy Forests Initiative. He wanted the people who would watch him on the news to see the destruction wrought by wildfire and, according to the President, by endless appeals and delays that prevent desperately needed fire protection measures from getting implemented.

Atop the platform, Bush gazed into the eyes of the television cameras. After some general remarks about fires devastating our forests and communities, he got to the meat of the speech. "In order to effect our healthy forest policy, we must cut through the red tape and endless litigation that blocks efforts to restore forest health," said the President. Continuing on this theme a moment later, he added, "So, for the good of Oregon's forests, and really for the good of her environment overall and for the good of your economy, I've directed the Secretary of Agriculture, the Secretary of the Interior, and the Council on Environmental Quality to do the following steps: first, to authorize thinning projects on an emergency basis in the most critical areas; second, to speed up the process of developing environmental assessments while considering the long-term threat that fire-susceptible forests pose to endangered species; and third, to expedite the appeals process.

"Listen, we want our citizens at the local level to have a voice. We want there to be an opportunity for our citizens to speak out. That's the great American way. But we must discourage the endless delays that prevent good forest policy from going forward. And Congress should pass legislation that will ensure that vital forest restoration projects are not tied up in courts."

Bush had pieced together the clues and identified the perpetrator: environmentalists miring worthy projects in the mud of frivolous lawsuits, endless administrative appeals, excessive study, and drawn-out public comment. Thus, while the Healthy Forests Initiative addressed forest fires, its even more ambitious aim was to "streamline" the process that leads to decisions about the management of fire in our federal forests.

I put "streamline" in quotes because to a large extent the term is a euphemism. Though some red tape and the occasional nuisance lawsuit are unfortunate realities, "streamlining" often goes beyond smoothing over such rough spots in the bureaucratic process. Frequently the term is code for avoiding accountability, for sidestepping laws and regulations that protect our health and natural resources by subjecting projects that may harm the environment to thorough study, public review, and challenges from citizens. However, it will get annoying if I continue to put "streamlining" in quotes, so I'll stop now. But later in the chapter, when I examine streamlining in depth, just imagine quotation marks whenever I use that word.

At another point in his speech at the site of the Squires Fire, President Bush elaborated on what he views as bureaucratic obstacles to sound and timely wildfire management. "For example," he said, "a thinning project to prevent catastrophic fire in the area where we were just standing was proposed six years ago. They said, 'Well, what can we do to make sure this area is protected?' Yet, because of burdensome regulatory hurdles and meritless appeals and litigation, only a very small portion of this acreage was approved for thinning before the fires came through. And we saw the difference between an area that had been thinned and an area which had not been thinned. And that difference is catastrophic. That's reality."

Well, that's one version of reality, the version proclaimed by the President and shown on the news. But if the cameras had panned and moved in closer, a more complex and more accurate version of reality would have emerged, one that reveals some of the shortcomings of both the President's wildfire policy and his attempts to use the Healthy Forests Initiative to streamline the management of our federal forests.

———

Are forest fires a problem or not? Conditioned by sensational images of 50-foot flames roaring through the pines—perhaps first planted in our minds by the fire scene in the movie *Bambi*—most of us grew up believing that fires destroyed forests. Then, in recent years, experts began teaching us that fire is a normal and necessary part of almost all forest systems. Now, we're again hearing that forest fires are destroying forests. What gives?

Call it the human factor. In undisturbed forests that aren't populated by people, fires, even vast fires, are agents of renewal. They foster the growth of understory plants favored by many animals, create diverse habitats, stimulate seeds to burst from cones, and recycle nutrients. Nearly every forest in the lower 48 states has evolved with fire—even those in wet climates that only burn once every couple of centuries—and must burn periodically in order to prosper.

It is the presence of humans that complicates the relationship between forests and fire. Fires have grown increasingly troublesome during the last century as timber operations, ranches, reservoirs, roads, power lines, cabins, resorts, ski areas, houses, towns, and even small cities have developed among the trees. A fire that burns through an isolated wilderness is one thing; a fire that consumes houses and resorts is quite another. Furthermore, some forests have been so altered by the hand of man that they no longer burn in a natural, beneficial way. Given the human factor, these days nearly everyone, from timber company CEO to anti-logging protestor, agrees that we face a fire problem in some of our forests. They agree that something needs to be done soon. But they disagree in many respects about the source, the nature, the scope, and the solutions to the problem.

The modern era of fire management can be traced to the early 1900s, when the national forests and the U.S. Forest Service were established. The Forest Service was in charge of controlling wild-fires, but the steep cost of suppression led to a policy of letting fires in unsettled areas burn until natural firebreaks or the weather stopped them. Though it had been motivated by a desire to save money, the Forest Service had stumbled onto an ecologically enlightened approach to fire well before the vital natural role of fire was widely appreciated. This policy lasted until the 1930s, when worries that too much merchantable timber was going up in smoke ushered in an era in which firefighters tried to put out most fires whatever the cost.

During the 1940s, fueled by booming timber interests and the demonization of fire, firefighting escalated into the industrial-strength endeavor it is today. With a vigor that would have made Smokey Bear proud, the Forest Service and others suppressed so many fires that natural fire patterns changed on a significant portion of the nation's forestland. In many ways we're still in this stage, but it is starting to be leavened by a more sophisticated and ecologically appropriate modus operandi. Whether we ever embrace natural wildfire to the extent practicable in our fire-averse society remains to be seen.

The widespread suppression of fires is one of the main reasons that some forests no longer are in a condition to burn naturally. In a number of forest systems each mild fire makes the forest less prone to massive conflagrations. The relatively small and cool ground fires remove undergrowth and debris from the forest floor and clear out small trees, thus eliminating the "ladder" fuels that carry fire up into the crowns of big trees—and it is crown fires that can blow up into massive conflagrations. In a classic case of unintended consequences, widespread suppression of fire has produced many dryland forests that are now far more vulnerable to fire because they're choked with undergrowth and ladder fuels. In recent years the damaging role of suppression has been widely recognized by scientists, land managers, and politicians, though the latter's resolve to let appropriate fires burn often wilts in the heat of the moment.

While pointing a finger at fire suppression, the Administration hasn't been acknowledging the harmful role that development of the forests has played. Livestock grazing has removed much of the grass and other fine fuels that under natural conditions would carry ground fires. Timber operations have diminished the fire-resistance of forests by logging so many of the big trees, which are the very ones most likely to make it through a fire. Logging also involves extensive road-building, which greatly increases the presence of people in the woods. People start 90 percent of forest fires, accidentally or intentionally, according to a Forest Service study conducted in the late 1990s, though in the West, lightning ignites most fires. Furthermore, clear-cuts can heighten the risk of wildfire because a few years after being shorn they turn into highly flammable thickets of shrubs and soon they grow into stands of densely packed young trees. For one to three years after logging, a site is littered with extremely combustible piles of slash—trimmed-off branches and other non-merchantable wood. If fire strikes before the slash is burned off or removed, the intensity of the blaze can rev up dangerously. As participating scientists wrote in their final report to Congress on the Sierra Nevada Ecosystem Project, "Timber harvest . . . has increased fire severity more than any other recent human activity"—and that would include suppression.

Though its impact largely is indirect, real estate development also greatly exacerbates the problems associated with wildfires by putting so many people and buildings in harm's way. In recent years new homes have proliferated in the so-called Wildland-Urban Interface—rural areas and the margins of towns where houses and subdivisions border or extend into the surrounding forest. The presence of homes and other structures, most of which have not been adequately prepared to withstand fire, greatly increases the need for suppression. Like building on active flood-plains, putting houses in forests (especially dry-climate forests) without adequate preparation for disaster ignores the realities of nature. Either owners need to get their properties ready to withstand fire or society should consider the wisdom of rampant building in fire-prone forests.

The President and Administration officials are among those who have noted the drawbacks of fire suppression and acknowledged the need for low-intensity, ground-hugging fires. Yet this has not stopped them from demonizing fire. They've merely narrowed the focus of their antipathy to large, high-intensity fires. They condemn all such blazes as burning unnaturally hot due to the unnatural buildup of flammable material, but for the most part this unnatural buildup of fuels has occurred only in some dry forests. In the majority of our forests, huge, hot (but not unnaturally hot) fires are natural, although they may happen only once every hundred or two hundred years. Even our unspoiled drier forests that have benefited from regular, cleansing ground fires will naturally experience stand-replacing blazes once in a great while, and the results are not ecologically devastating, as the Administration contends. To the contrary, those big fires play an important ecological role. Consider the Biscuit Fire, which the President and other Administration officials often have bemoaned as a disaster.

In May 2003, I ventured into the half-million acres that fell within the perimeter of the Biscuit Fire, the largest blaze of the notorious 2002 fire season and the largest ever in the state of Oregon. It occurred in the rugged Siskiyou Mountains, in extreme southwest Oregon. Contrary to popular belief, rain doesn't drench all of Oregon all of the time, and this part of the Siskiyous falls into the category of hot, dry forest. My guide to the Biscuit was Tom Atzet, a highly regarded Forest Service ecologist who has been working in the area since 1974. As we drove up a gravel road along the Illinois River, heading into the Siskiyou National Forest and the eastern reaches of the burn, Atzet spoke in his soft voice about the role of big fires.

"Even in the areas where we have relatively high-frequency,

low-severity fire [such as the Biscuit site], we have these fires every two or three hundred years that are just barn burners, even though we've had the primary system uninterrupted"—meaning the forest remains undeveloped and hasn't suffered unduly from fire suppression. I asked him what would happen if we suppressed all the barn burners. "You'd eliminate the extreme ends of the natural fire process," he said. "There's a saying in ecology that the extremes determine the range of species."

Atzet went on to explain that big fires change ecological relationships, set up new possibilities. "Sometimes," he said, "Fire is like a reset button." We switchbacked a bit farther up a mountainside, then Atzet continued. "We couldn't live without high-severity fire. The ecosystem requires a certain amount. You have to realize that change is probably the crucial thing, what really drives the ecosystem." He spoke of big fires producing new winners and losers and he asserted that such dynamics could help plants and animals adapt to new challenges, such as global climate change. "One of the reasons that mortality is such a good thing ecologically is because you're always allowing species to put out new combinations of DNA to be tested for what we're going into. If we were able to stop mortality, we'd be out of luck." He concluded by stating that if we allow only cool fires we're missing half the lesson of reintroducing fire to our forests.

Several miles along, Atzet pulled off the road and parked. As we tromped up a steep hillside toward one of his research plots, he pointed at the incense cedar, Douglas fir, Jeffrey pine, and madrone whose green needles and leaves shaded us. When we stopped to pant for a while, Atzet pointed out the fawn lilies, trillium, manzanita, and grasses at our feet, sprouting from the blackened soil. Yes, blackened soil—we were in the fire zone. In fact, the part of the Biscuit site through which we were traveling was among the most fiercely burned. Yet here was this beautifully singed slope, which the fire had cleared of brush and some small trees—a perfect job of thinning. It was even better than mechanical thinning, said Atzet, because a cool fire like that one burns down the undergrowth and small trees and serves up their nutrients to the soil. "There probably will be a flush of resources for those [plants] that survived," said Atzet. "They'll get a kick in the butt." He warned that if a fire is too severe, it burns up the nitrogen and that vital nutrient will go up in smoke, but clearly that hadn't happened where we were hiking. In fact, it hadn't happened on the vast majority of the landscape affected by the Biscuit Fire. As we drove on that day, continuing through the area that surveys have identified as among the most badly burned, we saw many untouched and lightly scorched sections along with many thoroughly cooked stretches. Surveys show that other places hit by the Biscuit Fire, especially within the Kalmiopsis Wilderness, had fared even better.

All in all, the half million acres overrun by the Biscuit Fire bore little resemblance to the wasteland that one might expect to encounter after listening to the President. "I flew over the Biscuit Fire today when we were coming in. It's devastating," said Bush in his August 22, 2002, speech. A moment later he added, "These fires destroy critical wildlife habitat, and they leave behind long-lasting environmental damage." A few minutes later he returned to the theme, generalizing about big fires like the Biscuit: "The catastrophic wildfires kill the oldest trees, those which we long to preserve. They kill just about everything that grows in the soil," said the President. "The fires that ravaged the West have destroyed endangered species habitat. They damaged fisheries. They've eroded soil." He goes on, but you get the idea; Bush and his Administration portray blazes like the Biscuit Fire as utterly ruinous.

In my tour of the Biscuit Fire I could readily see that the White House portrayal is inaccurate, but I didn't know just how inaccurate until I saw the postfire studies conducted by the Forest Service.

They revealed that only about 16 percent of the Biscuit's 500,000 acres had burned severely, about 23 percent moderately, about 41 percent lightly, and about 20 percent very lightly or not at all. Maybe the aftermath of the Biscuit will teach us to stop condemning big fires, but history says otherwise. Remember the doomsday wailing when a huge blaze swept across much of Yellowstone National Park in 1988? Naturally, the park recovered and is doing better than ever, yet that example (and plenty of others) hasn't prevented many people, including those in the Administration, from wailing as loudly as ever about the big fires of 2002.

The media unwittingly have aided and abetted the White House in its demonization of big fires. Television in particular took the grim-enough reality of the 2002 fire season and hyped it into supercharged tragedy. Though the Biscuit Fire and the other blazes of 2002 didn't cause nearly as much ecological damage as claimed by the Administration, it still was a rough fire season by modern standards. The total area within the boundaries of the fires reached 7.2 million acres before the rain and snow of winter finally put out the last flames, making it one of the worst years since the advent of large-scale fire suppression. (In the presettlement era, however, according to fire ecologist Steve Arno, some 18 to 25 million acres of western forest burned each year—"burned" meaning fire passed through the area, turning some trees to ash and leaving others healthy and alive.)

Bad as the fires were, television made things worse by fanning the flames of public perception. Evening after summer evening newscasts showed footage of howling fires licking high into the sky, devouring 100-foot pines, houses, and whatever else stood in their paths, yet no camera crews rushed to film the lightly scorched and unburned areas within the boundaries of these big fires. Viewers were introduced to families who had fled their homes and communities just ahead of the oncoming flames. Cameras captured haggard firefighters trooping through the woods and we heard grim reports of firefighters who had died battling the blazes. We were at war and fire was the enemy. This exaggerated image played right into the Administration's hands, and ever since it's been using the 2002 fires as a scare tactic to try to alter some of the rules that govern our public forests. Likewise, the Administration cited the wildfires that swept Southern California in 2003 as a reason to retool our forest fire policies, even though most of the California fires burned in brushy areas and had nothing to do with forests.

———————

If you cut through the rhetoric of the Administration's approach to forest fires, its essential message comes down to two things. The first is the need to streamline the decision-making process so that projects aimed at reducing the threat of forest fires—mostly thinning—get expedited. The second is the need to thin our forests. "Thin" is jargon for logging some of the trees and removing much of the brush in a forest that has become choked with too many trees and too much undergrowth. Under natural conditions, thinning gets taken care of by the agents of change, such as wind, insects, disease, and especially fire. But according to the President, 190 million acres of public forest have grown unnaturally dense, so fires will burn with unnatural intensity and produce unnatural consequences. So, as Bush said in his August speech, "We must thin, and we must quickly restore the areas that have been damaged by fire. People who fight fires and who study forests, who know a lot more about this subject than I do, agree."

Actually, most forest scientists disagree with much of the Administration's approach. They would agree that there's an important role for thinning to play, but they also would agree that Bush's promotion of thinning as almost a panacea is mistaken. Depending on how a particular thinning project is designed, it can involve clearing out the mostly worthless brush and small trees, which is good for fire protection but of little interest to the timber industry—or it can involve cutting a considerable number of valuable medium and large trees, which is bad for fire protection but of great interest to the timber industry. And the Administration is continually devising avenues by which logging companies can get to the bigger trees. Critics point out that the timber industry gave $294,000 to the Bush-Cheney 2000 campaign, $8,000 to the Bush-Cheney Recount effort, $350,000 to the Bush-Cheney inauguration, and $2,742,236 to the Republican National Committee during the 2000 and 2002 election cycles. Critics also note that one of the main architects of Administration forest policy is Mark Rey, Undersecretary, Natural Resources and Environment, of the U.S. Department of Agriculture and the person who oversees the Forest Service and our national forests. Prior to being appointed by Bush, Rey spent nearly 20 years working for timber industry trade associations.

To get an on-the-ground look at the interplay between thinning and fire, I traveled to that ridge within the burn area of the Squires Fire where Bush introduced the Healthy Forests Initiative. This fire also serves as exhibit A in the White House's campaign for thinning. I headed that way one morning in May 2003, in the company of David Calahan, a logger turned soldier turned firefighter who retired a few years ago after decades of fighting fires in southern Oregon. He has devoted much of his retirement to activism regarding local forestry issues. A resident of the rural valley threatened by the Squires Fire, he helped fight the blaze as a volunteer.

The Bureau of Land Management had gated off the road that President Bush and company had used to drive up to the top of the ridge, so, with the permission of the landowner whose property lies below the ridge, Calahan and I hiked through the tall grass of a spring pasture for a few minutes to reach the BLM land where the fire had occurred. Where the grass gave way to woods we crossed into the BLM property. Not 100 yards from the pasture we encountered ponderosa pines and Douglas firs whose trunks had been scorched: the first evidence of the Squires Fire. A minute later we labored up a steep hillside that had burned severely. Reduced to blackened poles bearing a few blackened branches, all the trees had been killed and the understory had burned to the ground. Calahan looked around and allowed that he wouldn't have wanted to be on this slope when that blaze had roared through.

As we continued up toward the top of the ridge, he talked about the three elements that determine the intensity of a wildfire, a list I since have heard from many professionals involved with forest fire. "First is weather. Fire is mostly driven by weather," said Calahan, breathing hard as we labored up the steep pitch and talked at the same time. "Second is terrain. Third is fuel." Forest policy focuses on fuel—trees, shrubs, grasses, and whatever else can burn—because it's the only element over which humans can exert at least some control.

After a few minutes we crested the ridge and emerged onto a logging road that followed the spine of the ridge to the north. The top of the ridge measured only about 50 feet across, so as we walked along the dirt road we could look down either side of the hill. The patchiness of the Squires Fire was immediately evident. We saw everything from areas as cooked as used charcoal to pockets of green trees and undergrowth that had gone untouched, though these were scarce in this area.

After walking several hundred yards we came to the site where President Bush had delivered his speech. We saw the ghost forest of standing dead trees that had served as the backdrop for some of the photos. The President's favorite adjectives did indeed suit that fried hillside; the fire had been devastating and catastrophic on that site. The fact that the hundreds of spindly, burned trunks were packed in close to each other served notice that this spot had not been thinned, and the lack of thinning, the President had emphasized, is why it had burned so destructively. In a different speech supporting Congressional legislation similar to the Healthy Forests Initiative, given on May 20, 2003, Bush again cited the Squires Fire as proof of the worth of thinning. "Nine months ago I stood at the scene of the Squires Peak Fire in Oregon," said Bush. "On one side of a dirt road, where small trees and underbrush had been removed before the fire rolled through, the forest was green and alive. On the other side of the road, where a similar thinning project had been stalled by lawsuits, the landscape was charred and the trees looked like matchsticks. The contrast between these two sides of the forest was startling, and it was tragic."

In search of that contrast, Calahan and I walked across the dirt road and looked down the slope on the other side of the ridge: the thinned area to which Bush was referring above. Sure enough, the trees were much farther apart and the forest floor bore the unmistakable evidence of thinning: stumps, which ranged in size from small to medium, plus the stubble of sawn shrubs. But it was not, as advertised, "green and alive." Far from it. The area had burned badly, though not as badly as the unthinned section. Calahan surveyed the trees and estimated that 80 percent were dead. "Isn't it kind of ironic," said Calahan, "that they're taking photos in one direction and immediately behind them is an example of a thinned forest that burned heavily, too?" Ed Reilly, an environmental planner for the local BLM district, later told me that the fire had blown up that thinned slope, and that the treatment had helped prevent total destruction. Even so, thinning was clearly not the silver bullet the Administration continually makes it out to be. At the time of the fire the site was at its most fire-resistant stage, yet the large majority of the trees had died anyway.

Heading back the way we'd come, still looking down the side of the ridge that had been thinned several years earlier, Calahan and I stopped about 150 yards from the platform site. "It killed everything here," said Calahan, gazing at a firescape every bit as devastated as the platform-backdrop area. Every ounce of green and brown had been burned away and all that remained—standing trees, downed trees, stumps, soil—was black. We saw several other similar scenes, in which thinned and cleaned-up sites at the peak of their ability to withstand fire had burned as severely as the unthinned site at which Bush made his speech. "So this [thinned area] was just how the BLM wanted to leave it but now it's toast, total toast," said Calahan of one spot. "It's simply a matter of Mother Nature kicking up her heels."

Back at his house Calahan and I looked at a White House paper on the Squires Fire, complete with photos, that focused on the Spencer Lomas timber sale, the 430-acre section that provided some of the President's photo ops. As the paper notes, 80 of those 430 acres hadn't yet been logged and thinned when the fire roared through. "As the accompanying photos of the Squires Fire show," reads the paper, "the difference in fire behavior between thinned and unthinned areas was dramatic. Although tree loss was minimized in the treated areas . . . in areas that were left untreated, the fire burned tree canopies and destroyed most trees."

After we looked at the White House photos, Calahan brought out some of the postfire photos he'd taken on some of those 80 unthinned acres. Contrary to the Administration's claims about the untreated acres, the photos showed lightly burned forest that was, in fact, "green and alive." "Much of that area burned just as sweet and clean as you'd ever want," said Calahan. "The fire stayed on the ground, moved around, left patches totally unburned, did no harm." Why did much of this unthinned forest not go up in flames? Who knows? Maybe the fire burned through there in the cool of the night, or when there was less wind, or at a downhill angle.

The upshot? "There were lots of places that were untreated and burned badly and lots of places that were treated and burned badly," said Calahan. "Every kind of example you'd want was right there. It just depends on where you point your camera."

Nearly all forest scientists agree with Calahan's general point: that forests and fires and the effectiveness of thinning are more complex than the impression given by Bush. On September 24, 2002, near the end of the fire season, a dozen fire researchers and ecologists, among them some of the field's most eminent authorities, sent a letter to the President urging him to respond to the problem of wildfire with "thoughtfulness and care." They write, "The fires are traceable to differing factors in different regions and forest types." They go on, "We have no simple, proven prescription for meeting this challenge throughout the West. In semiarid ponderosa pine forests effective restoration may result from cutting small-diameter trees [i.e., thinning] in overly dense stands." But, they add, "The value of thinning to address fire risks in other forest ecosystems is still poorly understood. Although a few empirically based studies have shown a systematic reduction in fire intensity subsequent to some actual thinning, others have documented increases in fire intensity and severity."

Intuition suggests that removing more fuels always would reduce the intensity of fire, but reality and intuition don't always match up, as noted by Norman Christensen, one of the authors of that September 24 letter to Bush. Christensen is Dean Emeritus and Professor of Ecology at the Nicholas School of the Environment and Earth Sciences at Duke University, the chair of the National Commission on Science for Sustainable Forestry, and the former chair of a review panel that examined fire management in Sierra Nevada national parks and of a panel that studied the ecological effects of the 1988 Yellowstone fires. "One of the things that some of us are concerned about is that there has been relatively little study of fire behavior relative to thinning," says Christensen. "There's a kind of commonsense aspect to this, that if you thin the fuels you're going to have more favorable fire behavior.

But some of the studies . . . suggest that it's a bit more complicated than that, and that particularly thinning of larger trees can create air circulation situations that can improve the movement of a fire." Other scientists have pointed out that taking the bigger trees opens up the canopy and lets more sunlight reach the forest floor, drying out the understory fuel and making it more flammable.

Nearly everyone agrees that it's helpful to remove small trees, maybe seven inches in diameter and less, from those overly dense forests that naturally burn at frequent intervals, but the necessity for thinning in wetter forests that burn infrequently and the effects of thinning trees larger than about seven inches in diameter are uncertain. Critics of the Administration's efforts point out that, as a way to pay for thinning, the President wants to allow timber companies to take large trees while they thin because the small trees have little economic value. This means that the Administration's thinning program, by permitting too many big trees to be cut, could backfire and make forests more vulnerable to fire. And if the Administration ends up allowing what amounts to commercial logging in the name of fuel reduction—which critics think will happen in many cases—that will aggravate the fire situation considerably, as many logged sites quickly grow into tinderboxes of shrubs and densely packed small trees. None of this even mentions the general ecological damage that increased logging can cause.

———————

As this book was going to press, Congress passed a bill, the Healthy Forests Restoration Act, that incorporated some of the environmentally harmful features of Bush's Healthy Forests Initiative but omitted some as well. Passage of this compromise legislation consigns the Healthy Forests Initiative per se to the past tense, but it's still important to dissect this former initiative for three reasons. One, many of its features did make it into the Healthy Forests Restoration Act. Two, the Healthy Forests Initiative provides an instructive example of the White House's streamlining efforts. Three, examining the life of the initiative reveals the direction in which the Administration would like to take forest policy—and, as members of the branch of government that turns laws into reality, the President and his appointees still have plenty of power to determine what happens out in the woods. As the provisions of this act get translated into on-the-ground actions, many of the controversial elements of the initiative will likely surface again.

For example, the act only partly settles one of the most contentious parts of the debate over fire policy: it's not just whether to thin and how to thin that generates the controversy, but where to thin. The President and his appointees justify their approach in large part as the best way to protect people and property from wildfire. They often evoke the terror and loss associated with the 2002 and 2003 fires that razed buildings and threatened towns. In a May 2003 Internet Q&A session with citizens, Interior Secretary Gale Norton said, "We give our highest priority to areas where homes are threatened." Yet the Administration does not, in fact, concentrate on protecting homes and people as much as many people think it should.

For example, the Administration and the Healthy Forests Restoration Act focused on federal lands, primarily national forests, and underplayed the fact that even if we bulldozed every acre of federal forest down to bedrock, it would provide only a modest amount of protection to communities. The critical area in which development and forest mingle, which I earlier labeled the Wildland-Urban Interface, is also known as the Community Protection Zone or the Red Zone. One widely recognized definition of this zone includes the community plus a half-mile buffer that has been thinned, mowed, cleared, and otherwise fireproofed. The Wilderness Society mapped the location of Community Protection Zones across the nation. They discovered several striking facts. For one thing, many of the zones are in the South and East, not just the

West, as is often assumed. Also, the total area of the zones—
11,782,095 acres (the size of Maryland and Massachusetts com-
bined) and rapidly counting—surprised people. But what really
raised eyebrows was the fact that a mere 15 percent of Community Protection Zones lies on or adjacent to federal forests.
Slightly more than 85 percent lies on or adjacent to private, state,
or other nonfederal forests. This means that thinning national
forests and other federal lands, regardless of the effectiveness of
thinning, will not help the vast majority of people and communities in Red Zones. The Wilderness Society study recommends that
we "get federal money to local communities, where the money
can be spent on planning and implementing locally based, collab-
orative, community-protection strategies." Many state and local
governments, conservation organizations, forest scientists, firefighters, and others second the motion.

The Healthy Forests Initiative, however, would have given only
minimal support for people and towns in that 85 percent of the
interface that isn't on or next to federal property, and the new legislation doesn't seem to do much better. "Unless you're providing
people the resources or allowing federal resources to be spent to
treat those lands, you're not getting the job done," says Marty
Hayden, legislative director of Earthjustice, a nonprofit environmental law firm. An alternative wildfire plan, proposed by Representatives George Miller (D-CA) and Peter DeFazio (D-OR),
offered significant direct federal aid to private landowners to protect their properties from fire, but the Administration and the
Republican-controlled House did not give the Miller/DeFazio bill
the time of day. In his May 20, 2003, speech about the Healthy
Forests Initiative, the President said, "The communities from
Georgia to California that are at significant risk for those fires
need our help. And today we pledge it, we pledge our help." But
his words ring hollow for all those communities in the nonfederal
portion of the Red Zone.

Even those communities that are neighbors to federal forests haven't been getting the amount of help from the Administration that the President's pledge suggests; a great deal of funding for hazardous fuel reduction has been going to projects outside the interface. That amount should rise under the Healthy Forests Restoration Act, which declares that at least half the funding should be spent in the Community Protection Zone. Yet many politicians, academics, environmentalists, and people who live in the Red Zone think the amount that goes to the interface should be raised considerably, to the 70 to 85 percent range.

Though the government does not gather much information about mechanical thinning projects, anecdotal information indicates that at least some and perhaps much thinning is occurring outside the Red Zone in the backcountry, where timber companies can find bigger trees and bigger profits. Some argue that these backcountry projects fireproof the forest so that fires can't start in the wilds and spread into communities, but this justification is, well, thin. As noted, thinning may actually make matters worse in some forest types, and cutting trees big enough to be commercially valuable likely increases fire danger in any forest system. Also, mechanical thinning is very costly and, in some places, impractical due to the terrain, so it would be prohibitively expensive (and ecologically destructive) to thin enough of the backcountry to provide a significant fire protection benefit. Besides, the Forest Service's own studies show that the best way to protect the Red Zone is to do treatments there. Homeowners should thin or clear the trees and undergrowth within 100–200 feet of their houses, landscape with fires in mind, build homes out of less flammable materials, and use common sense, such as removing dead leaves from the roof and mowing tall grass around the house. But this and similar work in the Community Protection Zones doesn't come cheap; it would probably cost about $18 billion to mechanically thin all the nation's Red Zones. Considering that the federal budget for fuel reduction projects has been running about $400 million a year, anyone who honestly makes community protection the highest priority would be directing most of the money to the Wildland-Urban Interface. The Healthy Forests Restoration Act authorizes an annual expenditure of $760 million, which is officially what the Administration has requested in the President's proposed FY 2005 budget. But it reaches $760 million via some accounting magic—the actual amount is $200 million to $300 million less.

Perhaps we should expand the definition of "community protection." Wallace Covington, a Professor of Forest Ecology at Northern Arizona University and Director of the university's Ecological Restoration Institute, makes the point that it's somewhat artificial to separate communities and the Red Zone from the larger forest system in which they are embedded. "Communities are in the forest because they are emotionally, economically, and socially linked and dependent on the forest," he said during Congressional testimony in 2002. "When we consider the areas that need immediate treatment we should consider the human community 'impact area.'" Covington and others point to community watersheds, as well as forest recreation sites, such as ski areas, hiking trails, and resorts that are important to a community's economy and culture.

However, Covington's approach has an Achilles' heel: money. If there isn't enough money in the federal fuel reduction budget to treat the Red Zone in a timely fashion, where would the funding for all those outlying areas come from? Municipal budgets couldn't begin to come up with the billions of dollars that would be required. States have been putting significant money into fire protection, but these days most states have budgets that are on life support and they can't come close to managing the job on their own. Individuals in the interface are doing well just to deal with their own properties and won't be heading into the watershed with a chain saw anytime soon. And the White House doesn't seem inclined to increase the federal contribution. Undersecretary Rey states that he will resist handing out more money for fire protection until he's confident that the money will be wisely spent. "Wisely spent" is streamlining code. It means, as Rey made clear, that he believes that environmental regulations need to be trimmed before funding levels rise so that we don't spend too much money on scientific reviews, citizen appeals, and other processes that he considers unnecessary. The one party that could benefit from insufficient funding for interface treatments is the timber industry; it could bolster its case to do the thinning with the proviso that it's allowed to make a profit by logging big trees outside the Red Zone.

The Administration's low-budget approach does not bode well for Red Zone communities. Just ask the people of Summerhaven. In the summer of 2003 the Aspen Fire burned down hundreds of homes in that little town, which borders national forestland near Tucson, Arizona. According to the *Arizona Daily Star*, Summerhaven had asked the Forest Service in 2002 to create a quarter-mile buffer around the community, but the agency had replied it didn't have the $1 million needed to do the work.

But if there's not enough money for fuel reduction at this time, hard-nosed prioritizing will be necessary. Clearly, it's not appropriate to put scarce funding into commercial timber operations in the backcountry that happen to be labeled as fuel reduction efforts. But it also would be difficult to justify thinning in popular recreation areas ten miles from town, à la Covington, while overstocked forests still hover on the edge of the community. Covington's vision makes sense, but its full realization must wait until funding materializes. In the meantime, most observers think that we should be mainly protecting communities and that we should branch out to only the most crucial outlying areas, such as vital watersheds, key ecological areas, and a smattering of small sites (like ski areas) of surpassing economic value to communities.

———————

If the Administration is casting its gaze beyond the Community Protection Zones, just where is the Administration looking to thin—and log?

Everywhere.

Okay, that's a bit of an exaggeration, but not much. Just listen to the Administration chorus. In his May 20, 2003, speech, Bush said, "One hundred and ninety-five million acres are vulnerable to devastating forest fires." The front page of a White House paper on the Healthy Forests Initiative proclaimed, "Currently, 190 million acres of public land are at increased risk of catastrophic wild-fires." This exact phrase was delivered at a September 2002 Congressional hearing in testimony given by Mark Rey and Rebecca Watson, Assistant Secretary, Lands and Minerals Management, for the Department of the Interior. The front page of a White House fact sheet on the Healthy Forests Initiative said, "Currently, 190 million acres of public land and surrounding communities are at increased risk of extreme fires." In her May 20, 2003, Q&A, Secretary of the Interior Norton said, "An estimated 190 million acres of federal forests and rangelands face high risk of catastrophic fire." The thing is, the entire national forest system, which encompasses the bulk of America's public forests, consists of 191 million acres.

So, the President and other Administration officials maintain that pretty much all our national forests are in dire straits and desperately need to be thinned. In his August 22, 2002, speech introducing the Healthy Forests Initiative, Bush laid out the magnitude of the task: "Some will say, 'Well, there's thinning taking place,' and let me just put what's taking place in perspective to reality. At the rate in which we're thinning our forests it will take a century, one hundred years, to restore America's two hundred million acres of federal forestlands to healthy and safe conditions. That's too long, as far as I'm concerned." For his part, Rey said, "What we probably need to do is to effectively treat closer to ten million acres a year." Rey allows that they probably won't treat every one of those 190 to 200 million acres. For example, he says they won't thin or log in wilderness areas except in cases in which endangered species are at risk from fire. But Rey, too, asserts that all these 190 million acres need treatment. And he speaks of "playing the odds" in not prioritizing treatment of those forest types that burn infrequently, which implies that in time he'd like to get around to those lower priorities, too. This in turn implies that the Administration might encourage the thinning and logging of the vast majority of those 190 million acres.

My first clue as to the extreme inaccuracy of the Administration's figure of 190 million acres came from my own environs. I live in the Willamette Valley, in Oregon, in a town sandwiched between the Coast Range and the Cascade Range. Millions of acres of national forest lie nearby. Much of it is jungle-thick, all right—with ferns, rhododendrons, salmonberry, vine maple, and all the other native understory plants that belong there. This is not unnaturally dense for this neck of the woods. Furthermore, northwest Oregon is much wetter and cooler than the ponderosa pine and other dry-climate forests where the big fires hit in 2002—the forests that the Administration typically uses as its model for a "normal" forest. Forests in northwest Oregon don't experience cool, ground-hugging fires, as unmanaged dryland forests do. The same is true for the similarly wet forests on the west side of Washington and in the northwest corner of California. In general, it takes prolonged, extreme drought, the sort experienced maybe once every couple of centuries, to create the conditions for wildfires in these parts. And when the time finally comes for these forests to burn, they will—there's no practical way to stop them, short of heavily thinning and logging everywhere. Society just needs to protect the communities within these forests, preferably via Red Zone preparations rather than firefighting.

When wet forests finally dry out and burn, they tend to burn on a vast scale. This is fine from an ecological perspective, but if the area is populated, big fires can create problems for people, such as regional air pollution and a sudden, widespread loss of recreational opportunities all at once. In some places society needs to strike a compromise between ecological health and social needs. One possibility would be to create fuel breaks to try to prevent an enormous number of acres from burning in any one year. This point has been raised by Rey, who, unlike Bush and most others in the Administration, acknowledges the variety of forest types and the fact that thinning isn't appropriate for all of them. But Rey, too, misses or ignores the essential point: fire in most of these wetter forests would not be catastrophic. Such blazes might be big, depending on fuel breaks, and in patches they might be severe, but they wouldn't fit the definition of "catastrophic," meaning unnaturally big, hot fires that result from unnaturally overgrown conditions.

As the dozen forest scientists wrote in that September 24, 2002, letter to the President, "Indeed, many forests in the West do not require any treatment. These are forests that for thousands of years have burned at long intervals and only under drought conditions, and have been altered only minimally by twentieth-century fire suppression. These forests are still 'healthy' and thinning would only disturb them, not 'restore' them." In an attempt to determine how much forestland remains healthy and how much is dangerously overgrown and primed to burn unnaturally, in 2002 the Forest Service published a study of the condition of forests in the 15 western states, where most public forestlands are located. The report estimates that 28.5 million acres fall into what the researchers term "Class 3," which means their natural fire regimes are "significantly altered," they have high fuel loads, and they're too overgrown to safely use prescribed fire and should be treated by mechanical thinning. These Class 3 acres are the ones that would burn catastrophically. Many scientists question the methodology and results of this Forest Service study and think it overestimates the amount of forest that is unnaturally overgrown, but for the purposes of this discussion let's assume that the study's figures are correct.

That means we're down to less than 30 million acres of dangerously fire-prone forest, aside from what little such forest might exist on public lands beyond the West. That's a far cry from 190 million. But even the 28.5 million figure is less than it seems. For one thing, about a third of the acres studied by the researchers were on nonfederal lands. Christensen roughly estimates the actual amount of federal forest in imminent danger to be 15 to 20 million acres.

Let's say that 20 million acres of public forests are grossly overgrown due to human interference and are unnaturally susceptible to fire. Most of these are ponderosa pine and other relatively dry forests found in the Intermountain West, between the Rockies and the Cascades; in the Sierras; and in the Southwest. Are these then the places that we should thin or otherwise treat? Probably, though to some degree the answer depends on the details of how thinning and other activities would be carried out. But before scientists and managers wrestle too much with that problem society has another question it must answer: how much can we afford to treat?

"Mechanical thinning is an incredibly slow and expensive process," says Christensen. He estimates the cost at $1,000 to $2,000 per acre. One U.S. Forest Service estimate puts it at $1,685 an acre. Let's use the figure of $1,500 per acre. If we used the Administration's figure and thinned 190 million acres, it would cost $285 billion. Even if we use the far more realistic estimate of

20 million acres, that would still bear the unnerving price tag of $30 billion. Remember that the Administration's FY 2004 budget provided only about $400 million for fuel reduction. Worst of all, that outlandish expenditure on thinning would buy only temporary relief, because very quickly the brush and young trees would grow up again. Christensen warns that you can't think of forests as static. "We may make it fireproof for a year or two," he says, "but it will very quickly become fire-prone again." Even though maintaining thinned areas is cheaper than doing the initial work, especially when prescribed fire can be used, this still means we'd have to spend billions on maintenance every decade or so—or tens of billions, if we go with the White House's acreage estimates.

———

Consider some of the aspects of the Healthy Forests Initiative that we've discussed. Whether to thin. Where to thin. How to pay for thinning. Whether the federal government should provide more funding to states and locals so they can treat the 85 percent of the Community Protection Zones that fall outside federal jurisdiction. The accusation that some thinning operations actually are just commercial logging operations wearing lipstick. The fact that the Administration is demonizing big, severe fires, which are ecologically vital in many forests. The Administration's claim that 190 million acres of forest are at high risk of catastrophic wildfire.

In my view, the points of contention listed above—and by no means is it a comprehensive list—demonstrate that many provisions in the Healthy Forests Initiative fell onto a continuum that ranged from debatable to dubious. At the very least, I think anyone but the most biased observer would have to admit that the initiative's provisions were not inarguably correct and above questioning. Yet the Administration built its case for streamlining fuel reduction projects on the implicit premise that the initiative's approach to wildfire management was one of indisputable goodness. In its push to exclude these projects from scientific and public review and appeal, the White House in essence was saying that the Administration's versions of thinning and other fire protection treatments were so obviously right that they should largely have been exempt from the oversight provided by environmental laws and implemented without challenge.

This righteous point of view lies at the heart of the streamlining debate, whether dealing with fire policy, water pollution, endangered species, or any other issue. Scratch the outer layers of the debate and you'll find sincere efforts to improve the administrative processes that attempt to balance protection of the environment with the needs of natural resource businesses. But dig down to the core of the streamlining movement and you'll find people in government and industry who see nearly all administrative appeals and lawsuits as pointless, as obstacles designed to delay or even thwart plainly desirable projects that serve the public interest.

This point becomes even clearer when one considers a general observation about this Administration and streamlining. It's almost never about simplifying processes so that government, citizens, and public interest groups can more easily increase environmental protections. For example, some highly imperiled species of plants and animals have been languishing for years, even decades, as candidates for listing under the Endangered Species Act, but you don't see the White House working to streamline their addition to the list. On the contrary, the Administration is busy wrapping yet more red tape around the process in order to delay new listings. When this White House speaks of streamlining, it is talking about simplifying processes in ways that make it easier for industry to operate. So it's misleading when the Administration portrays streamlining as merely improving government processes for all concerned; it's a one-sided proposition.

The perspective of hard-core streamliners, which defines any contrary viewpoint as an impediment, emerges when advocates of streamlining tell horror stories about whirlwinds of red tape and blizzards of lawsuits. Remember, these anecdotes highlight actions by environmentalists that the streamliners have singled out to epitomize heinously obstructive behavior. A 2002 article about environmental reviews by Margaret Kriz in *National Journal,* the nonpartisan magazine that covers government and politics, sketches a classic case. According to Kriz, Bush officials were quick to cite as a horror story the effort to build a new and larger bridge across the St. Croix River in Stillwater, Minnesota. Currently cars and trucks must crowd across a narrow, 70-year-old bridge, sometimes causing traffic jams and, according to city officials and developers, hampering development. Yet, say the streamliners indignantly, despite the obvious need for a new bridge, for 30 years—30 years!— environmentalists have used the review process mandated by federal law to block construction. Clearly, assert the streamliners, the Stillwater Bridge exemplifies the kind of open-and-shut case that should be freed from cumbersome reviews of its environmental impact. (Under a 2002 executive order issued by Bush, the Department of Transportation has put the bridge on a short list of priority projects slated for rapid review and, presumably, rapid implementation.)

But one person's obstruction is another person's determined stand for conservation. As Kriz notes in her article, environmental groups claim the new bridge would harm wetlands, sully the bluffs along the St. Croix (a federally designated "wild and scenic river"), and foster urban sprawl. The National Park Service, which oversees wild and scenic rivers, has expressed some of the same concerns. You can almost hear the environmentalists indignantly noting that for 30 years—30 years!—developers and the local growth machine have used their deep pockets and political clout to keep trying to build this bridge. Clearly, the environmentalists would assert, the Stillwater Bridge exemplifies the kind of contentious case that should be subject to thorough reviews of its environmental impacts.

When proponents talk about streamlining they're often eyeing the National Environmental Policy Act (NEPA)—the Stillwater Bridge being a case in point. Passed by Congress in 1969 and signed into law by President Nixon in 1970, NEPA is the nation's keystone environmental statute and is often referred to—by its admirers—as the environment's Magna Carta. More than 80 countries have adopted similar laws.

The essence of NEPA is that it requires government agencies—and, by extension, business—to look before they leap. Prior to NEPA's passage, agencies authorized resource development and industry would implement the projects. Only later (if ever), after damage had been done, would anyone acknowledge and try to remedy the problems caused by, say, clear-cutting steep slopes or dumping toxic mine wastes into a river.

Under NEPA, agencies and industry, prior to acting, must study the possible environmental effects of projects that involve federal agencies, federal funding, or federal permits, and then make public the results of those studies. When proposed actions plainly won't cause significant harm, the agency can allow them to move forward without putting them under the NEPA magnifying glass. This exclusion generally is reserved for minor projects. Bigger or less predictable projects that may cause significant harm must undergo Environmental Assessments (EAs), which involve a thorough examination of the project's environmental outcomes. If the results of the EA aren't conclusive or indicate significant environmental damage, or if an even more in-depth study is mandated by regulation, the agency must conduct an Environmental Impact Statement (EIS). An EIS rigorously reviews all the relevant science, generates a menu of options and the environmental effects each would produce, and makes all this information public. However, a NEPA analysis itself does not give the thumbs-up or thumbs-down to a project; it simply provides the knowledge that policy makers and citizens need in order to pass judgment on proposals.

Ideally, knowing that NEPA awaits, businesses would make sure that a project is environmentally sound before they even propose it. If that ideal isn't achieved and the NEPA process reveals that undue environmental harm will occur, the agency and the business involved can use NEPA analysis to modify the project in ways that avoid that harm. If the proposed action isn't modified or isn't improved enough and will still cause significant environmental harm, then NEPA provides the information with which someone can challenge the project under other laws. For example, if an Environmental Impact Statement shows that a proposed real estate development will significantly degrade critical wetland habitat used by a bird on the endangered species list, then the project may be challenged via the Endangered Species Act.

In a minute we'll delve into the ways in which the Administration is attempting to streamline the use of NEPA as it applies to wildfire management. But first it's important to understand that streamlining has reached well beyond fire issues and that its proponents intend to take it even further. As in the Stillwater Bridge case, the President signed an executive order in 2002 to speed up NEPA reviews for federal bridge and highway projects. (This despite the testimony from the Transportation Department's Inspector General that delays usually stem from funding problems or sheer complexity rather than from any unreasonable burden imposed by NEPA.) The Administration has ordered the agencies to expedite NEPA reviews of oil and gas exploration. The White House also tried to exempt from NEPA a variety of commercial and military activities in the deeper parts of the ocean that still fall within U.S. jurisdiction, but a federal judge ruled that the act's environmental oversight applied all the way out to the 200-nautical-mile limit of the nation's Exclusive Economic Zone. More broadly, through the Council on Environmental Quality, the Administration convened a NEPA task force that may make far-reaching changes to this foundational law.

Streamlining reaches beyond NEPA, too. For example, the White House backed the Army Corps of Engineers' controversial plan to expedite issuing permits that allow developers and others to discharge fill or dredged material into wetlands and streams without giving public notice, taking public comment, or undergoing rigorous (or any) oversight by the Corps. John Studt, at the time the chief of the Corps' regulatory program, portrayed the new rules as changes that would improve environmental protection while speeding up development. In an e-mail to his staff he wrote, "The harder we work to expedite issuance of permits, the more we serve the Nation by moving the economy forward." However, a constellation of critics lambasted the plan, most notably the U.S. Fish and Wildlife Service, the Department of the Interior agency that is the federal government's premier advisor on matters of ecology. In a memo, the Service stated that the Corps lacked "sufficient scientific basis to claim" that the expedited permits would "cause only minimal impact on the nation's natural resources." Going further, Fish and Wildlife asserted that the new rules would result in "tremendous destruction of aquatic and terrestrial habitat." Unfortunately, Secretary of the Interior Gale Norton neglected to deliver the Service's report and it didn't see the light of day until after the Corps rendered its decision. Interior spokesman Mark Pfeifle said the failure to forward the report was inadvertent.

I could cite example after streamlining example, but even a comprehensive list—besides pummeling you into despair or putting you to sleep—wouldn't convey the full impact. You have to see the ways in which the Administration's many and varied relaxations of the rules interact. The subject we are about to plumb in depth—streamlining in the name of reducing hazardous fuels in our forests—leads into a representative example of the potent synergy being pursued by the White House. As you'll see, the Administration would like to exclude from environmental review and appeal a great many thinning/logging projects that are labeled as hazardous fuel treatments—some legitimately so and some not so legitimately. The environmental impact of these projects might get evaluated at a different stage, such as when a forest plan is revised. (A forest plan is the master document that guides everything that happens in a particular national forest.) But in 2002 the Administration proposed changing the rules so that forest plan revisions no longer had to be accompanied by an EIS. No worries, said the Administration, projects can still be evaluated on a case-by-case basis. Yet most of the projects are excluded from review because they've been labeled as hazardous fuel treatments, salvage operations, efforts to address insect infestations, and so on. At each stage these projects escape scientific and public scrutiny.

One would think that projects can at least be appealed, and thus held accountable, but that's no longer necessarily true. In 2003 the White House revoked the right to appeal many of them. The Forest Service used to guide logging and thinning by marking which trees were to be cut, but in 2003 the Administration did away with that accountability tool for some timber sales, so in those cases logging companies and their contractors pretty much can cut whatever they want within the boundaries of their sales. The White House even argues that a project signed off on by a cabinet secretary or undersecretary can be immune from appeals. If all these bits and pieces of streamlining came to pass—and some already have—there would be far fewer circumstances left in which agencies and industry would be required to do thorough environmental analysis or cases that citizens would be able to appeal.

Not surprisingly, the timber industry expressed approval of all these proposed changes. Environmentalists expressed no surprise at the timber industry's approval, noting that in numerous substantial ways the proposed changes are nearly identical to items on the wish list presented in 2000 in Senate testimony by Steven P. Quarles, a representative for the American Forest & Paper Association, an industry organization. Sally Collins, the Forest Service's Chief Operating Officer, told *The Washington Post* that any similarity is a coincidence. Also not surprising is the fact that 107 Democratic Representatives sent a disapproving letter to the President in which they accused the Administration of proposing a "planning rule that renders the public planning process virtually meaningless." It goes on to state, "The proposed rule . . . diminishes opportunities for public comment on and availability of documents, further obfuscating what guides the agency on forest planning." Referring to the Administration's intent to ease environmental oversight during the creation and revision of national forest management plans and to two other White House ideas to streamline forest protections, those 107 members of Congress wrote, "The cumulative effect of these proposals is a radical rewrite of national forest policy to the detriment of the public. In the name of 'healthy forests' and 'streamlining,' your Administration has proposed far-reaching and unjustified policy changes that deviate from the letter and spirit of laws governing forest management to create an opaque system marked by unbridled agency discretion to log our forests." Finally, there was one surprise: a letter from 11 Republican Representatives citing concern about the White House's plan to change forest management. The GOP members especially worried that the Administration's rules would cause a retreat from sound science. But the objections from members of his own party didn't deter the President any more than the Democratic complaints did, and he moved ahead with the proposed changes.

———

Many people in the conservation community worry that streamlining constitutes an end run around popular environmental laws that this politically sensitive Administration is afraid to tackle head-on in the spotlight of Congress. Others think that even sincere efforts to speed up NEPA analysis or other environmental reviews may result in environmental harm. However, many people in the corporate world are cheering the Administration. They say that all the analysis and public comment that NEPA and other laws require are expensive, time-consuming, and fraught with uncertainty, which makes it difficult for them to plan. The Administration is careful not to badmouth these laws, but when it speaks of "red tape" and "endless litigation," it's speaking largely of the processes generated by NEPA and company. The Administration says that it doesn't want to change these processes fundamentally, it simply wants to "improve" and "modernize" them—to streamline them.

Vague terms, such as "public input" and "modernize" convey general impressions but do little to clarify policy. Looking at concrete examples usually yields a clearer understanding, and in this case there's no better example than the Healthy Forests Initiative and its legislative spinoff, the now-defunct McInnis/Walden bill, which rattled around Congress during the summer of 2003.

The first thing people noticed about the treatment of the National Environmental Policy Act under McInnis/Walden was the gaping hole where NEPA's heart used to be. This bill would have enabled agencies to ignore all alternatives to their proposed action when they do an environmental analysis. Typically, NEPA reviews provide a number of alternatives, including no action, from which the agency can choose, and which provide the public with options to support or challenge. Council on Environmental Quality regulations state that the evaluation of alternatives lies at the "heart of the environmental impact statement" and provides "a clear basis for choice among options by the decision maker and the public." With an agency offering just one plan, "the best thing for the environment is obviously whatever the agency thinks," says Marty Hayden of Earthjustice sarcastically. "It's the agency's project and they don't need to look outside the box. When Congress passed NEPA, one of the big reasons for it was to take the blinders off agencies and make them look at alternative approaches and make them share those approaches with the public and take public comment on them."

In many cases the Healthy Forests Initiative recommended bypassing the rigorous scrutiny available under NEPA by providing what is known as a Categorical Exclusion (CE) for most fire management activities. Under NEPA, minor projects that have no significant environmental impact, such as building an outhouse in a national park or cutting roadside brush in a national forest, can be excluded from environmental review and appeals. The Administration has pushed for CE status for many hazardous fuel reduction projects, including thinning operations. It asserts that these projects are obviously beneficial and so similar to other fuels projects that have satisfied environmental reviews that there's no need for extensive study or a right to appeal by the public. As we've seen, this is far from proven.

As for granting CEs to proposed projects similar to fuel reductions projects that already have passed thorough environmental review, the idea has basic merit. "You're supposed to use Categorical Exclusions under NEPA when you're doing the same kind of activity over and over again on a routine basis where you can accurately predict the results," says Undersecretary Rey. Rey notes that since 1995 the U.S. Fish and Wildlife Service has been carrying out fuel reduction projects as CEs. The Administration compared these Fish and Wildlife projects with fuel projects conducted by the Forest Service and other agencies that had been subjected to Environmental Assessments. Rey says that most of the projects were comparable and he and the Administration concluded that in the future all such projects should be granted Categorical Exclusions. "If a project doesn't raise any red flags," he says, "there's no reason to grind your way through an environmental assessment and spend one hundred thousand dollars of taxpayers' money."

It's no doubt true that some treatment projects are similar enough that if you've studied one you've studied them all, but there's a danger in shoehorning too many projects into a single category. For example, I asked Tom Atzet, the Forest Service ecologist who took me on the Biscuit Fire tour, how much grouping for fuel reduction projects he'd recommend for the Siskiyou National Forest. He allowed that one probably could lump together projects slated for sites that were alike in terrain, microclimate, vegetation type, soil type, and other important ways and not conduct separate environmental reviews for each place. But he warned that forests harbor a great diversity of sites and that it would be easy to overdo lumping and end up neglecting important environmental studies. The Administration's plan could lump together far too many projects that have significant differences. This could lead to thinning in inappropriate places, such as sensitive plant habitat or in an animal migration corridor. More dangerous, it could give CEs to thinly disguised commercial logging sales and treatments that are being done in places that need no treatment. Add up all the problems and questions surrounding fuel treatment projects and it's clear that many fuels projects are prime candidates for NEPA review, so that potential environmental consequences can be determined, and for appeals under NEPA, in case the public disagrees with the ways in which the agencies and industry intend to address those potential consequences.

When they hear the word "appeals," most people think of an appeal of a lower court's decision to a higher court, but in the context of NEPA we're talking about administrative appeals. Here an agency, as part of the NEPA process, issues a decision document that describes in detail the actions that the proposed project will entail. If citizens object, they have 45 days to file a written appeal with that agency. The agency then has up to 65 days to vote up or down. If the agency decides that the appeal has merit, then the agency can take more time as it decides how to modify the project or even to drop it. A cornerstone of the NEPA process, the right to appeal gives the public a say without going to court. As U.S. District Court Judge Donald Molloy said of the right to appeal in a 2002 court case, "Ultimately its force is to allow the democratic process of participation in governmental decisions the full breadth and scope to which citizens are entitled in a participatory democracy."

The Administration acknowledges the importance of citizen participation, but it says that the process has gotten out of control, that environmental organizations are drowning agencies with meritless appeals that delay or even kill worthy projects. In particular, the White House and the timber industry often single out the frequent appeal of fuel reduction projects by environmentalists. Many observers, however, disagree. Hayden notes that even if the Forest Service really were beset by hordes of frivolous appeals, it wouldn't matter because "there's a 37-cent answer": write a letter denying the appeal. A frivolous appeal by definition has no merit, so the Forest Service can reject it out of hand. And it doesn't have to worry about being sued, because such a meritless complaint won't get anywhere in court.

Frustrated by what they claimed was an abuse of the appeals process by environmentalists, several of the Administration's staunch allies in Congress directed the General Accounting Office, Congress's investigative arm, to study the matter. The GAO's findings must have come as a bit of a shock for both the White House and the members of Congress who requested the study. The 2001 report discovered that of the 1,671 fuel reduction projects proposed by the Forest Service for FY 2001, only 20 got appealed—

just over 1 percent. And those 20 appeals came not only from conservation groups but from individuals, industry, and recreation organizations.

Displeased with the GAO report, the Forest Service slapped together its own study on appeals in a few days in August 2002. The report found that nearly half of 326 mechanical fuels decisions in 2001 and 2002 that were subject to appeal were appealed, but it was widely denounced by academics and environmentalists as at least sloppy and at worst biased. Researchers at Northern Arizona University, who are conducting the most encompassing, in-depth study ever of Forest Service appeals, concluded that the Forest Service study used incomplete and selective data. Though the Northern Arizona University study isn't finished as of this writing, some of its early findings bear mentioning. For example, it found that private individuals filed 35 percent of all Forest Service appeals, more than any other category of appellants. Environmental groups came in second, with most of their appeals coming from a few local and regional organizations. Furthermore, the data shows that the number of appeals has been declining. Many observers also note that factors other than appeals often contribute to delays, such as poor preparation of NEPA documentation and insufficient funding for the agencies conducting the analysis.

The Administration's claim that America is suffering from an epidemic of environmentalist appeals that hinder fire protection projects received another major blow in May 2003. Several members of Congress who share the White House's penchant for blaming fire problems on the litigiousness of conservation groups asked the GAO to do another report on appeals of fuel reduction projects. Claiming that the 2001 GAO report didn't approach the problem in the right way, the members of Congress directed the GAO to come at the issue from another angle. Nonetheless, the second report confirmed that appeals were not a significant source of delay. It found that the vast majority of such projects—76 percent—sailed through unappealed. Of the appeals, 79 percent got processed within the prescribed 90-day time frame.

Streamliners expressed two basic objections to these results. One, many of the projects included in the study were exempt from appeal by CEs and therefore shouldn't be counted as unappealed. This objection makes little sense, given that the point of the study and the subject of the debate is the number of fuel reduction projects that get held up by appeals—why they do or don't get held up seems irrelevant. Two, streamliners make the case that even delays of 90 days are too long during this forest fire crisis. This objection springs many leaks. The forest fire issue reached crisis levels years ago and will remain there for years to come—90 days here or there will have little influence.

Meanwhile, lost in the debate are the reasons for appeals. As noted earlier, doctrinaire streamliners treat all appeals as meritless obstacles, but many are legitimate challenges to dubious or even unlawful projects. Sometimes the two or three months spent considering an appeal result in a much better project or even the cancellation of a destructive project. This is hardly wasted time. In fact, in the case of dubious or unlawful projects, the blame for wasted time lies with the agency and company that proposed a harmful project in the first place.

In his 2002 ruling affirming the public's right to appeal logging plans, District Court Judge Donald Molloy writes, "It is presumptuous to believe that the agency's final decision has a perfection about it that would not be illuminated by interested comment, questioning, or requests for justification of propositions asserted in it. Congress wanted the opportunity for full democratic participation in Forest Service decision-making when it created a statutory right to an administrative appeal. Neither the Secretary of Agriculture, the Undersecretary of Agriculture, nor the Forest Service can take away a right the Congress granted or a process Congress demanded."

If appeals aren't the problem for which the Administration's solution is searching, perhaps lawsuits will serve. "There's just too many lawsuits, just endless litigation." So said the President in a speech about the Healthy Forests Initiative in 2002. Lawsuits do have the potential to be the bête noire that could justify radical streamlining, because citizens always can sue concerning a project they don't like, even if it's shielded from appeals by a Categorical Exclusion. Alas, this angle doesn't pan out either; the 2003 GAO report finds that only about 3 percent of fuel reduction projects were challenged in court, and many of these likely involved harmful projects that needed to be blocked or altered.

Why is the Administration working so hard to undermine the public's right to challenge federal forest policy and timber projects? The success of those challenges, says Andy Stahl, Executive Director of Forest Service Employees for Environmental Ethics. He notes that legal actions are the main reason that the timber industry is no longer clear-cutting an unsustainable 12 billion board feet a year, as it was during the 1980s. By alleging that litigation is the main reason that much-needed fire protection projects aren't moving forward, the Administration hopes to make it more difficult to challenge Forest Service projects of all sorts in the courts.

For the moment let's take the Administration's quest to streamline at face value and put aside the likelihood that in many cases streamlining deserves those quotation marks I tacked onto the word at the start of the chapter. And let's overlook the majority of projects, which, contrary to the claims of the White House, proceed at a reasonable rate that's consistent with thorough environmental review. That still leaves numerous proposed projects that do indeed drag on for too long before getting resolved. These include activities that most conservationists strongly support, such as fuel reduction efforts in the Community Protection Zone.

One can cite many reasons for the tie-ups—and I have mentioned some of them—but one major factor hasn't come up yet, and that's trust in the public. In many cases the Administration is trying to streamline citizens and public interest organizations out of environmental deliberations rather than trying to include them more. Administration officials often speak of collaboration, but in action that generally means cooperating with business and with only those locals who want to develop resources without being hindered by NEPA and other federal statutes. If the Administration were willing to broaden its perspective and honestly try to balance the viewpoints of business and all citizens, including the welfare of the general public, it might find that many of the entanglements that hamper some projects would unsnarl.

A walk in the woods above Ashland, Oregon, introduced me to an instructive example of successful collaboration that demonstrates the value of a good-faith NEPA process. The town of Ashland lies in the Siskiyou Mountains of southern Oregon, just a few dozen miles from the sites of the Biscuit and Squires Fires. On the hills bordering the town sprawls "the forest at Ashland's doorstep," as locals affectionately call the 15,000 acres of handsome woods, most of it old-growth, that constitute the town's watershed. Most of the watershed lies within the Ashland Ranger District of the Rogue River National Forest.

The watershed is important—as the main source of water for Ashland, as habitat for an exceptionally diverse array of plants and animals, as a wildlife corridor, as an accessible recreation area, as an essential part of Ashland's self-image, and as a key part of Ashland's Community Protection Zone. Not surprisingly, considering that the exceedingly valuable watershed was badly overgrown after a century of fire suppression and extra crispy from several years of drought, the folks at the Ashland District Ranger's office decided in 1996 to carry out a fuel reduction project in the watershed. They called it the HazRed Timber Sale Project, or HazRed for short. The first action would target some 8,000 trees larger than 20 inches in diameter, with more commercial logging to follow.

As one observer put it, "the community freaked out." One of the people accompanying me on my walk, Liz Crosson, outreach coordinator for the Klamath-Siskiyou Wildlands Center, phrased it less dramatically, simply noting that many community members, from the Chamber of Commerce to the hard-core environmentalists, opposed the Forest Service's plans. "It had a lot of commercial logging in it that we felt was detrimental to the health of the watershed," says Crosson. Logging rare old growth in a critically placed wildlife corridor in a town's watershed struck many citizens as a terrible idea. Though HazRed aimed to remove some small trees and brush, its emphasis on cutting many medium and big trees convinced locals that the project was something more than a genuine fuel reduction effort. Because the Forest Service had launched this project with little local consultation and because it was a project that most observers branded as clearly inappropriate for this watershed, it sparked what seemed destined to be a stereotypical tussle, the kind that usually leads to delays, appeals, and bitter lawsuits.

Thanks to NEPA and an enlightened district ranger, the citizens of Ashland and the Forest Service avoided that bruising and unproductive scenario. Using the knowledge and maps created by the assessment process under NEPA, locals tromped through the forest and became firsthand familiar with the details of the project. They saw the big trees—thousands of them—marked for cutting with a swipe of blue paint. "I think getting out there is what galvanized the community," said another of my walking companions, Joseph Vaile, staff biologist at the Klamath-Siskiyou Wildlands Center. Citizens deluged the Forest Service with negative comments.

At that point it could have turned into the all-too-common pitched battle but, largely thanks to that district ranger, conflict gradually became collaboration. "I think it's important to note," says Crosson, "that we had a district ranger [the main decision maker at the district level] at the time, Linda Duffy, who was extremely open and wanted to emphasize public input. She really helped facilitate a process that is what I think NEPA is truly meant to be." Seeing how unhappy the community was (and perhaps recognizing the dubious nature of the project), Duffy scrapped HazRed. She walked the project area with her staff and eventually they unmarked about 4,000 of the trees originally targeted for cutting. The community found this an improvement, but citizens still thought that it was inappropriate to have large-scale commercial logging in the watershed, even to create fuel breaks, so they filed an appeal under NEPA.

In response, Duffy decided to do a full-fledged Environmental Impact Statement—that most famous and, in streamlining circles, most despised of NEPA documents. But instead of viewing the EIS as an impediment to an unquestionably righteous project, she took the high road. She arranged a series of meetings with locals and ended up discussing the draft EIS with hundreds of them over a period of six months. A delay? Yes, but apparently she saw it as time well spent. She even allowed citizens to borrow keys to Forest Service gates so they could hike through the project area and see for themselves the changes encompassed by the new plan, which she named the Ashland Watershed Protection Project. But it was more than a change in name. It reflected many of the concerns of the people of Ashland and, though it still included some logging, it got their approval. And by most everyone's measure the project is much the better for having been subjected to this process. Sure, it took several years, but it wouldn't take nearly that long next time, not if the agency has learned from the experience and starts out on the right foot, trusting the public and sincerely working with them instead of against them.

As I hiked through the watershed with Vaile and Crosson I saw hundreds of brush piles; leftovers from some heavy-duty thinning. But few big trees had been cut and the forest looked great. Vaile and Smith were visibly pleased at the result of the first round of the fuel reduction treatment. They said that the brush piles will be cleared away at the earliest opportunity. With the forest thinned and the slash gone, the Forest Service can do some prescribed burning and at long last return fire to its watershed. If it hadn't been for NEPA, the Ashland watershed would not be enjoying such robust health.

Maybe the best way to "streamline" NEPA and other environmental laws would be to embrace them.

CHAPTER 3

The Best Offense
Is a Bad Defense

Nothing about the assortment of people gathered inside the courtroom on the afternoon of October 15, 2001, was out of the ordinary—just the usual mix of judges, lawyers, legal assistants, court staff, and onlookers. But it was noteworthy that a certain party had decided not to show up at the hearing.

People had assembled in the Ninth U.S. Circuit Court of Appeals in San Francisco to hear arguments regarding the appeal of a lower court's preliminary injunction that had stopped the Roadless Area Conservation Rule from taking effect. A policy announced by President Clinton on January 5, 2001, the Roadless Rule aimed to protect 58.5 million acres of unroaded national forestlands from road building, logging, and other forms of development. On January 8, 2001, timber giant Boise Cascade and several other plaintiffs had filed suit in a U.S. District Court in Idaho against the federal government regarding the Roadless Rule. The next day the state of Idaho had filed a similar lawsuit. After months of legal maneuvering, the District Court had issued a preliminary injunction, finding in favor of Boise Cascade and Idaho. That decision had been immediately appealed to the Ninth Circuit—but not by whom you'd think.

On that October afternoon in San Francisco the three judges on the Appeals Court panel sat at the front of the courtroom. Attorneys for Boise Cascade and the state of Idaho sat behind the table for the plaintiffs. However, the three chairs behind the defense table were not occupied by attorneys representing the original defendant, as one would have expected. That defendant, the U.S. government, was the certain party that had decided not to appeal the case. Instead this important appeal had fallen to conservation interests, represented in the Ninth Circuit courtroom by two lawyers from Earthjustice and a professor from Vermont Law School. Without them this matter would not have been properly adjudicated because the Bush Administration had chosen not to mount the wholehearted defense to which the Roadless Rule was entitled—including the filing of an appeal that held great promise.

Patrick Parenteau, the professor sitting at the defense table that day, notes that this is not how the American justice system is supposed to work. It is based on an adversarial approach. "The truth is found through the vigorous representation of opposing points of view," said Parenteau, slipping into law professor mode. "This is the foundation of our justice system. And that was missing here. The court was not getting the benefit of vigorous representation of opposing points of view in the [Roadless Rule] case."

The Department of Justice officially refused to discuss its reasons for not appealing the case and defending it in the Ninth Circuit, though a Justice Department attorney told me that "such decisions often are political." Critics think the reason the Administration didn't show up in San Francisco is simple: it dislikes the Roadless Rule and wishes it would go away because it interferes with the Administration's plans to open some of those public lands to development. But it doesn't want to oppose the rule openly because it's popular; a *Los Angeles Times* poll conducted before the Justice Department's no-show found that 58 percent of Americans supported the Roadless Rule. Even in the famously conservative Rocky Mountain states, where the effects of the rule would be most widely felt and many environmental protections rate lower than head lice, a majority favors the rule, according to the *Times* poll. Given such public support, how could the White House try to do away with the Roadless Rule without arousing public resistance and without being blamed for trying to do away with the Roadless Rule? Early on the Administration had contemplated a head-on attack. On the day he took office, Bush suspended the Roadless Rule. Observers thought he might try to get rid of it, but he backed off, apparently due to the negative reaction of Congress and the public. And not only did he back off, but in May 2001, the Administration promised to uphold the rule with only minor changes. So how does the Administration get to appear to keep its promise while still undermining the Roadless Rule? Simple: let Boise Cascade and the state of Idaho do the attacking in court and then make sure the Department of Justice doesn't put up much of a fight.

Not that Justice couldn't have put up a good fight. On the contrary, the evidence convincingly demonstrates that it would have won in the Ninth Circuit if it had tried. One of Boise Cascade and company's main arguments, for instance, was that implementing the Roadless Rule would cause "irreparable harm" to those 58.5 million roadless acres. The timber company's lawyers asserted that human intervention, especially fire suppression, had so altered these roadless forests that only active management—i.e., road-building and logging—could save them from ecological catastrophe. If this sounds familiar, it is because Boise Cascade's claims paralleled those made by the President in his Healthy Forests Initiative. Not surprisingly, Boise Cascade's arguments shared many of the same flaws as the Healthy Forests Initiative; in fact, this line of reasoning makes even less sense when discussing only roadless areas. By definition, most of these areas are largely untouched and have been subject to little of the human intervention that seemed to worry Boise Cascade. To argue that such natural areas need active management in order to remain healthy is to argue that forests that survived just fine for millennia before the advent of industrial forestry suddenly can't get along without our help. Occasionally, active management in roadless areas may be justified, such as in a dry, unnaturally overgrown forest where fire would threaten the survival of a population of endangered species or when the area is close to a town. But there was no need to kill the Roadless Rule to achieve these limited ends, especially considering that the Roadless Rule to some extent allowed for active management under such exceptional circumstances.

Boise Cascade also asserted that the rule was developed without adequate comment from interested parties, such as themselves. They wanted an extension in order to have more time to prepare their comments and they felt the maps showing the precise location of the proposed roadless areas were not provided soon enough and were not easily accessible. Environmentalists countered by noting that public comment was voluminous.

In the months following the October 1999 publication of the Clinton administration's Notice of Intent to prepare a Draft Environmental Impact Statement (DEIS), some 16,000 citizens attended 187 public meetings regarding the Roadless Rule. By May 2000, when the Forest Service published the DEIS, more than 500,000 comments had been received. After the release of the DEIS, the Forest Service held two more rounds of public meetings: about 230 at which the Forest Service explained the Roadless Rule and the DEIS and about 200 meetings at which they gathered oral and written comments from citizens. In addition, more than 1.1 million people sent written comments on the DEIS to the Forest Service. It was one of the largest expressions of public interest ever concerning an environmental policy—and the overwhelming majority of the comments favored the Roadless Rule.

All those supporters of the Roadless Rule would have been dismayed had they known how little the Administration did to defend the Roadless Rule; they would have been positively outraged at the times the Administration openly sided with Boise Cascade. In papers filed with the District Court in Idaho, the Department of Agriculture (USDA), which includes the Forest Service, agreed with the plaintiffs' criticism of the public comment process. Setting aside the fact that USDA's claims regarding the inadequacy of the public comment process were questionable, it is not common practice for the defense to argue the plaintiff's case. Communications not intended for the public made even clearer the Administration's desire to undo the Roadless Rule. In memos, faxes, and other internal documents brought to light in a Senate staff report prepared in October 2002, it became apparent that the White House never thoroughly explored the pros and cons of the Roadless Rule. These communications reveal that while supposedly reviewing the rule the Administration mostly discussed ways in which it could derail it without leaving any fingerprints.

Many current and former Forest Service personnel were disappointed by the White House's refusal to argue the merits of Boise Cascade's lawsuit. Among them was Mike Dombeck, Clinton's last Chief of the Forest Service. Head of the Forest Service when the Roadless Rule was created and a named defendant in the suit, Dombeck sent a letter to USDA Secretary Ann Veneman ruing the "lackadaisical and half-hearted" defense of the rule. He also criticized the Administration for not coming to him and to the Forest Service staffers who developed the Roadless Rule for help "in either fashioning the strategy to be used in defending against legal challenges or in developing the arguments presented in any of the filings made thus far."

The most damning evidence demonstrating that the Administration could have mounted a potent defense of the Roadless Rule surfaced because someone else did mount a potent defense. Though the Justice Department skipped the hearing at the Ninth Circuit Court of Appeals, those three lawyers representing environmental interests did take seats at the defense table. Earlier that year, when it had become apparent that the Administration had no intention of defending the Roadless Rule, the court had allowed environmentalists to intervene and argue the merits of the government's case. So they argued the merits—and they won. December 12, 2001, in a two-to-one opinion, the Court of Appeals sided with the defense and lifted the preliminary injunction that had stymied implementation of the Roadless Rule. However, as of this writing, the Roadless Rule still was in limbo due to other court challenges.

———

The Bush Administration has used such legal strategies so often that observers have coined a term for it: "sue and settle." Strictly speaking, the term alludes to cases in which an aggrieved party sues the federal government and the Administration, despite having a strong case, agrees to a sweetheart settlement that gives that party what it wants. But broadly speaking, the term also encompasses other forms of courtroom capitulation on the part of the government, such as simply mounting little or no defense, as in the case of the Roadless Rule, or not appealing a strong case to a higher court, again, as in the Roadless Rule.

Often the sue-and-settle approach has the disorienting effect of pitting the Administration against its own agencies and experts. Take the case of the California red-legged frog, once the Golden State's most abundant frog and likely the title character in Mark

Twain's short story, "The Celebrated Jumping Frog of Calaveras County." Largely a victim of urban sprawl and the concomitant draining of wetlands, the frog landed on the threatened list under the Endangered Species Act in 1996, by which time it had been eliminated from more than 70 percent of its historic range. In order to protect the frog, in March 2001 the U.S. Fish and Wild- life Service, which oversees endangered species matters, declared 4.1 million acres in California to be "critical habitat." This means that any company or person seeking to build on or otherwise de- velop a portion of that critical habitat must first convince Fish and Wildlife that the development won't drive the frog closer to extinc- tion or impede its recovery. Though critical habitat designation doesn't prevent development, many home builders detest it because it may cut into their profits by keeping them away from certain coveted wetlands, making them build fewer homes on a given piece of land, or forcing them to buy land elsewhere to mitigate the dam- age they do where they're building.

In June of that same year business interests led by the Home Builders Association of Northern California sued the government, largely on the basis that Fish and Wildlife had underestimated the economic impact of protecting the frog. (It's worth noting this argument, since opponents repeatedly and mistakenly criticize the Endangered Species Act for not taking economics into account. As the Home Builders' suit demonstrates, the act does indeed consider the economic costs of protecting species. It does so when critical habitat is designated—after which actual economic harm may occur—and not at the time a species is put on the list, which in itself carries no economic burden.) In 2002, after closed-door meetings between the Administration and the business interests that had brought the lawsuit (conservationist lawyers asked to be included but were refused), the Administration settled. It agreed to slash the amount of protected habitat from 4.1 million acres to

200,000 acres and those 200,000 acres were public lands that couldn't be developed anyway. Quoted in a story in the *San Jose Mercury News* before the Administration's deal with the plaintiffs, Fish and Wildlife spokesperson Pat Foulk had said, "We stand by our science. We don't think it's going to create the level of hardship the plaintiffs have indicated." But instead of defending its own agency's position, the White House thrust aside the studies and expertise of the Fish and Wildlife Service and sided with industry.

As Administration officials are quick to point out, other presidents have used settlements, both for and against environmental interests. But the current Bush Administration has carried the practice to new heights—or depths, depending on one's point of view. This White House uses sue-and-settle techniques more frequently than its predecessors, often to decide cases of immense magnitude, which wasn't common under past administrations. Vital environmental policy is being decided behind closed doors in settlements between the Administration and industry, policy that many critics think should be debated fairly and decided openly. Citing 11 cases that came up during the first 16 months of the Bush White House, a report from the office of Senator Charles Schumer (D-NY) says, "If these cases are representative of DOJ's [Department of Justice's] current approach on environmental laws, it sends a dangerous message to environmental opponents. It tells them that if they do not like an environmental law or regulation, rather than challenge it in a public legislative or regulatory forum, they should sue. The failure to appeal just the cases in this report alone leaves far-reaching decisions on the books that reinterpret core legal principles . . ."

The list of sue-and-settle cases collected by Schumer's office is one of several compilations that support the idea that the Bush White House sues and settles frequently and on matters of enormous consequence. Here's a handful of examples:

In the 1990s, in an effort to protect a wide range of sensitive Pacific Northwest plant and animal species, the Forest Service and BLM started conducting surveys of lands proposed for logging to make sure that timber operations would not unduly jeopardize these species. The day after Christmas in 2001, Douglas Timber Operators sued to eliminate the survey rule. Eventually an agency employee who disapproved of secrecy leaked the fact that the Administration was talking behind closed doors with the plaintiffs to settle the case. A lawyer representing several environmental groups that had intervened in the case asked to be included in the discussion, but was rebuffed. On the other hand, another party, which had intervened on behalf of the timber industry, was welcomed into the settlement talks. Soon those people invited to the table reached a settlement that required the Forest Service and BLM to examine the option of dropping the survey rule. Such "examinations" usually mean that change is coming. Sure enough, in May 2003, the Administration unveiled its proposal to generally discontinue the survey requirement.

On Earth Day 2001, Secretary of the Interior Gale Norton appealed to voters concerned about the environment by announcing that she would allow to proceed an already planned and supposedly finalized phaseout of snowmobiles in Yellowstone and Grand Teton National Parks. But just two months later, in settling a lawsuit brought by snowmobile manufacturers, the Administration agreed to stop the phaseout and conduct further study of the rule, per the request of the snowmobile interests. Further study despite the fact that the National Park Service had studied the issue for many years, held 22 hearings, and received hundreds of thousands of comments from citizens, more than 80 percent of whom favored banning those highly polluting, wildlife-disturbing machines from the two parks. The snowmobile manufacturers hired William Horn to provide some clout for their legal and lobbying campaign; now a high-profile lawyer, Horn was Interior Secretary

Gale Norton's boss when she worked at Interior during the Reagan administration. Horn arranged closed-door settlement talks between the manufacturers and Interior. In the end, the Administration imposed a few restrictions on snowmobiles but pretty much gave the manufacturers what they wanted; snowmobiles by the thousands would continue to throng Yellowstone during the winter and we would likely once again see fume-shrouded park rangers wearing respirators at the entry stations. Even the National Park Service's own final report on the issue states that phasing out snowmobiles is "the environmentally preferred alternative that preserves the parks in the best possible condition while allowing for current generations to experience and enjoy the parks." However, as this book went to press, a federal court rejected the Administration's policy, calling it "completely politically driven." In this case the Administration did feel motivated to mount an appeal, so the ultimate outcome remains uncertain.

In a practice called "mountaintop removal," coal mining companies, especially in West Virginia and Kentucky, blast the tops off mountains and dump the debris into the valleys below, burying streams and woods. Citizens sued to restrict mountaintop removal, but lost in Circuit Court. Bush's Department of Justice argued that the Circuit Court's decision was wrong, yet, illogically, asked the U.S. Supreme Court not to take the case on appeal. By not challenging the Circuit Court decision, the Administration not only lent support to mountaintop removal, but implicitly approved a far-reaching precedent that could bar citizens from suing state officials in federal court. This would be a serious setback, given that many state governments lack the means to deal effectively with big business and that state governments often are cozy with industry.

For years the state of Wyoming, looking out for its livestock interests, has demanded that the federal government vaccinate elk on the National Elk Refuge, fearing the elk would transmit a disease to cattle. The U.S. Fish and Wildlife Service refused. It doubted the safety and efficacy of the vaccine and figured its alternative approach was better. Wyoming disagreed and sued, arguing the broad point that states, not the federal government, have ultimate authority to manage wildlife on National Wildlife Refuges. Both the District Court and the Court of Appeals found against Wyoming, but a small part of the case survived and went back to the District Court. Told by the court to work it out, the Administration and Wyoming fashioned a settlement that overrides the expert opinions of refuge staff and allows the state to carry out its elk vaccination program.

These cases typify the Administration's record. Tellingly, among the many such cases I examined, the Administration always sued and settled in a way that favored industry. I didn't find a single example in which a matter dear to corporate interests was undercut by a weak defense (when a strong defense was available) or a pro-environment settlement that the Administration had negotiated in closed-door meetings attended only by environmentalists.

Perhaps more than any other issue, the designation of wilderness is being profoundly altered by the Administration's sue-and-settle machinations. This comes as no surprise when you consider the pro-development resumes of Bush himself, Vice President Cheney, and many of the President's appointees. Timber companies, real estate developers, and other business interests may chafe under regulations that restrict their activities, but they particularly abhor wilderness. These industries need land, and a wilderness designation goes beyond restricting them to shut them out almost entirely. Energy companies, ever popular with this Administration, have an especially big stake in preventing the establishment of additional wilderness. Oil and gas outfits covet BLM lands, and of the BLM's 264 million acres only about 6.5 million acres—about 2.5 percent—currently are protected as wilderness. But millions of additional acres have been identified as potential wilderness, and some of the White House's most problematic sue-and-settle actions have been aimed at not realizing that potential.

The settlement that may open the floodgates for development of the greatest amount of wilderness-quality lands involves a case in Utah. The Administration settled it on April 11, 2003, but to understand the case we must go back four decades. As farms, ranches, cities, suburbs, roads, power lines, canals, logging, mining, factories, ski areas, golf courses, and myriad other forms of development spread throughout the U.S., citizens in the middle of the twentieth century awakened to the fact that, outside Alaska, wild America was quickly vanishing. This realization led Congress to pass the Wilderness Act, in 1964. The act enabled Congress to formally confer wilderness status upon unspoiled federal lands, providing permanent protection from development of the sort listed above.

Sometimes, typically prompted by constituents, members of Congress introduce their own wilderness bills. Other times agencies, such as the National Park Service and the Forest Service, inventory their lands and recommend some areas for wilderness status. The recommendations get passed on to the appropriate secretary, who passes them on to the President, who in turn can pass them on to Congress for a final decision.

However, the Wilderness Act didn't explicitly order the BLM to join its brethren agencies in inventorying for wilderness-quality lands. And the BLM of the time, oriented to serve the needs of livestock and mining interests, didn't go out of its way to suggest setting wild places off-limits from development. Congress mended this hole in the fabric of wilderness protection in 1976, when it passed the Federal Land Policy and Management Act. Section 603 of the act instructed the BLM to search all its acres for places worthy of being designated as wilderness. Given the BLM's orientation toward resource extraction, Congress worried that the agency might drag its feet, so they added a deadline; the BLM had 15 years, until 1991, to complete the inventory and pass its recommendations to the President. The President in turn had until 1993 to forward his recommendations to Congress. Any lands they identified as likely candidates would be declared Wilderness Study Areas (WSAs), which meant that, until Congress decided their fate, they had to be protected from any development that could render them unsuitable for wilderness designation.

The BLM didn't exactly tackle the wilderness inventory with zeal. It eliminated many tracts from consideration with little thought to their wilderness potential, such as big chunks of the Southwest underlain by coal deposits. Even when it did look it sometimes pronounced as unsuitable lands that conservationists felt would make excellent wilderness. And, as Congress had feared, the BLM did indeed stall and delay; despite the marching orders from Congress, the agency straggled into 1991 without having completed the inventory. Controversy swirled around the process, especially in Utah.

In 1991, at the end of the 15 years, BLM's Utah office had identified only 3.2 million acres of WSAs—and that number would have been much smaller if not for environmentalist lawsuits. Many people believed that millions of additional acres deserved WSA protections and they set out to prove it. The Utah Wilderness Coalition conducted extensive surveys and in the mid-1990s came up with 2.5 million additional acres for a total of 5.7 million acres suitable for wilderness. Clinton's Secretary of the Interior, Bruce Babbitt, thought the coalition's findings merited attention and he directed the BLM to examine those lands to determine if they indeed rated WSA standing. This pushed the state of Utah over the edge and, before the coalition's claims could be explored, Utah sued.

In 1996 the case went before the U.S. District Court in Salt Lake City, where it was heard by a judge sympathetic to Utah's perspective—the former chief of staff for the notoriously antienvironmental senator from Utah, Orrin Hatch (R-UT). The judge agreed with the state of Utah and stopped the inventorying and the review of the coalition's findings. The judge ruled that Congress had given the BLM 15 years and no more to survey for wilderness. That decision not only undermined the surveys done by the coalition but, if allowed to stand, it would end forever the possibility of agencies identifying new areas with wilderness potential, even in lands acquired after 1991. The ruling also ignored the likelihood that the BLM hadn't done a thorough job of inventorying during those 15 years.

The law didn't seem to support the District Court's view that all identification of potential wilderness had to be completed by 1991. The government appealed and the Tenth Circuit Court took the case. In 1998 the Appeals Court reversed the District Court and threw out almost all of its case. The BLM then proceeded to check the coalition's inventory. The agency found that the coalition had been almost exactly right; the BLM identified an additional 2.6 million acres beyond their original figure of 3.2 million, for a total of 5.8 million—100,000 acres *more* than the coalition had found. So 5.8 million acres of BLM lands in Utah were tentatively protected.

One part of the state of Utah's suit survived. Not agreeing or disagreeing with Utah, the Appeals Court said that the state could pursue the portion of its lawsuit that challenged BLM's right to protectively manage lands identified in the inventory as having wilderness characteristics while deciding whether to designate them as WSAs. Apparently, the state of Utah didn't see much hope in

pursuing the matter, however, and let it lapse. The case disappeared until spring of 2003, when conservationists heard through
the grapevine that the state of Utah and the BLM were about to
settle the wilderness case. Earthjustice attorneys representing a
variety of environmental groups asked to participate in the settlement discussions. Because the case had far-reaching implications
and dealt with fundamental statutes, the environmentalists felt
that it should be discussed in public and not behind closed doors.
But the Administration and the state of Utah were not legally bound
to open the doors and they kept them firmly closed until April 11,
2003, when the settlement came out into the daylight.

How sweet it was, from Utah's point of view. The agreement
gave the state exactly what it had asked for in the only part of the
suit that the Appeals Court had allowed Utah to pursue; no longer
can the BLM protect the wilderness character of lands until their
eventual status is decided. "The settlement is an utter capitulation
to the state of Utah," said Jim Angell, one of the Earthjustice
lawyers working on the case. "There's nothing in this settlement
that Utah gave up."

But the Administration didn't stop there. "Utah got more than
it ever asked for in its original lawsuit and more than it could have
won," said Angell. "And it gives the state of Utah things the Tenth
Circuit had already held they couldn't possibly even pursue." For
example, despite the court's earlier ruling that Utah didn't have
the right to sue to stop inventories, the settlement surrendered the
authority of the BLM to inventory wilderness and create new
WSAs, except for those areas identified before 1993. "This was
not a conflict being resolved," said Angell of the settlement. "This
lawsuit really was a vehicle for a fundamental reinterpretation of
the law, a way to get to a place the Administration wanted to get
to." An example of where they wanted to get to arose as this book
went to press, when the BLM sold oil and gas leases in and around
Desolation Canyon—a prime expanse of wildland that almost

surely would have been protected had all the wilderness-quality land in Utah been set aside. Many more such sales are expected.

———————

The fact that settlements can be larded with policy provisions that stray from the original lawsuit is just one of the attractions of the sue-and-settle approach. Settlements also enable the Administration and the plaintiffs to keep everyone else in the dark while decisions are being hammered out. Often citizens and environmental groups don't hear about a settlement until it is done. Even when the public interest attorneys get wind of an impending settlement they're usually shut out of the process; not only does the Administration refuse to let them participate in the talks but in many cases the Administration won't provide documents or even reveal when it and the plaintiffs are meeting. When conservation groups seek documents under the Freedom of Information Act (FOIA), frequently the Administration stonewalls, ignoring the 20-day deadline because they know they'll get at most a slap on the wrist. Late in August 2003, the Wilderness Society and Earthjustice brought suit against the Department of the Interior, accusing it of illegally withholding documents regarding the settlement deal it had made behind closed doors. At the time of this writing, the Wilderness Society had been waiting for nearly eight months and had received an inadequate response from Interior. In other wilderness cases conservation groups likewise have been left empty-handed and have had to resort to lawsuits to try to get documents from the Interior Department concerning agreements made behind closed doors.

There's an even more basic reason that the Administration finds settlements attractive. "If these cases got litigated," said Angell, "industry would have little chance of winning on the merits of the claim. If they settle, and basically the government gives them what they want, it's harder to overturn." It's difficult for citizens and public interest groups to object to a settlement, as they have few levers. Courts have a strong inclination to approve settlements and move on to the rest of their crowded dockets. From the judges' point of view a settlement means that the two opposing parties have agreed to a solution, so why rock the boat? Sometimes courts will scrutinize a settlement to determine how well it serves the public interest and occasionally they'll disapprove a settlement on those grounds, but the default position is approval.

Settlements are especially unlikely to get overturned when industry challenges an environmentally friendly policy that is not required by law. The plan to banish snowmobiles from Yellowstone and Grand Teton National Parks provides a classic example. It came from the Clinton-era Park Service, not from a statute enacted by Congress. Common sense and ample science supported the ban on snowmobiles, so if the case had gone to court the government—or environmentalists intervening on the public's behalf—almost surely would have won. But when Bush came into office and arranged a settlement with the snowmobile manufacturers to lift the ban, those who supported the ban had less leverage than if they had been backed by legislation. After all, lifting the ban wasn't illegal, it was just a choice not to help the environment. Yellowstone may yet be free of snowmobiles, but only because the pre-Bush Park Service compiled such a strong body of evidence about the problems snowmobiles cause. As of this writing, federal judges in different jurisdictions are batting the case back and forth like a tennis ball and it's anybody's guess who will win.

Settlements also allow the Administration to tie the hands of its agencies. For instance, the BLM typically has broad discretion to manage some of its holdings as wilderness, but the Utah settlement severely limits that discretion. And the settlement not only limits the agency's discretion during this Administration—when the Bush White House and Bush's appointees are there anyway to make sure no wilderness gets designated—but it limits the discretion of the

BLM under future administrations. If a post-Bush administration directs the BLM to pursue wilderness in violation of the settlement, Utah can take them to court to enforce the settlement. A settlement resembles a binding contract and leaves little room for renegotiation or for revisiting the merits of the original case.

Take all the elements of the Utah settlement together and it could open millions of unspoiled acres to development. The prospects for wilderness dim further when you couple this settlement with other Administration sue-and-settle cases and with the widespread opposition to wilderness by members of Congress from the West. Most potential wilderness lies in the West and custom dictates that Congress not declare wilderness in a state unless its Congressional delegation approves. Earthjustice is appealing the Utah case, and its case seems sound, but in the meantime the Administration is opening these wild BLM lands to oil and gas exploration, mining, grazing, off-road vehicles, road-building, and other development that would degrade them and render them unsuitable for wilderness designation. As projects move off the drawing board and onto the ground, environmental groups will seek injunctions to try to stop the degradation until the appeal of the Utah case gets decided, but the volume of projects could overwhelm the overextended legal resources of the conservation community.

Many advocates of unfettered development insist that we already have enough wilderness in America. After all, Congress already has designated 662 wilderness areas encompassing 106 million acres. But a closer look at the numbers reveals a different story. A bit more than half of those protected wild acres sprawl across Alaska; only about 2 percent of the lower 48 has been designated wilderness. According to the Wilderness Society, 75 percent of the lower 48's 2 percent is scenic but often harsh and relatively unproductive desert and mountain country. And that 75 percent is not very diverse, representing only a small portion of the nation's ecoregions. In terms of both quantity and quality, then, America doesn't have much land left, especially biologically diverse land, that hasn't felt the touch of industrial society. The Wilderness Society calculates that only 200 million or fewer acres remain that may be suitable for wilderness, and that number is constantly dwindling. And the amount of untamed land will shrink rapidly if the Bush Administration succeeds in its anti-wilderness sue-and-settle campaign.

Does it matter if we never designate another acre of wilderness in the United States? Critics portray wilderness as nothing more than the playground of an elite minority of white-wine-sipping, Eddie Bauer–clad environmentalists. These critics would say that 106 million acres—even given the caveats noted above—are more than enough. Advocates would retort we don't have enough wilderness, that we need wilderness more than additional oil wells or outlet shopping malls. These advocates would state that the image of wilderness as a playground for the elite is a propaganda stereotype. They also would say that "playground" is a misleading word because the wilderness experience often goes beyond ordinary recreation and engages visitors on a more profound level. Hearing the howl of a wolf pierce the night while you're sleeping under the stars stirs primeval feelings, deeply meaningful feelings that you don't get from everyday outdoor pastimes like riding bikes or pitching horseshoes in the park. Advocates also would say that wild places have intrinsic worth apart from any service they provide for humankind.

Hardheaded critics who scoff at the notion of intrinsic worth or deeply meaningful primeval feelings may find the practical ecological value of wildlands and water more compelling. Entire books recently have been written expounding on this rapidly expanding body of knowledge, so I can't begin to do the topic justice in this space. But here's a short list of services provided by wilderness and other undeveloped and less developed areas: forests help stabilize the climate by sequestering carbon dioxide; wildernesses serve as reservoirs for genetic diversity of plants and animals; healthy estuaries serve as breeding and rearing waters for many commercial fish species; undeveloped lands maintain soil productivity; intact forests help control floods; and unspoiled wetlands help purify drinking water.

If ecological value doesn't sway those critics, perhaps the economic value of wilderness will. Let's examine outdoor recreation in a different light—as big business. All those hikers, kayakers, campers, anglers, climbers, backpackers, canoeists, and others who revel in the wilds spend a lot of money on gear and travel, and the people who revel in making profits by selling that gear and travel have come to realize that the existence of wilderness is important to their financial well-being. The Outdoor Industry Association (OIA) underscored this point in May 2003, just a month after the state of Utah and the Administration made their anti-wilderness deals. Twice a year, some 16,000 to 17,000 people in the outdoors business, most of them members of the OIA, gather in Salt Lake City for the Outdoor Retailer Show. But in May they threatened to move the show in order to put pressure on Utah to moderate its antagonism toward wilderness. This sent a tidal wave through the convention and visitor business in Salt Lake City, as the Outdoor Retailer Show brings in at least $24 million a year in direct visitor spending. That $24 million represents about 10 percent of the city's total convention business, making the show Salt Lake's single most important convention. OIA's displeasure definitely got the attention of Utah, though it remains to be seen whether wilderness will benefit.

Those holdouts who remain unconvinced that undeveloped lands have significant worth may want to consider an example that combines the spiritual, recreational, ecological, and economic benefits, and on a large scale. Surprisingly, America has a drinking problem. According to an article in *Orion* written by Gretchen C.

Daily and Katherine Ellison, at the start of this millennium some 36 million of our citizens were getting their drinking water from systems that didn't meet EPA standards and contaminated water was killing as many as 900 Americans a year and sickening about one million others. The problem mostly stemmed from deteriorating mechanical water systems.

Daily and Ellison cite the prime example of the New York City metropolitan area and water for the area's nearly ten million people. By the mid-1990s, the future looked dim for New York's drinking water and the city government was staring down the barrel of a $6 to $8 billion price tag for a new filtration plant plus $300 to $500 million a year in maintenance expenses. In a fit of imagination, it instead looked to the source of its water. For nearly a century New Yorkers had been getting exceptionally pure water from a 2,000-square-mile upstate watershed of mountains, wetlands, streams, and valley farms. The water was so clean that, unlike most large U.S. cities, New York never had needed to run it through a filtration plant. But an outbreak of subdivisions, roads, and second homes in the watershed and rising levels of chemicals in the runoff from farms and timber operations began contaminating that sweet water. But New York realized that by spending $1.5 billion to buy land and take other steps to protect the watershed from development, it could avoid building that painfully expensive filtration plant. Preventing overdevelopment in the watershed also preserved the area's spiritual, recreational, and ecological benefits. Even the most hardheaded wilderness critic would have to admit that the New York case was a good deal.

Often the wildcard in sue-and-settle cases, as in any litigation, is the judge. Though well-drawn federal environmental laws clearly lay out the intent of Congress, even the most scrupulous judges still have ample room to interpret because statutes typically eschew detail. The Clean Water Act, for instance, states that it applies to "waters of the United States"—a broad term that, according to Vermont Law School's Patrick Parenteau, could be construed to include or exclude 80 percent of U.S. waters. For these reasons, on-the-ground conservation and environmental health consequences sometimes depend at least in part on the nature of the person sitting on the bench.

A 2003 study of the National Environmental Policy Act (NEPA) showed that a large majority of the judges of all political colors rejected the Administration's anti-NEPA arguments, but judges appointed by Republican presidents were more likely than those appointed by Democratic presidents to agree with a point of view antagonistic to NEPA. This difference of opinion was dramatic in the courts of appeal, where panels of three judges hear appeals from lower courts. When a majority of the three judges owed their appointments to Republican presidents, the anti-NEPA arguments prevailed in 60 percent of the cases. When a majority came from Democratic presidents, the anti-NEPA arguments won only 11 percent of the time. Such partisan patterns have been confirmed by other studies.

The Bush Administration is emphatically aware of the pivotal role judges can play and has made a concerted effort to nominate candidates for federal court judgeships who share the President's political philosophy. However, confirmation hearings have featured relatively little public discussion of the views that those nominees hold on the environment, focusing instead on hot-button issues, such as abortion. Social liberals have accused the Administration of nominating only antiabortion candidates; the Administration has denied that it uses abortion as a litmus test. Whether judicial nominees' views on abortion are indeed a litmus test lies beyond the scope of this book, but there is one litmus test that the President usually employs, yet it goes largely unnoticed. Nearly all his nominees to the federal courts believe, often fervently, in curtailing the power of the federal government. This belief manifests itself as a distaste for regulation, including environmental regulation. And some of these nominees, like some of their like-minded brethren already sitting on the federal bench, appear to view cases through a lens distorted by that distaste.

William G. Myers III personifies the anti-federal-regulation nominees that Bush is shepherding toward lifetime positions as federal judges, though he's more rabid than most. Nominated late in 2003 to the Ninth Circuit Court of Appeals, which decides many important environmental cases, Myers's confirmation seemed far from assured as this book went to press. But his record indicates that the Ninth Circuit will be getting an extreme ideologue if the Senate does confirm him. For most of his career he has been an attorney and lobbyist for the livestock and mining industries. He is renowned for his inflammatory remarks, such as equating the federal government's management of public lands with "the tyrannical actions of King George in levying taxes [against the colonies]" and "the biggest disaster now facing ranchers is not nature, but a flood of regulations designed to turn the West into little more than a theme park." Appointed by Bush to his current position as the senior solicitor for the Interior Department, Myers has used his time there to try to implement his antiregulatory rhetoric, working to ease grazing restrictions on public lands, facilitate mountaintop mining, keep snowmobiles in Yellowstone, and lift the ban on importing endangered wild animals—dead or alive—as hunting trophies or commercial products. At the time of this writing, Myers had just emerged from one ethics investigation by the Interior Department's Inspector General and was still entangled in another. The Inspector General's office cleared Myers on charges that he'd violated his recusal agreement, though the investigation revealed that he had indeed met repeatedly with his former industry clients. The pending investigation involves charges that Myers gave special treatment to a high-profile rancher who allegedly is a chronic violator of federal grazing regulations.

Speaking of the pending nominees who have made dubious remarks, William Haynes II deserves special mention. Picked by Bush to sit on the Fourth Circuit Court of Appeals, Haynes currently serves as the Defense Department's top lawyer. In a 2002 case in which conservationists sued the Defense Department over the bombing of an island important to nesting migratory birds, Haynes and his defense team argued that nature lovers actually benefit when the bombs kill birds because it makes the surviving birds less common and "bird watchers get more enjoyment spotting a rare bird than they do spotting a common one." Does it surprise you that Haynes lost this case?

Americans who think that the federal government has an important role to play in regulating environmental protections should keep their eyes on the E. Barrett Prettyman Courthouse, near the Capitol in Washington, D.C. This building houses the U.S. Court of Appeals for the District of Columbia Circuit. Often characterized as the second-most important court in the nation, after the U.S. Supreme Court, it probably ranks ahead of the Supreme Court when it comes to environmental affairs. As Chris Mooney notes in a 2003 article in *The American Prospect*, Congress has granted the D.C. Circuit exclusive jurisdiction over numerous major environmental issues. In addition, many regulatory cases can be appealed either to the local Circuit Court or to the judges in the Prettyman Courthouse. Since the 1980s, when President Reagan stacked the D.C. Circuit with antiregulatory true believers, litigants looking to avoid environmental restrictions usually have chosen to go to the D.C. Circuit when possible. Retirements and Clinton appointments moderated the court somewhat, but as of mid-2003 it still was considered fairly hostile to regulation. Senator Charles Schumer (D-NY) called the D.C.

Circuit "the court of first resort for corporations that wanted to get relief from government actions." And, with few exceptions, this is where those cases get decided once and for all. Mooney cites the fact that in 2001, the D.C. Circuit heard 480 cases dealing with agency regulations yet the Supreme Court delivered opinions on only three appeals that came up from the D.C. Circuit. By the time this book comes out, Bush probably will have filled vacancies that existed at the time of this writing, most likely with judges whose presence will strengthen the D.C. Circuit's antiregulatory character.

The gravest danger to environmental protections posed by the D.C. Circuit and all the other federal courts lies not in particular decisions about particular regulations but in their undermining of the legal bedrock that supports many environmental laws. For instance, going against decades of mainstream legal thought, some current U.S. Supreme Court justices and a smattering of lower-court federal judges have questioned the reach of the Commerce Clause as the constitutional source of Congress's authority for many environmental laws. If Congress loses this authority, most pollution legislation would become the province of the states, which, as discussed earlier, probably would lead to an overall weakening of safeguards, especially in the long run. (In the short run, given the Administration's antienvironment perspective, many states probably would provide stronger protections than the federal government.)

The Fourth Circuit Court of Appeals provides a glimpse of what the future may hold if anti-federal forces come to dominate the judiciary. In West Virginia companies are mining coal by blasting the tops off mountains—a practice descriptively called "mountaintop removal." This crude method of mining wreaks havoc on the environment and local communities. The debris removed from the top of the mountains is dumped into the valleys, polluting streams and ruining wildlife habitat. Citizens sued the mining companies under the Clean Water Act and won in lower court. But a panel of three Fourth Circuit judges, all appointees of President Bush senior, reversed the decision despite the law's long-standing prohibition of such actions. The Fourth Circuit didn't even look at the merits of the case. The judges ruled that the mountaintop removal case was a state matter and that the West Virginia citizens didn't have the right to sue in federal court.

The attacks on the applicability of the Commerce Clause and similar efforts to erode the rationales that support most environmental legislation have been the work mainly of judges appointed by Presidents Reagan and Bush senior. Their success has been modest to date, but if Bush junior appoints enough like-minded judges, that success rate could rise quickly. Combine the President's current and impending judicial appointments, the Administration's sue-and-settle offensive, and other quiet courtroom stratagems and you have the ingredients of serious environmental setbacks. This is only compounded by a Congress led by vehement foes of the environment, such as House Majority Leader Tom DeLay and Chairman of the Senate Committee on the Environment and Public Works James Inhofe. At the moment the judicial branch provides the best chance for environmental protections. Pro-environment litigants have been winning high percentages of their cases, but now settlements often are depriving environmental advocates of the chance to try cases on their merits and an influx of antienvironment judges may lower the winning percentage among the cases that do get fairly tried. Increasingly, the scales of justice are being weighted against the environment.

CHAPTER 4

There Ought to Be a Law Enforcer

Bob Danko took pains not to badmouth Hatfield's Ferry, the nearby power plant. Southwest Pennsylvania is coal country, has been for generations, and the plant burns literal mountains of coal. That makes Hatfield's part of the King Coal culture that clings to people in these hills like smoke, even though there isn't all that much mining going on anymore—much of the coal powering Hatfield's Ferry comes from across the border, in West Virginia. Danko also supports the plant because of its employment opportunities; given the long-standing misery of the local economy, every family-wage job matters. Still, once he'd expressed his loyalties, Danko, simultaneously reluctant and eager, began telling me about some of the health problems that he attributes in part to the pollution coming from what is one of the dirtiest power plants in America.

Danko was sitting across from me at his kitchen table in Masontown, a municipality of some 4,000 on the east bank of the Monongahela River. Born a couple of miles from that kitchen, Danko serves his community as the county treasurer. Looking over Danko's right shoulder and out his kitchen window, I could see the twin smokestacks of Hatfield's Ferry, a literal stone's throw away if you have the arm of a major-league outfielder. Those looming towers and the enormous facility they crowned have been part of Masontown's landscape since 1969, when the plant was built on the "Mon," as locals call that workhorse river. Danko's wife, Marsha, joined us as the conversation turned to the downside of living under the influence of an old, coal-fired power plant, the kind of soot-belching industrial behemoth that people associate more with Dickensian England than with twenty-first-century America.

At first the Dankos spoke of relatively minor issues, such as the noisy emission releases in the middle of the night and the sticky residue that settles on their house, their cars, and anything else exposed to the airborne assault from the plant. But soon they talked about what really worried them, about the many and various illnesses that had inflicted their family, friends, and neighbors since the pollutants started billowing from the Hatfield's Ferry stacks. The Dankos readily acknowledged that not all of the pain and suffering could be pinned on the power plant, but they are convinced that Hatfield's Ferry deserves a significant portion of the blame.

Representatives of Hatfield's corporate parent, Allegheny Energy, say that their network of generating stations are in compliance with federal and state air pollution laws. They point out that their plants fall under the acid rain trading program, which allows energy companies to reduce acid rain–producing emissions anywhere in their system as long as they meet an overall quota. This overall cap on pollution levels was set pretty high, so Allegheny has managed to stay under the maximum by upgrading one of its West Virginia plants, where it cost the least to install modern control equipment. Allegheny also notes that even though the most effective pollution-control technology hasn't been used at Hatfield's, the plant's emissions aren't as bad as they once were.

However, the Allegheny representatives did not point out that these improvements have been minimal and those towering smokestacks at Hatfield's Ferry continue to release a toxic torrent into the air above Masontown and vicinity. For example, in 1990 Hatfield's emitted 163,432 tons of sulfur dioxide and by 2002 that figure had only dropped to 158,712 tons, a reduction of less than 3 percent. And during some of that 12-year span Hatfield's sulfur dioxide emissions were considerably higher, reaching 185,496 tons in 2001. Even the relatively low 2002 amount makes Hatfield's Ferry the second-dirtiest power plant in the nation in terms of sulfur dioxide. A study by the U.S. Public Interest Research Group calculated that 91 percent of those sulfur dioxide emissions could be cleaned up if Allegheny Energy installed scrubbers at Hatfield's.

After the Dankos had told me about the people they know who had gotten sick or died from illnesses that may have been caused or aggravated by air pollution from Hatfield's, we fell silent for a moment. Then Bob looked at me and said quietly, "There ought to be a law."

Actually, there is a law. And it should have cleaned up most old, coal-fired power plants by now. It just isn't being seriously enforced. Under the Bush Administration, many environmental laws aren't being adequately enforced, let alone vigorously enforced. During their nomination hearings, one Bush appointee after another swore that he or she would carry out the laws of the land, even the ones with which they disagree, but too often that has not been the case. Lax enforcement is another tactic that the White House uses to undercut popular environmental protections without having to openly attack them. The Administration knows that frontal assaults on valued environmental laws probably wouldn't succeed and certainly would carry a considerable political price.

For example, the White House isn't likely to try to repeal the Clean Water Act, one of our country's seminal environmental laws. Yet the Administration does little to make polluters obey the Act, according to a 2003 EPA study, as reported in *The Washington Post*. This internal EPA document reveals that to a significant degree 25 percent of major industrial facilities are not complying with the pollution requirements of the act. A couple of hundred of the facilities exceeded the limit for contaminating waterways by more than 1,000 percent. Yet such egregiously illegal behavior drew little response from the Administration. Even against facilities in "perpetual significant noncompliance" during the last two years, EPA took enforcement action only 32 percent of the time. And fewer than half the companies that EPA targeted ever paid fines. Besides, the fines averaged $6,000—chump change that won't deter future violations, and deterrence is a key to effective enforcement. Two studies done in 2002 by the U.S. Public Interest Research Group showed similar results.

J. P. Suarez, former Assistant Administrator for Enforcement and Compliance Assurance for the EPA (this Bush appointee left early in 2004 to become a Wal-Mart executive), told the *Post* that the agency intends to press the states to handle enforcement. In theory this is the way it often should work, but it's an open secret that many states do a poor job of monitoring industry and insisting on compliance. It's also well established that often the federal government, and especially the current Administration, likewise do a poor job of pressing the states. A 2001 audit by the U.S. Office of Inspector General found that when the feds stop pushing, many states slack off. The Administration possesses the ultimate power to enforce the Clean Water Act and many other environmental laws, but that authority does little good when it is not used.

It's also difficult to enforce the law if you don't have enough enforcers. The White House has cut the enforcement budget at EPA and other natural resource agencies. Soon after Bush took office the Administration moved to lop some 270 of the agency's enforcement positions. Congress restored some of those cuts, but in the next fiscal year the President's budget again called for drastic reductions, this time looking to ax about 200 additional enforcement jobs. Once more, Congress restored some of these crucial staffers, but despite the legislative branch's efforts some of Bush's proposed cutbacks took place and the number of enforcement personnel at EPA fell to its lowest level in recent years.

Further evidence of slack enforcement crops up in research compiled by the Environmental Integrity Project, a new nonprofit that watchdogs enforcement of U.S. environmental laws. EIP is headed by Eric Schaeffer, who served as EPA's Director of the Office of Regulatory Enforcement until 2002. His organization found that in fiscal year 2002—the first full fiscal year under Bush—the penalties leveled against polluters by EPA fell dramatically. In the three years prior to Bush the amount of money recovered from polluting companies in federal court averaged about $103 million annually. In 2002, under Bush, that figure dropped to $51 million. EIP's work and other studies further indicate that more often than in the past the current Administration has pursued minor violators and less often has pursued transgressions committed by Fortune 500 companies. As reported in *The Sacramento Bee* in July 2003, EPA agents say that before Bush came into power they targeted "the most significant and egregious violators." EPA officials challenge EIP's findings, but in these matters EPA's credibility has taken a tumble, as evidenced in the rest of that *Bee* article.

The story reports that the Bush EPA intentionally exaggerated the strength of its antipollution enforcement record. Suarez said that "the 674 enforcement cases initiated in 2002 were the highest ever." But the press release touting this supposed accomplishment did not reveal that 190 of the cases involved counterterrorism and not pollution. The *Bee* reports several other sleight-of-hand embellishments, as well. For instance, EPA agents said that high-level EPA officials pressured them to open weak cases just to fatten the agency's stats. One senior agent told the *Bee* that "we were encouraged to do that—find anything that's got any breath to it and put a case number on it. We were approaching the end of a fiscal year. They wanted to make it look like a good year." Mike Fisher, a lawyer in EPA's mid-Atlantic office, expressed his frustration in an e-mail acquired by the newspaper: "The press and the public deserve the truth about the [EPA's] Criminal Investigation Division's enforcement accomplishments." He referred to one of EPA's methods for inflating its record as "seriously misleading." EPA headquarters offers denials and excuses, but none is very convincing, especially as information in the *Bee* story counters nearly all of EPA's spin.

The Endangered Species Act ranks near the top of environmental laws that the Administration does little to enforce. This comes as no surprise. From top to bottom the President's environmental appointees dislike the ESA. In fact, in their pre-Administration jobs many current Bush officials worked to dismantle it. Interior Secretary Gale Norton, for example, whose agency is the primary enforcer of the Act, has a long history of antipathy to this keystone statute. In 1995, when she was Attorney General of Colorado, Norton even argued against the ESA in the U.S. Supreme Court. She attempted to strike at one of the pillars of the law by claiming that habitat destruction that harms endangered species isn't prohibited by the ESA. The Supreme Court did not agree with her.

Running counter to the prevailing hostility of Bush officials, an overwhelming number of Americans approve of the Endangered Species Act. A 2002 survey found that 78 percent wanted the government to maintain a strong ESA and 91 percent supported vigorous enforcement of laws that protect wildlife habitat. Such poll numbers motivate the Administration to try to skirt the ESA through limp enforcement rather than confronting it.

Consider the representative case of the manatee, the beloved "sea cow" found along Florida's coast. In this instance, the Interior Department did not enforce a deadline for proposing a new array of actions to protect these marine creatures, whose numbers have dropped to only about 3,000. Instead, the Administration is instituting guidelines that allow more development in manatee habitat and that don't include the needed measures, such as establishing speed zones for watercraft. (Many manatees are killed when struck by boats—95 in 2002.) Under a court settlement, Interior agreed to establish protected areas for the manatees, but it didn't do it. Instead, the Administration asked the judge to revoke or delay the settlement. The judge declined, the Administration appealed, and then the judge threatened to cite Norton and other officials with contempt of court for not enforcing the settlement agreement.

The Administration often uses underfunding to avoid implementing portions of the Endangered Species Act, as evidenced by the way the Department of the Interior is starving the budget for establishing critical habitat for listed animals and plants. Forced by court orders, the Interior Department (whose political appointees frequently and publicly bad-mouth the critical habitat provisions of the ESA) has allocated the legal minimum for critical habitat; anything less would likely result in Interior Secretary Norton being cited for contempt of court. But the agency has made no effort to get enough money to fully fund critical habitat needs, which are estimated to be more than ten times the amount requested by Interior. And it's not just ESA enforcement that suffers from chronic underfunding; the Administration is reducing the budgets of many enforcement programs that it doesn't like. The landmark environmental laws that most Americans cherish are losing their muscle due to a lack of exercise.

———————

Before going to southwestern Pennsylvania I'd been in Washington, D.C., walking the corridors of power. I'd talked with many people in government about environmental laws, about the regulations meant to implement those statutes, and about the politics that suffuse the environmental policy landscape. Sometimes as we discussed the fine print of regulations or theories about harnessing the market to serve the environment, I felt the people and places that need protection fading into abstractions. Perhaps that's partly because few policy makers live next to a toxic-laden Superfund site or get out to see river valleys buried under mining waste or are present at dams when their turbines chew up thousands of migrating salmon.

I doubt that many of the people in the Administration who decide whether and how vigorously to enforce environmental laws realize that some of the electricity that illuminates Washington, D.C.—even the White House—comes from dirty power plants like Hatfield's Ferry. And I'm sure that few if any of them have visited with the citizens in places like Masontown and vicinity, whose health and welfare subsidize the cost of that electricity and the profits made by the power plant's owners. Yet when the Administration decides to hamstring enforcement of laws, real people and actual places suffer. Electric power may flow from generators in heartland regions like southwestern Pennsylvania to Washington, D.C., but an even greater power flows in the opposite direction, and sometimes that power is used to thwart the law rather than enforce it.

The morning after leaving Washington I stood beneath rows of power lines, just a few hundred yards from where they emerged from the Hatfield's Ferry power plant. The loud hissing and snapping of the thick cables gave me the impulse to duck, even though the lines stretched across the blue sky perhaps 100 feet overhead. I'd been taken there by Farley Toothman, my guide for the morning. Toothman, whose family has lived in the area for several generations, is a tall, square-jawed man in his late forties who used to work as a coal miner but later became a lawyer. When we spoke he was in his eighth year as a member of the Board of Commissioners for Greene County.

Also in our party were Lisa Marcucci, a resident of a county to the north and a leading voice in citizen protests against two old, coal-fired power plants in her area; Marcucci's father, Vic Graves; and Chris Gardner, an assistant to Toothman. As we stood beneath the wires and gazed at the plant, everyone talked about the corrosive nature of some of the pollutants that spew from the smokestacks and settle on the surrounding area. Marcucci said that she'd read a BMW manual that advises owners to maintain the finishes on their cars by protecting their Beamers from air pollution, singling out fly ash, a by-product of old coal-burners like Hatfield's Ferry. "If you work down there," Toothman added, "the company will pay to repaint your car once in a while and they'll wash your car for free in their truck wash anytime. Now lungs they don't do anything about." An Allegheny Energy representative told me that fly ash has been drastically reduced in the last few years since Hatfield's installed electrostatic precipitators at the plant. I phoned some locals to get their opinions and each of them said there seemed to be as much fly ash as ever coating their cars, lawns, and houses. As she was talking to me, Marsha Danko looked out her window and said that fly ash was pouring out of the Hatfield's smokestacks as we spoke.

Before we'd met up with the others and driven to the source of all that power and pollution, Toothman had taken me through the western reaches of Greene County. Driving fast and talking faster, the energetic commissioner provided a running commentary on the sights out our windshield and background information about his county and its pollution issues. He said he'd been elected on an economic development platform, but he'd quickly realized that "one of the most important things that impacts our ability to do economic development are the things that environmental problems are doing to the people of Greene County." He said that the incidence of cancer and asthma among the 40,000 inhabitants of the county is way above the national average. And while asthma pales in comparison with cancer, it's not a minor matter. "Superintendents say that the single most important thing affecting their ability to educate kids in our communities is asthma, because they miss so much school," said Toothman. Regarding pollution in general in Greene County, he added, "This is a social justice issue, because Greene County is the poorest county in the commonwealth of Pennsylvania. We're obviously an easy target for dumping everything."

After Toothman and I had joined the others and the five of us had toured some more, he headed off to another engagement. The rest of us lunched at a café in downtown Carmichaels, a town of just over 500 people about four as-the-soot-flies miles from Hatfield's Ferry. After lunch, we walked a block down to the Borough Building. Marcucci had arranged a meeting with several longtime residents of the area. She said that when word got around that I was coming to southwestern Pennsylvania to talk with people about some of the health issues related to the power plant, a number of people volunteered to get together with me, including the three women I met that day in the Borough Building. That surprised Marcucci, who said that typically folks in these parts don't open up to strangers. "They heard that someone was coming who wanted to listen to them and they want to talk," said Marcucci. "I think the suffering has reached a peak."

We sat in the modest building's main room, a plain, slightly cluttered place about the size of a large living room. Photos, presumably of community people and events, and several American flags adorned the walls. We sat in folding chairs around a table and a desk. The three women who came to share their experiences were in their sixties and seventies and had lived in these parts for all or most of their lives. They were Mary Lewis, Charlotte O'Rourke, and Ruth Enci.

Lewis, O'Rourke, Enci, and Marcucci are well aware that not every death and illness that occurs in their area can be attributed to pollution. And they know that of the deaths and illnesses that do stem from pollution, not all can be blamed on air pollution. And they agree that of the health problems caused by air pollution, not all can be laid at the doorstep of Hatfield's Ferry or the old, coal-fired power plants in Ohio, West Virginia, and elsewhere whose emissions drift into Pennsylvania. But they suspect that far too many deaths and illnesses are connected to what comes out of those smokestacks.

After introductions and some small talk, Lewis plunged into the matter at hand. She explained that she and her husband, Bill, had been living outside the area over which the toxic plume from Hatfield's Ferry usually drifted. But in September 1993 they had moved to a farm close to the plant. By January 1994, Bill had such severe respiratory problems that he went to the hospital, "and he's been on a breathing machine every night since," said Lewis. "Before moving to the farm he was healthy as a horse." Lewis herself used to walk miles every day checking parking meters, but she has developed breathing problems and now finds it difficult to walk any distance. As if leafing through a family album of tragedies, Lewis continued, describing the serious ailments that had stricken several of her eight children.

O'Rourke, too, wanted to talk about her husband. Staring down at her hands, she began speaking but got choked up by the memory and had to stop. We waited in silence as she composed herself. Then, in a soft voice, she said, "He was a healthy man. He drove for the dairy for years. Never had a problem. All of a sudden he started complaining of back pain, and we found out that he had renal cell carcinoma. Renal cell carcinoma is not a real common kind of cancer." She recollected that a woman down the road got it, too, but quickly had the infected kidney taken out and survived. "My husband lived from August of that year until July of the following year. He became paralyzed in February. It's a very, very painful cancer and incurable unless they find it right away and remove it."

O'Rourke remembered the oncology ward where her husband had died, at a hospital in Pittsburgh. The ward was small and she had assumed that the few beds would be taken by people from Pittsburgh and other population centers. To her surprise, several of the other cancer patients had been people she knew, people who lived near her. "That's when I first realized something was going on," she said. "It struck me that there's something screwy going on here, with all those people from my small area of Masontown. It gives me goosebumps just to think about it." A little later O'Rourke reflected on how much her reaction to the news of cancer had changed over the decades. "It was rare for anybody to have cancer," she said. She remembered when she used to feel stunned whenever she heard about someone she knew having cancer, but she said it has become sadly routine. She added that often it was young people, not just the elderly, to which the others nodded in agreement.

At this point O'Rourke turned to me and handed me three sheets of paper. It was a list, she said. She and a friend of hers had sat down and compiled a grim ledger of people in Masontown who had died from cancer or who had cancer. "And that's only the beginning," she said. "We just thought of people we know. I think something must be going on here. There shouldn't be that many people having cancer here." I looked at the top page. Gene

Franks, Jr. Jim Girard. Lola Cappellini. Alphonso Ciarmella. David Mallick. Felicia Yanosik. Edna Kimmell. And on and on. Later I counted the names. There were 70. And how many people did they know in this town of 4,000? Perhaps a few hundred? That's a mind-boggling percentage. At our meeting Enci borrowed a sheet of paper from me and began writing her own list. And Toothman later told me of someone in his county who, like O'Rourke and her friend, had compiled a list of people she knew who had died of or had cancer, and that total reached 43.

"It's not only the cancer," said Enci, "but the high rate of MS [multiple sclerosis]. We have whole families with MS. It's not just one child but all of them." Lewis, O'Rourke, and Enci conferred regarding the timing of the MS explosion and decided that it has been during the last ten to fifteen years. Enci continued, "Almost every week you hear of someone getting MS or some other kind of muscular disease."

"Lupus, too," said Lewis and O'Rourke in near unison. "My daughter-in-law," said Lewis, "the one who works at the Dairy Queen, she was just diagnosed. My granddaughter that we raised just was diagnosed with lupus, too. She went from a size eighteen dress down to a six." This drew audible gasps from a couple of people. The three older women assured me that none of this was going on before Hatfield's Ferry went online.

"I think another big thing here and probably in Masontown is the high occurrence of asthma," said Enci. "On a day like today [high air pollution readings], in the afternoon so many senior citizens can't even be outside because they can't get a breath of air."

"I keep all of my doors and windows closed," said O'Rourke. "I never open them. I just don't want to breathe the air."

I mentioned Toothman's comment about kids missing school due to their asthma and all three women said oh, yes, so many children have it. I asked if asthma was common before the power plant was built.

"We didn't even know what asthma was," said Enci. Marcucci told us that in her kids' elementary school there's a whole cabinet filled with inhalers, about 100 of them, for all the kids who have asthma. Marcucci said she heard from an expert that the invisibly small particulates in the air pollution from the plant constitute the biggest danger. "They lodge the deepest in the lungs," said Marcucci. "And once they're in your lungs they never go away. So I worry about my two little boys, age ten and six. They're breathing these fine particulates and they have asthma now. Is that telling me that they're going to be candidates for worse disease later because they're reacting so young, and those particulates are in their lungs and staying there for all their lives?"

Despite her fears, Marcucci expressed a desire to accommodate the power plants. "I don't want to put the plants out of business. I mean, it would be foolhardy to think that we don't need electricity. But I'm so frustrated and angry that every advantage is given to industry and not even a consideration is given to people's health. The Constitution says equal protection under the law. Well, I don't think the people are getting equal protection." The others agreed with this point.

"It's people's livelihoods," said Enci. "And I like that little switch on the wall. But we shouldn't have to pay with our health."

The three women went on to discuss the plethora of friends and family who suffered from pneumonia, Alzheimer's, asthma in adults, and allergies. As the conversation wound down, it turned to pain of a different nature as they talked about what they feel has been an abuse of their trust. The three older women and Marcucci all said that for many years they'd believed the assurances from the power companies, the state environmental agency, and the EPA that the power plant pollution didn't present any undue health risks. But too many years of death and disease, unanswered questions, and lack of action have eroded their trust. "Their bottom line is money," said O'Rourke, a hard edge in her usually soft voice, "and the government is right there with them." The others nodded in agreement.

"I feel betrayed," said Marcucci. "And I feel betrayed not only by the industry, but I feel betrayed by the agencies, both at the federal and state level, that were put there to protect us. They turned their backs on us."

———————

Those four women, and people all over the nation, have good reason to feel betrayed. Marcucci is right when she says that they've been let down by both the corporations that own the dirty power plants and by the government agencies that oversee air pollution. But before we examine the Administration's poor enforcement of the law that would help these people, we should step back from the emotionally charged conversation in the Carmichaels Borough Building and look dispassionately at some of the facts regarding the health effects of air pollution from old, coal-fired power plants.

Very briefly, here's how a coal-fired power plant operates: it pumps water from a river (or some other body of water) into huge boilers that are sometimes called "teakettle" units; the water inside the teakettles is heated to a boil by burning coal; and the steam from the boiling water turns the turbines and generates electricity. It takes a stupendous amount of coal to keep the temperatures inside those boilers as high as 3,000 degrees. Some of the by-products from burning all that coal heads out the smokestacks, but if the utilities use the right technology many of the most harmful of those unwanted wastes can be intercepted and disposed of properly. Those by-products include sulfur dioxide, nitrogen oxides, mercury, carbon dioxide, and tiny bits of matter—what we might call "soot" and what scientists call "particulate matter." Particulate matter consists of a mixture of different compounds and pollutants that either spew into the air from the smokestacks or form in the atmosphere through chemical reactions, often involving the sulfur dioxide or nitrogen oxides.

All of these pollutants can damage human health, the environment, or both. Carbon dioxide is the largest contributor to global climate change, which is changing the fundamental nature of the planet. Mercury enters the food chain, especially by accumulating in fish, and threatens the health of people who eat contaminated fish. According to a 2000 report from the National Research Council of the National Academy of Sciences, in utero children are the most vulnerable; the report estimates that 60,000 babies a year are born with neurological difficulties caused by mercury that their mothers ingested by eating affected fish. Sulfur dioxide and nitrogen oxides are the key components of acid rain, which has damaged many forests and increased the acidity of many streams, lakes, and wetlands, inflicting tremendous damage on aquatic life.

Particulate matter is one of the worst offenders; Lisa Marcucci is right to be gravely concerned about the effects of the microscopic emissions on her kids. Scientists, too, worry most about the bits of soot that measure less than 2.5 microns in diameter, which is more than 100 times smaller than the width of a human hair. They call this "fine" particulate matter or "fine particles." These miniscule invaders—usually composed of sulfate—get sucked deep into the lungs, evading the natural defenses that intercept larger bits of soot. Once embedded way down in the lungs, these chemicals interfere with the absorption of oxygen by the lungs and can cause decreased function, illness, and even death. In a handout about particulate matter I saw a typo in which "sulfur dioxide" mistakenly was written "suffer dioxide." Whether a Freudian slip or a random error, it certainly suggests the misery inflicted by these invisible pollutants.

For decades polluting industries and their champions in government have asserted that air pollution from power plants did not cause undue harm to human health. This denial ran counter to a long history of commonsense concern about pollution that possibly dates back as far as fourteenth-century England, when King Edward II is said to have ordered the torture of subjects who sullied the air with coal smoke. In modern times some extreme instances of lethal pollution have dramatically demonstrated the dangers of air pollution. For a few days in 1948, in Donora, Pennsylvania (only a few dozen miles from Carmichaels and Masontown), pollution shrouded that town of 14,000, making half of them sick and killing perhaps 20. In 1952, in London, coal smoke settled onto the city for several days, killing some 2,400 people.

These mid-century disasters prompted authorities to try a traditional technique lyrically captured in the phrase "dilution is the solution to pollution." Utility owners extended their smokestacks to send their emissions sprawling across the landscape, assuming that they would disperse widely and prevent future catastrophes. This strategy indeed may have prevented another Donora, but soon scientists began seeing evidence that the dispersed pollution was killing and sickening people, just not in the concentrated way that occurred in Donora and London. Through the 1970s and 1980s research pointing the finger at air pollution and the byproducts of coal combustion mounted, but industry and its government friends continued to deny the problem. In the mid-1990s denial became exceedingly difficult after two major studies, one by Harvard and one by the American Cancer Society, found strong connections between particulate matter and significantly increased levels of mortality and cardiopulmonary disease. Studies rolling in from around the world showed similar results. Nonetheless, industry and its government supporters blasted these studies as "junk science" and sued to try to stop EPA from using this information to set tougher standards.

Finally, the issue was taken on by the Health Effects Institute (HEI), a nonprofit research center funded by both industry and the EPA that was created to help settle disputes over health science and related policy. HEI reanalyzed the Harvard and American Cancer Society studies and reported back in 2000 that the two studies and their conclusions were accurate. Using the information from these and other studies, Abt Associates, a highly regarded consulting firm, then produced a report that is the basis for much of the information presented here. John Spengler, Professor of Environmental Health at the Harvard School of Public Health and a leading authority on air pollution, called it "the most rigorous look to date at the contribution of air emissions from the nation's power plants to fine particle levels and the impact of those emissions on human health."

And that impact is staggering. Abt Associates found that particulates from power plants cut short the lives of more than 30,000 people a year in the U.S. Abt Associates say "cut short the lives" instead of "kill" because in some cases the victims are gravely ill from an unrelated condition and the pollution only shaves a few weeks or months off their lives. On the other end of the spectrum, however, particulates lead to the deaths of young adults and even children—people who are just starting their lives. This undercuts a long-standing industry position that air pollution deaths are insignificant because they were merely shortening by a few days the lives of the dying—"harvesting," industry called it.

Other studies also suggest that the estimate of 30,000 deaths annually may be an underestimate. For example, emerging but extensive research indicates that particulate levels common in many cities are linked to heart attacks. More research is needed, but apparently the fine particles can trigger fatal attacks by changing the cardiac rhythms of people with existing heart problems. But even 30,000 is a fearsome number. To put it in perspective, consider that the September 11, 2001, terrorist attacks killed a little more than 3,000 people; that drunk drivers kill about 16,000 people a year; and that about 17,000 people annually are the victims of homicide.

Research demonstrates that the nonlethal havoc wreaked by particulate matter from power plants is enormous. Even limited research estimates that about 20,000 people a year are hospitalized for respiratory and cardiovascular problems. Serious asthma attacks annually send about 7,000 gasping people to the emergency room. Asthma attacks that don't require hospitalization or emergency room treatment take the breath away from people about 600,000 times a year. Eighteen thousand six hundred cases of chronic bronchitis occur each year. More than 5 million days of work are lost. And about 26,300,000 people a year have their daily activities restricted in minor ways. If all these statistics are starting to feel unreal, just think back to the people of southwestern Pennsylvania.

Fine particles pose particular risks for children. For one thing, kids' respiratory systems are still developing so they don't have as much resistance to environmental insults as healthy adults do. Children also inhale about 50 percent more air in relation to their body weight than do adults. And apparently the younger they are the more vulnerable they are, so babies suffer most of all. Kids who breathe too much particulate matter typically get hit with more than the average number of childhood illnesses, but more worrisome is the risk that their lungs may never develop properly. Studies also have found that infants subjected to highly polluted air die from respiratory problems 40 percent more often than infants living outside pollution hot spots. These bad-air sites also correlate with a 26 percent increase in the risk for Sudden Infant Death Syndrome. The harm that fine particles inflict on children made me think of Charlotte O'Rourke. Near the end of our discussion in Carmichaels she said, "If I could save people . . . that's why I want to help. To help the children we've been talking about."

If you live in the Southeast, the southeastern part of the Midwest, or the southern part of the Northeast, you may want to check out the map of the United States in the Abt Associates report that shows which parts of the nation have the highest death rates from power plant air pollution. The red that symbolizes annual death rates in excess of 40 per 100,000 adults covers most of Kentucky, Tennessee, North Carolina, and West Virginia, and sizeable portions of Alabama, Georgia, Mississippi, South Carolina, Virginia, Ohio, Indiana, and Illinois—and the southwest corner of Pennsylvania. Pennsylvania is number one when it comes to annual deaths from power plant pollution—2,250—but Kentucky suffers from the highest death rate—44.1 per 100,000. The orange and yellow that signal death rates of 30 to 40 adults per 100,000 and 20 to 30, respectively, flare out a few hundred miles in all directions from that red core. The entire western half of the country plus a narrow northern band that stretches from Minnesota to Maine show on the map as a nice, healthy dark blue and sky blue, signifying death rates of 0 to 1 and 1 to 10, respectively. Why the colorfully distinct difference? The reason readily appears if on top of the death-rate map you lay a map showing the locations of old, coal-fired power plants, plus a swath to the east of the plants depicting the area to which the prevailing winds carry air pollution from the plants. The maps bear a revealingly close resemblance to each other.

According to 1998 figures, power plants account for 67 percent of all the sulfur dioxide and more than 25 percent of the nitrogen oxides emitted in the U.S. That's about 13 million tons of sulfur dioxide and 6 million tons of nitrogen oxides. And old, coal-fired plants put out the lion's share of the pollutants, including the particulates, that come from the nation's power plants. These antiquated facilities typically disgorge sulfur dioxide and nitrogen oxides at a rate four to ten times higher than that of new coal plants or old coal plants retrofitted with modern pollution controls.

As that last line reveals, I've been using the phrase "old, coal-fired power plant" loosely, and it's time to sharpen the definition.

When I say "old, coal-fired power plant" I'm referring to facilities that are indeed old (in the 30- to 50-year-old range as a rule), but I'm not referring to all coal-fired power plants of this advanced age. (The typical life span of these power plants is 35 to 40 years.) Some of these facilities have been retrofitted with the best available pollution-control technology, which typically reduces sulfur dioxide and nitrogen oxide emissions by more than 75 percent. Though these updated plants hardly measure up to solar or wind power in terms of pollution, they are far cleaner than the old, coal-fired facilities that have avoided upgrading. So, when I say "old, coal-fired power plant" I'm talking about the several hundred troglodyte facilities in the U.S. that haven't been brought up to date, though they would have been cleaned up some time ago if only the law had been enforced.

That law is the Clean Air Act, passed by Congress in 1970, and an amendment to the act called New Source Review (NSR). New Source Review in part required companies building new power plants and certain other facilities, such as oil refineries, to use the best available technology to control certain air pollutants. Because this aspect of NSR is fairly simple and easily enforced, and because installing effective control technologies is relatively inexpensive when they're included in plant designs from the beginning, companies generally complied with this part of the law. So, power plants constructed after 1970, even the coal-fired ones, generally emit significantly less pollution than pre-NSR plants. However, another New Source Review provision "grandfathered" old power plants, permitting them to postpone installing the best control technology and to temporarily continue polluting at their pre-Clean Air Act levels. Despite the health risks to the public, Congress didn't think it fair to demand instant compliance, so they set up NSR to allow the utilities to comply gradually—a classic balance between economic concerns and health and the environment.

Here's how New Source Review was supposed to work. After

two or three decades coal-fired power plants start wearing out, losing their generating capacity. This means that the vast majority of the grandfathered plants, most of which were built in the 1950s and 1960s, were degenerating during the 1980s and 1990s. Congress figured that as the plants experienced diminished capacity the utilities would either decide to decommission the aging facilities or renovate them to restore or even expand their lost capacity. When the plants underwent modifications that restored or expanded capacity, the result would be more pollution, or "new sources" of emissions—hence the name New Source Review. When these additional emissions rose above a small threshold level, NSR kicked in and required utilities to add the latest pollution-control technology. Not only did this approach enable the utilities to postpone and spread out spending the hundreds of millions of dollars that it costs to retrofit a major plant, but it let them install the new technology while the plant already was undergoing renovation, which is much cheaper than doing a retrofit in isolation.

With New Source Review in play, Congress calculated that after a decade, maybe two, nearly all of the old, coal-fired plants (and other polluting industrial facilities) would shut down or modernize and public health and the environment would be much the better for it. But things haven't worked out that way.

The old, coal-fired plants have turned out to be cash cows. They have fully capitalized their construction costs, so continuing to wring profits out of their paid-up old hides thrills managers and owners who otherwise are looking at spending maybe $1 billion to build a new plant. In addition, the major expense for the old plants is fuel, and coal is inexpensive. And because these elderly facilities haven't been forced to abide by pollution standards, they can burn the cheapest, high-sulfur coal, fattening profits even further. In addition to simply wanting to save money, the utilities that own old, coal-fired plants are fighting to retain their "pollution subsidy" because it helps them remain competitive in an electricity market that is swelling with excess capacity as new, efficient, and much cleaner gas-fired power plants come online.

That same competitive market belies one of the rationales that the Administration and the utilities use to fight New Source Review. They claim that the cost of pollution-control equipment would get passed on to consumers. But even the usually pro-utility Department of Energy found otherwise in a study in 2000. Their research showed that even if every coal-fired power plant larger than 25 megawatts installed the best available technology for sulfur dioxide and nitrogen oxides by 2010, the impact on ratepayers would be minimal. In the deregulated markets, competitive pressures would keep the price down, so it is the owners of the plants who would take most of the financial hit. This likely explains their fierce opposition to New Source Review.

Reluctant to put their cash cows out to pasture, many utilities have engaged in a great deal of repairing and replacing in order to keep those plants humming. If the EPA under President Reagan had wanted to enforce New Source Review, the agency could have made a strong case that those major repairs and replacements should have triggered NSR and compelled the utilities to install modern pollution controls. However, Reagan's EPA didn't enforce NSR, so the electric power industry didn't have to fight NSR and they simply ignored it for most of the 1980s.

Preliminary bouts over New Source Review took place in the late 1980s and early 1990s, but the main event didn't occur until the mid- and late-1990s. The slugfest revolved around the extent to which utilities could modify their old plants without NSR kicking in and mandating that they add new pollution-control technology. Following the appearance of New Source Review, EPA issued regulations stating that "routine maintenance, repair, and replacement" would not trigger NSR and compel the utilities to install modern pollution controls or forego the modifications. But anything more than minor work on the plant would initiate NSR requirements. EPA looked at the "nature, extent, purpose, frequency, and cost" of a project to determine whether it was routine maintenance. This was another compromise intended to make life easier for the industry without sacrificing the health and environmental benefits of NSR.

Many utilities returned the favor by developing an organized strategy to take advantage of the routine maintenance provision. They dubbed this strategy "life extension" or "life optimization." The idea was to milk an extra decade or two out of these aging plants by doing extensive repairs and replacements while avoiding NSR and the expensive pollution technology it required. Some utility employees spoke candidly about this strategy—at least, they did when they weren't addressing an environmental agency. In 1995, in front of the Public Utilities Commission of Ohio, for example, a plant manager for Ohio Power said: "The company has recognized for some years the benefits of extending or optimizing the lifetimes of several of its older coal-fired generating units . . . and has developed and begun to implement life-optimization programs to accomplish that objective. The life-optimization programs extend over several years, and require significant capital expenditures during those years. Without those expenditures, the units' lives could not be extended, and they would most likely achieve more traditional lifetimes, on the order of 35 to 40 years. As a direct result of the life-optimization programs, the company expects those units to achieve, instead, lifetimes on the order of 50 years for certain of those units and of 60 years for others."

Members of the utility industry even discussed ways to keep their intentions quiet. The minutes from a 1984 industry gathering reveal several ruses that power companies should employ, according to a consensus of the conference participants. They agreed that companies should call their projects "upgraded maintenance programs"; that they should "downplay the life extension aspects of these projects (and extended retirement dates) by referring to them as plant restoration (reliability/availability improvement projects)"; and that they should address these matters "at the state and local level and not elevate [them] to the status of a national environmental issue." (Meaning, I take it, that the conferees were advising companies not to approach EPA for a permit, because the agency might bring New Source Review to bear.)

Life extension projects do not sound like routine maintenance to me. Nor did they seem minor and ordinary to the utility employees and utility equipment vendors who have testified in various settings that these so-called routine maintenance projects were neither routine nor mere maintenance. Nor did these projects sound routine to EPA, which was reinvigorated under the Clinton administration and ready to do some enforcement. So, in 1996, EPA for the first time began seriously investigating potential NSR violations, and found them in droves. American Electric Power replaced 11 furnaces at its Tanners Creek plant, in Indiana, and called it routine maintenance. The Southern Company built brand-new units at two of its plants and called it routine maintenance. Allegedly, 18,000 tons of sulfur dioxide a year were spewing into the skies of Kentucky from American Electric Power's Big Sandy plant due to some modifications that the utility called—you guessed it—routine maintenance. New emissions exceeding 60 to 140 tons annually (depending on the pollutant) are supposed to initiate New Source Review.

EPA discovered hundreds of projects at old, coal-fired plants that should have been subject to New Source Review requirements. Awash in damning information, EPA finally set out to enforce the law. Starting in 1999 and continuing into 2000, EPA sent referrals to the Department of Justice to take action against nine utilities and 51 of their coal-fired plants, including some of the biggest power companies in the nation. Late in 1999, Justice joined with attorneys general from a number of northeastern states and filed enforcement actions against several companies whose plants are among the most flagrant violators. The legal battle was on.

The power industry has built its defense around the interpretation of "routine maintenance" and around what kind of modification should prompt New Source Review. This generally has proved feeble. Though it never got finalized, regulatory language drafted by EPA in 1994 equated "routine" with "minor." This clearly reflects Congressional intent, which is crucial in interpreting laws. In a case involving NSR, the U.S. Court of Appeals for the D.C. Circuit held that "the clear language of the statute unavoidably imposes these costs except for *de minimis* increases." This means that the act plainly states that when old power plants make physical changes or modifications they must install modern pollution control equipment, unless those changes are trivial and result in only minimal increases in emissions.

Many observers were astonished by the utility industry's brazenly self-serving interpretation of NSR requirements. "People like me and others at EPA looked at [the power companies] as if they were delusional," said John Walke, Director of Clean Air Programs for the conservation group Natural Resources Defense Council (NRDC) and an attorney at EPA prior to coming to NRDC, in 2000. " 'Are you insane?' we asked. 'The factors laid out couldn't possibly lead you to believe that these activities which you are undertaking, which cost tens of millions of dollars, and increase pollution by hundreds of thousands of tons, and have never before been undertaken, are routine maintenance.' " Eric Schaeffer, EPA's Director of the Office of Regulatory Enforcement at the time the NSR lawsuits got filed, makes the point, "Most of the projects our cases targeted involved big expansion projects that pushed emission increases many times over the limits allowed by law." In other words, though some projects to modify coal-burning power plants may indeed fall on the borderline between true routine maintenance and changes that should trigger New Source Review upgrades, the projects that EPA began prosecuting at the end of the Clinton administration involved some of the most blatant offenders, plants whose modifications crossed far over that borderline.

Lately industry has added a new element to its defense, asserting that neither the magnitude of the modification nor the increase in harmful emissions matters. The salient point, say the power companies, is whether those modifications raise the plant's capacity and emissions above the level of the plant's original maximums. Thus a doddering plant whose capacity and emissions have diminished over the years could undergo massive renovation that greatly increases both its capacity and the emissions generated by that restored capacity and still be exempt from New Source Review. This defense also lacks merit and has been largely rejected by courts.

In a landmark NSR case, a Federal Appeals Court writes that even though the "statutory scheme intends to 'grandfather' existing industries, the provisions concerning modifications indicate that this is not to constitute perpetual immunity . . ." "Perpetual immunity." This fine phrase captures the essence of the situation that Congress sought to avoid and that industry is trying to create. Not only did Congress legislate an end to power plant modifications that greatly increased pollution, but they intended for New Source Review to phase out or dramatically clean up old, coal-fired power plants. Congress didn't want these dirty holdovers to be around for decades, enjoying perpetual immunity, even if their emissions never increased above their original maximum, pre-Clean Air Act levels. Those levels harm far too many people and ecosystems and were granted only temporary immunity as a bridge to ease the industry's transition to much cleaner power. Congress wanted to see a big decrease in air pollution, and reasonably soon.

In 2000, the EPA and the Department of Justice successfully

settled a few of the first batch of NSR cases. In those settlements the utilities agreed to install state-of-the-art pollution controls. At last, the enforcers were getting the job done. It appeared that Mary Lewis, Ruth Enci, Charlotte O'Rourke, Lisa Marcucci, and all the other suffering folks were likely to get the relief Congress had wanted them to have so many years before. Then George W. Bush took office and his EPA took its foot off the accelerator and hit the brakes.

"One of the first things that happened was an intense lobbying effort by industry to try to shut down the enforcement cases," says Walke. As an example of the lobbying, Walke cites the effort by the National Coal Council. Not a trade association, as its name suggests, the National Coal Council is an official federal advisory committee that counsels the Department of Energy (DOE). "Federal advisory committees are supposed to be well-balanced, representative," said Walke. But the coal council is "stacked entirely with coal producers, people from electric power plants that burn coal, rail companies that haul coal, and so on, across the board. It's like a good old boys club to promote the coal industry."

The coal council was working on a report that in part addresses New Source Review during the time that Vice President Dick Cheney and his now infamous energy task force were meeting. (This is the task force that excluded everyone except industry representatives and was taken to court for refusing to let the public know who those representatives were, let alone what they talked about.) Papers obtained by the Natural Resources Defense Council in a Freedom of Information Act request revealed that among the industry executives who met with the task force were officials from the Edison Electric Institute, the National Mining Association, the North American Electric Reliability Council, and the Southern Company, one of the nation's biggest utility owners and one of the leading defendants in enforcement cases. The minutes from the council's meetings suggest that coal industry representatives and Department of Energy members on the council came up with the idea of releasing a draft of the coal council report early in order to influence Cheney's task force. It turns out that the council subcommittee that produced the report was headed by Bill Brownell, an attorney at Hunton & Williams, a big D.C. law firm that is serving as the chief litigation counsel for a number of utilities in pending NSR cases. Brownell himself is a defense attorney for several of those power companies. "So here you have a defense attorney," said Walke, "who's serving on a federal advisory committee to the Department of Energy presenting a report to the Cheney energy task force calling for the enforcement cases against his clients to be abandoned by the government."

The utilities that own coal-burning power plants have backed up their lobbying with hefty campaign contributions. They gave $126,000 to the 2000 Bush-Cheney campaign, $300,000 for the Bush inauguration, and $1,540,000 to the Republican National Committee during the 2000–2002 election cycle. Much of the money came from the companies whose plants are the targets of the pending enforcement cases. In addition, high-level officers from three energy companies facing NSR lawsuits served on Bush's Energy Department transition team. The utilities also have an important connection inside the EPA: Jeffrey Holmstead, EPA's Assistant Administrator for the Office of Air and Radiation, a key office for air pollution issues. Prior to being appointed to the office by President Bush, Holmstead, an attorney, represented the Alliance for Constructive Air Policy. This industry group has 16 members, 13 of them power companies. Among these power companies are several that EPA has taken to court for violating New Source Review and others that worry about being taken to court for violating New Source Review, including Allegheny Energy, the owners of the Hatfield's Ferry plant.

In November 2003 the public interest group Public Citizen accused Holmstead of misleading two Senate committees in sworn testimony in 2002 when he asserted that EPA enforcement staff had told him that the Administration's proposed softening of NSR rules would not weaken the pending enforcement cases. But Public Citizen notes that, on the contrary, EPA enforcement staff had told Holmstead that softening the rules would indeed undermine the cases, an account corroborated by Eric Schaeffer and Sylvia Lowrance. Lowrance worked at the EPA for 24 years, retiring from the very position now held by Holmstead. Lowrance quit quietly, but has since criticized the Bush EPA's enforcement record. Holmstead disputes the accounts of Schaeffer and Lowrance and declares that his testimony was entirely accurate.

Given the ties between the National Coal Council and the Administration, it came as no surprise when the White House supported the council's viewpoint and recommendations. The D.C. grapevine whispered that the report from Cheney's energy task force would recommend giving the coal council its way by dropping the NSR enforcement cases. However, this didn't happen. Some observers think that then–EPA Administrator Christie Whitman, despite having often toed the White House line on New Source Review, fought against a total dereliction of duty regarding enforcement of NSR. After all, as governor of New Jersey, Whitman had fought vigorously against air pollution from dirty power plants. For example, in 1999, Whitman added New Jersey to the list of plaintiffs in an EPA lawsuit against American Electric Power, Inc., alleging New Source Review violations. In a press release, Whitman said, "We've done much here in New Jersey to ensure that our residents can breathe clean air. All of our efforts are fruitless, however, if New Jerseyans must breathe the dirty air coming into our state from midwest coal-burning power plants. This legal action will require that these power plants clean up their emissions and stop polluting our air." Other observers think that the Administration backed off because their pro-industry bias would be blatantly exposed if they simply folded the tent on all the strong enforcement cases entrained by the previous administration.

Whatever the reason, instead of dropping the pending enforcement cases the White House decided to use more subtle means to disable NSR. When the Cheney energy task force issued its report in May 2001, it included three recommendations related to New Source Review. One directed EPA to overhaul the NSR regulations, a subject I'll get to presently. Another instructed EPA and the Energy Department to review the impact of NSR on the nation's capacity to generate electricity. The White House and industry maintained that New Source Review enforcement was preventing much-needed expansion of the power industry. Experts from across the political spectrum disagreed with this assessment. PA Consulting analyzed the U.S. power market and found that more than enough new capacity was being built. The consulting firm's report stated that "with the current wave of new plant announcements, it is even likely that the industry will overbuild." The libertarian Cato Institute, no friend to the environment, agreed, estimating that so much new capacity is scheduled to come online by 2004 that there may be an "electricity glut." Even the Administration's own Department of Energy, one of the main opponents of New Source Review, conceded that capacity is booming. A DOE document notes that "during the past several years, there have been significant increases in new plant capacity additions, with 2001 being a record year for new capacity additions. With the demand expected to be considerably less than the amount of initially proposed new capacity construction over the next several years, many of these plans are gradually being delayed or canceled." The third recommendation directed the Justice Department to examine further NSR investigations and current enforcement actions while Justice reviewed the merits of the New Source Review enforcement cases.

In the coded language of Washington, D.C., ordering a reexamination of NSR strongly implied that the White House found NSR wanting and was looking for a new legal interpretation more to its liking—and to the liking of the utilities. Supporters of New Source Review found this effort absurd and asserted that the enforcement cases were obviously consistent with the law and regulations. Nonetheless, the Justice Department proceeded with a review that was scheduled to take 90 days. It ended up taking eight months, and during that time the White House's challenge of NSR had a chilling effect on the pending enforcement cases. Administration officials openly advised power companies to delay settling, advice that some utilities gladly heeded.

The review vindicated the supporters of New Source Review. Much as the Administration wanted to find a reason to drop the pending enforcement cases, the law didn't allow such wiggle room. The Justice Department report said in summary: "EPA reasonably may conclude that the enforcement actions are consistent with the Clean Air Act and its regulations." But officials in the Department of Justice emphasized that their report only applied to cases already filed, not to the future. Quoted in *The Boston Globe,* Viet Dinh, the Justice Department official who oversaw the report, said that "it examines only currently pending enforcement actions to determine their lawfulness, and expresses no opinion on how the Clean Air Act should be enforced in the future." This wasn't exactly a ringing endorsement of NSR; indeed, it sounds more like a grudging admission that the Administration couldn't find any legal flaws in the pending cases and an implication that, despite the lawfulness of the NSR cases, the Administration isn't exactly champing at the bit to file any more of them. In fact, as of this writing, nearly three years after Bush assumed the Presidency, his EPA has not filed a single new NSR-related lawsuit.

Instead, the White House has attempted to gut New Source Review. As I mentioned earlier, the Cheney-led energy task force recommended that EPA revamp New Source Review, a recommendation that Bush subsequently ordered the agency to carry out. I'll examine the EPA's rule-makings in a moment, but first, note the effect that just the knowledge that revamping was underway had on enforcement of NSR. Thomas Sansonetti, Chief of Environmental Matters at the Department of Justice, has repeatedly stated his intention of vigorously pursuing the pending cases. "We're going full steam ahead," he told *Daily Environment Report.* "We're actively pursuing all cases. When companies refuse to settle, DOJ will take them to trial." Be this as it may, the Administration's well-known efforts to undercut New Source Review and the barrage of negative comments about NSR from Bush officials affected the lawsuits.

Eric Schaeffer witnessed the impacts firsthand. "It is no longer possible to pretend that the ongoing debate with the White House and Department of Energy is not affecting our ability to negotiate settlements," he wrote in February 2002. "Cinergy and Vepco [two major power companies being sued by EPA at that time] have refused to sign the consent decrees they agreed to 15 months ago, hedging their bets while waiting for the Administration's Clean Air Act reform proposals. Other companies with whom we were close to settlement have walked away from the table. The momentum we obtained with agreements announced earlier has stopped, and we have filed no new lawsuits against utility companies since this Administration took office. We obviously cannot settle cases with defendants who think we are still rewriting the law."

The drag on enforcement efforts grew stronger as industry began leaking details from EPA's revamping effort and after EPA officially presented its proposed changes, in June 2002. In Senate testimony in July 2002, Eliot Spitzer, Attorney General of New York state and one of the driving forces in the NSR lawsuits, stated his belief that the EPA proposals were undermining the pending enforcement cases:

It would be naive to believe that industry will not try to use the "NSR reforms" in court to justify their past conduct. We are already seeing the effects of this Administration's misguided and illegal policy changes: settlements are stalled, judges are wondering about the impact of the reforms on their cases, and industry lawyers are already arguing in court that the cases should not go forward. Whether or not the rollback will affect the existing cases is an issue of first impression for the courts because of the unprecedented nature of EPA's action. Never before has EPA—or Congress, for that matter—undertaken such a clear retreat on environmental protection. Conducting such a rollback while enforcement cases under the old rules are pending is not only unprecedented but was unimaginable, at least before this Administration came to power. Simply put, the existing NSR cases are in jeopardy and we are fooling ourselves if we believe that the federal government will be filing more cases after rewriting the regulations to legalize the conduct at issue.

In the end, the White House was not able to orchestrate a retreat on all the pending cases. By summer 2003, the Justice Department and EPA had settled five major New Source Review cases, all on terms favorable to clean air and people's health. The companies agreed to abide by NSR provisions and install state-of-the-art pollution controls on their old, coal-burning plants, reducing particulate emissions significantly. The Administration has taken credit for these environmental victories. Speaking of the settlement with Southern Indiana Gas and Electric Company, Inc., Sansonetti told *Business and Legal Reports,* in June 2003, "This excellent settlement shows how the Department's aggressive enforcement can help bring industry into compliance with our environmental laws, ultimately making for cleaner air for all citizens to enjoy." In the same article, J. P. Suarez, the former EPA Assistant Administrator who took a job with Wal-Mart, said, "EPA continues to aggressively enforce the nation's environmental laws, and as a result of our actions, the people of this great country can be assured of cleaner air."

Pious words from these two Bush appointees, but difficult to take at face value given the White House's push to bury New Source Review. Most of the credit for these welcome settlements belongs elsewhere than with the top echelons of the Administration. Many observers cite the public outcry and Congressional backlash prompted by the White House's evident desire to torpedo the pending NSR cases. These critics feel that the furor caused Bush to back off for political reasons, and that seeing their champion retreat in turn convinced some utilities to settle. People close to the agencies say that all of us who breathe should thank the career civil servants at the Department of Justice and EPA who, despite the anti-NSR emanations from the White House, have persisted in enforcing the law. Finally, we owe our gratitude to Eric Schaeffer and the 15 people who worked on his staff when he was Director of the Office of Regulatory Enforcement at EPA.

And work they did. When George W. Bush emerged as the Republican presidential candidate about a year before the 2000 election, Schaeffer feared that his growing enforcement of New Source Review would be cut off at the knees if Bush won the election. Schaeffer knew that as governor of Texas, Bush had not vigorously pursued efforts to reduce emissions from grandfathered coal-burning power plants. So Schaeffer shifted into high gear and urged his staff to work 70-hour weeks in order to get as many enforcement cases as possible into the pipeline. They were working even on the day of Bush's inauguration.

Schaeffer continued at EPA for a year under the Bush regime, but when the weak enforcement of NSR that he had feared came to pass Schaeffer resigned in protest. In his letter of resignation he wrote, ". . . I cannot leave without sharing my frustration about the fate of our enforcement actions against power companies that have violated the Clean Air Act." In his closing paragraph, Schaeffer cited Teddy Roosevelt, who said, "Compliance with the law is demanded as a right, not asked as a favor."

Late in 2003 it appreared that those five favorable settlements would be the only cases that would make it all the way through the pipeline. On December 31, 2002, and August 27, 2003, the Administration produced rules that tore the heart out of New Source Review and undercut the pending enforcement cases. In the fall of 2003 the Administration seemed to pull the plug on current NSR cases and likely future cases, including some 50 facilities (many of them coal-fired power plants) that the pre-Bush EPA had found in violation; the 70-plus power companies that had been under investigation; and hundreds of additional facilities that probably would have been investigated, given EPA's evidence indicating a widespread lack of compliance with NSR. The future of clean air looked dim.

Then came a Christmas present for people downwind of aging power plants and other polluting facilities. On December 24, 2003, two days before the President's new rules were to take effect, the Circuit Court of Appeals for the District of Columbia Circuit blocked the implementation of a key part of the White House's new rules: the provision that redefined "routine maintenance" in an industry-friendly way. The court is expected to make a final ruling in the summer of 2004, according to the EPA. Guessing at ultimate outcomes based on preliminary injunctions is always a risky business, but the court's language indicates that the state attorneys general, cities, and environmental organizations may prevail in the case. In making their ruling, the three judges of the Appeals Court wrote that the parties challenging Bush's new rule "have demonstrated the irreparable harm [of the rule] and likelihood of success on the merits." What will happen to the pending enforcement cases in the meantime remains to be seen. Some observers think the Administration will continue to let them languish, but in late January 2004, EPA Administrator Mike Leavitt announced the Administration's intention to aggressively enforce the existing cases until the final ruling is issued. Such a surprising reversal of the White House's long-standing antipathy toward enforcing New Source Review led many environmentalists to dismiss Leavitt's pledge as election-year politicking, and they suspect that little enforcement will materialize.

———————

Whatever the outcome of the case pending in the D.C. Circuit, the evolution of Bush's new NSR rules is instructive. The proposed changes that EPA developed at the behest of the Cheney energy task force were not developed entirely by EPA, though officially the agency was in charge of the process. Through a Freedom of Information Act request, the Natural Resources Defense Council uncovered a series of e-mails sent in the fall of 2002 that reveals political meddling by the Administration. High-level Bush appointees from the Department of Energy, the White House Council on Environmental Quality, and the Office of Management and Budget participated in this e-mail exchange, the point of which was to alter the NSR rules that EPA was drafting. The hub of the e-mails was the office of the General Counsel for the Department of Energy. They not only suggested fundamental changes in EPA's draft, but wrote their own version of key legal passages and substituted them for EPA's language, apparently with the approval of the Council on Environmental Quality and Office of Management and Budget officials in the e-mail loop. The substance of the DOE version adhered closely to the views of the power industry. Even the phrasing and words in DOE's e-mails echoed the language the utilities used in court cases involving NSR—court cases they lost, incidentally.

The proposed rules are too numerous and complicated to address comprehensively. Such voluminous regulation may seem odd coming from an Administration that supposedly advocates streamlining, but in this case the complications cater to industry. At an April 2003 conference on New Source Review, this point was made by Bruce Buckheit, Director of EPA's air enforcement division at the time. He noted that the rules, if adopted, would create "an additional layer of complexity that is beyond belief." He singled out the tangle of accounting rules and noted that they could lead to the kinds of accounting abuses that rocked the corporate world a couple of years ago. He concluded, "Think Enron."

In deference to the complexity, let's look at one representative change that was central to the D.C. Circuit's decision to issue a stay: a cost threshold for an expanded definition of what kind of modification qualifies as "routine" maintenance, repair, and replacement. Under this proposal a major piece of equipment could be installed in an aging plant provided that the cost didn't exceed 20 percent of the replacement cost of a "process unit," which includes the turbine, boiler, generator, and other components that transform coal into electricity. Here's an example of a past project that under the new rule would be exempt from New Source Review. The Tennessee Valley Authority's Allen Plant undertook a massive refurbishment in 1992 that required working ten stories above the ground to cut a 25-foot-diameter hole in the boiler wall. Plant managers had to build a special monorail and trolley system to move workers and equipment, and hired dozens of temporary employees. This project was unique in the 33 years of the plant's life. The total cost was nearly $11 million. Most important, the project resulted in a significant net increase of both sulfur dioxide and nitrogen oxides. Yet the Administration would have us consider this routine. EPA estimates that under the new rule more than 95 percent of the violations at issue in its enforcement cases would be exempt from NSR review.

The upshot of the President's NSR rules would be to allow plants to utterly reconstitute themselves over the course of several years without triggering NSR. The "perpetual immunity" warned against by the courts would come to pass. Contrary to the intent of Congress and the Clean Air Act, these grandfathered coal-fired power plants would keep harming people and the environment for years to come if the new rules go into effect.

The Bush Administration and its industry allies were not the only ones to criticize New Source Review and offer a detailed blueprint for reform. In April 2003, a panel of the National Academy of Public Administration (NAPA), a nonpartisan Congressional advisory body, released its two-year study of NSR. Like the White House, the NAPA report called for fundamental reform, but there the similarity ended. NAPA recommended strengthening New Source Review and criticized the Administration's attempt to weaken it. In essence, it urged government to quit fooling around and do what NSR review clearly was intended to do: clean up dirty old power plants and other aging sources of pollution. "Contrary to Congressional intent," said the report, "many large, highly polluting facilities have continued to operate and have expanded their production (and pollution) over the past 25 years without upgrading to cleaner technologies. The result: thousands of premature human deaths, and many thousand additional cases of acute illnesses and chronic diseases caused by air pollution."

The report was long and detailed, but its basic prescription would have given old, coal-fired plants ten years to comply with the law they've been dodging for decades, either by shutting down or installing best-available pollution controls. It would have protected human health and the environment and given industry the certainty it said it wanted—though I suspect some companies only want a certain kind of certainty. The NAPA report also notes that finally eliminating the pollution subsidy for old coal plants is a matter of fairness for those power companies that have built clean new plants or have invested in cleaning up their old plants.

Significantly, though the report called for reforms, it specifically would not have undermined enforcement efforts. "EPA and the Department of Justice should continue their investigations and enforcement actions to correct past violations of NSR," stated the report, "especially for changes at existing facilities. These actions will produce significant environmental benefits, deter future violations, and encourage other modified facilities to comply with NSR until Congress has adopted the Panel's other recommended reforms." However, this report, like all the other criticisms of Bush's proposed changes to NSR, had no discernable effect on the White House's view. Early in 2003, the Senate nearly stopped the new rules governing NSR from going into effect, but the effort lost 46 to 50. (Four Democrats expected to support it were out of town during the vote.) In August the President put the final stamp of approval on his industry-friendly version of New Source Review and the owners and managers of power companies popped open the champagne. But now they will have to wait for the D.C. Circuit's decision before they know if they popped those corks mistakenly.

In February 2002, the President rolled out his big gun aimed at air pollution, including New Source Review: his Clear Skies Initiative. The Administration trumpeted this program as "the most significant step America has ever taken to cut power plants' emissions" and stated that the proposal "will aggressively reduce air pollution from electricity generators and improve air quality throughout the country." The initiative relies on market-based mechanisms to essentially replace enforcement and make New Source Review and its lawsuits moot.

Most observers agree that Clear Skies would accomplish some significant reductions in power plant pollution. However, most also would agree that the claims made by the White House in the above paragraph are overstated. I will mention just a few of the many flaws critics have pointed out.

One, while the initiative would make some cuts in power plant emissions, it does not address emissions from the approximately 15,500 other large industrial facilities, such as oil refineries, that also pollute our air with fine particulates and other harmful substances. As noted earlier in this chapter, grandfathered coal-fired plants are the worst polluters, but taken together these non-power-plant sources are important and constitute a major gap in the Clear Skies Initiative.

Two, Bush's program covers sulfur dioxide, nitrogen oxides, and mercury, but it does not address carbon dioxide, which nearly everyone in the scientific community considers a key greenhouse gas that contributes heavily to global climate change. This despite the fact that during the 2000 campaign the President pledged to limit carbon dioxide emissions. The Clean Air Act does not address carbon dioxide, either, as global warming was not recognized as a problem when the Act passed in 1970. But many policy makers and scientists feel that as we proceed into the twenty-first century any laws reducing air pollution should reduce carbon dioxide, too. An increasing number of power companies agree because they want a predictable future for their investment decisions. In 2003, Michael J. Bradley, executive director of the Clean Energy Group, which consists of nine utilities, told *The Washington Post*, "One way to achieve business certainty is to have some sort of agreement on greenhouse gas. It's going to come down the road sometime, so you might as well take care of it now."

But most utilities, still myopically focused on the next quarterly report, oppose dealing with carbon dioxide anytime soon. *The*

New York Times reports that several major power companies hired Haley Barbour, formerly the Chairman of the Republican National Committee, to lobby Administration officials to in turn press Bush to renege on his promise. Among other actions, Barbour wrote Vice President Cheney in March 2001, to urge that the President back down from his campaign pledge on carbon dioxide emissions. A couple of weeks later Bush indeed went back on his word. The White House denies that the lobbying influenced the President.

Three, as noted earlier, the market-based mechanisms on which the Clear Skies Initiative relies often do not work as well as advertised.

Four, Clear Skies handcuffs states, preventing them from enacting stronger clean air laws—an odd provision from a President who claims to champion states' rights. Typically, the federal government sets minimum emission standards and allows states to set tougher ones, but Clear Skies offers no such choice.

The White House claims not only that Clear Skies will accomplish significant reductions in power plant pollution, which is true, but that it will achieve larger reductions and achieve them sooner than would the Clean Air Act. Few outside the Administration and the coal-burning utilities would agree with this assessment, but rather than wallowing in dueling numbers, perhaps some less direct but telling indicators are in order. Take the power industry's reactions to Clear Skies. A business article in the April 25, 2003, *St. Louis Post-Dispatch* captures the unabashed acknowledgment by many energy companies—especially those tied to coal—that Clear Skies would not be as stringent as the Clean Air Act. While writing about the rosy outlook for Arch Coal, Inc., the nation's number-two coal company, the reporter notes in a matter-of-fact way that among the factors buoying Arch Coal's expected rise in profits is help from the White House: "With the Clear Skies Initiative of President George W. Bush essentially giving coal-burning operations more time to clean up their emissions, federal and state environmental pressures have been relaxed."

Another indication of the relative rigor of the Clean Air Act versus Clear Skies comes from Congress. In mid-2003 some of Bush's loyal supporters in the Senate introduced a Clear Skies bill. However, an alternative bill, the Clean Air Planning Act, championed by Senator Thomas R. Carper (D-DE) and cosponsored by Republican senators Lincoln Chafee of Rhode Island and Judd Gregg of New Hampshire, also was knocking around in the Capitol at that time. The Carper bill would have regulated the same three pollutants as Clear Skies plus carbon dioxide and it would have reduced them further and sooner. Yet the Carper bill, though considerably stronger than Clear Skies, was not considered a tough piece of legislation. It was viewed widely as a compromise that fell between the weak provisions of Clear Skies and the aggressive provisions of a third Senate bill, the Clean Power Act of 2003, authored by Senators James Jeffords (Independent-VT) and Joseph Lieberman (D-CT), enthusiastic supporters of the Clean Air Act, and cosponsored by 18 other senators. The Jeffords/Lieberman bill would have produced many of the same results as a rigorously enforced Clean Air Act. In short, Clear Skies and the Clean Air Act lie at opposite ends of the spectrum.

The environmental advantages that the Clean Air Act enjoys over Clear Skies depend on the act being rigorously enforced, especially its New Source Review provisions. Because of Bush's poor enforcement record, a few pro-environment analysts have quietly suggested supporting Clear Skies to ensure that at least some reductions in fine particulates and other emissions can be achieved. This same cynical reasoning implicitly appears in the White House's Clear Skies literature. It makes the argument that in part the Clean Air Act won't result in pollution reductions comparable to those of Clear Skies because with the act "the regulatory development debate is usually very controversial," "compliance deadlines are often delayed," and "there is significant uncertainty in the outcome of the litigation." But these problems stem from lax enforcement. An Administration determined to protect the nation from air pollution would shrug off the controversy and would not tolerate delays in compliance.

As for litigation, despite overt hostility from high-ranking Administration officials, including the President, the few NSR cases that EPA and the Justice Department have prosecuted have resulted in environmentally favorable settlements. It seems increasingly clear that if the Administration presented a unified front, enforced the law energetically, and made it known that it intended to continue enforcing NSR energetically, the uncertainty would vanish, litigation would be less common, and delays would decline as pre-lawsuit compliance rose.

It also is becoming increasingly apparent that litigation over New Source Review stems not so much from problems with NSR as from industry's pretense that NSR is too murky to obey. In the summer of 2003, a federal judge decided a major, precedent-setting NSR case that the defendant, Ohio Edison Company, had refused to settle. (Ohio Edison is a subsidiary of FirstEnergy Corporation. According to the Center for Responsive Politics, in the 2002 federal elections FirstEnergy gave about $700,000 to Republican candidates and FirstEnergy's president, Anthony Alexander, and chairman and chief executive, H. Peter Burg, have been big fund-raisers for Bush.) Brought by EPA and three states, the lawsuit claimed that $136 million in improvements at Ohio Edison's Sammis Plant, in Ohio, had far exceeded routine maintenance and should have prompted New Source Review pollution controls. Judge Edmund Sargus, Jr., emphatically agreed, writing in his ruling: "By any standard, the enforcement of the Clean Air Act with regard to the Sammis Plant has been disastrous."

In his 109-page decision, Sargus agrees wholeheartedly with the government's case and bluntly dismantles the arguments made by Ohio Edison—essentially the same arguments advanced by the Administration. Here is the judge's comment on the key matter of recognizing which modifications of power plants should initiate NSR: "While the analysis required to distinguish between a modification sufficient to trigger compliance from routine maintenance, repair and replacement is complex, the distinction is hardly subtle. Routine maintenance, repair and replacement occurs regularly, involves no permanent improvements, is typically limited in expense, is usually performed in large plants by in-house employees, and is treated for accounting purposes as an expense. In contrast to routine maintenance stand capital improvements which generally involve more expense, are large in scope, often involve outside contractors, involve an increase of value to the unit, are usually not undertaken with regular frequency, and are treated for accounting purposes as capital expenditures on the balance sheet. As outlined in Section III, the only two courts which have addressed this issue have essentially adopted this same analysis."

Sargus follows with his evaluation of the modifications made by Ohio Edison that it argued were routine:

> *The eleven projects at issue in this case were extensive, involving a combined outlay of $136.4 million dollars. The vast majority of the expenditures were treated for accounting purposes as capital, as opposed to maintenance, expenses. Most of the work was performed by outside contractors, as opposed to in-house maintenance crews. The purpose of the projects was to extend the lives of units built before 1970, not simply to perform routine preventative care on components of the units. Finally, all of the projects involved replacement of major components which had never before been replaced on the particular units. As a result, the projects were not routine in any sense of the term, and could have been projected to significantly increase the emission of pollutants.*

At times one can sense the judge's impatience with what he obviously views as Ohio Edison's thin defense. At one point, discussing what Sargus calls "the plain language of the regulation" defining routine maintenance, repair, and replacement, the judge writes: "In view of this language, it is hard to fathom that Ohio Edison did not have notice that the sorts of projects undertaken at the Sammis plant would not be considered as 'routine.'"

Given that industry and the Administration share the same perspective on New Source Review, the White House should sit up and take notice of Sargus's decision. Not only do excerpts from his ruling like those quoted above destroy the Administration's technical reasoning about NSR, but other parts of the decision decry the industry/Administration position more broadly. For instance, Sargus says that he understands that, in their effort to make money, utilities would try to "influence the conduct of the EPA." "What should be unexpected and condemned, however," he writes, "is an agency unwilling to enforce a clear statutory mandate set forth in an act of Congress."

In his concluding remarks Sargus extends his general criticisms: "If any of the activities undertaken could be considered to be 'routine maintenance,' the regulation would vitiate the very language of the CAA [Clean Air Act] itself. Such a result could not have been intended by Congress."

The pro-environment analysts who reluctantly recommended accepting Clear Skies did not carry the day. Settling for second-best (third-best, actually) didn't seem to inspire many people, and during 2003 environmental and public health organizations and their Congressional supporters pushed for stronger measures, such as the Carper bill and the Jeffords/Lieberman bill, and opposed Clear Skies. Bush's program entered the fray with few cosponsors and many observers don't think it is going to replace the Clean Air Act anytime soon. Perhaps that's why the Administration resorted to deception to bolster its bill's odds.

By "deception" I don't mean garden-variety exaggerations or mere public relations effusion. Two more serious machinations surfaced in 2003. First, EPA officials at the agency's D.C. headquarters knowingly exaggerated the potential benefits that Clear Skies would bestow on Washington state, according to a report in *The News Tribune*, a Knight Ridder newspaper published in Tacoma, Washington. That report says that in EPA's state-by-state evaluation of the pollution reductions that Clear Skies would produce, the agency claimed Bush's initiative would reduce sulfur dioxide emissions by 87 percent in Washington. But Washington State's Department of Ecology and EPA's own regional office in Washington State repeatedly had informed the national EPA office that this figure was incorrect—wildly wrong, in fact.

All of those sulfur dioxide reductions had already been mandated under an agreement made while Governor Bush was still setting up ineffective voluntary pollution programs in Texas. Regardless, for months, EPA ignored its regional office and the Washington State government. Finally overwhelmed by reality, it acknowledged its error, but it still didn't earnestly correct it. The state-by-state analysis continued to claim an 87 percent reduction benefit; all EPA did was add a jargon-shrouded footnote that fell disappointingly short of a full correction. The Washington Department of Ecology informed EPA headquarters that far from reducing pollution, Clear Skies would, by overriding state regulations, lead to an increase of 34 percent in sulfur dioxide emissions, up to an 88 percent rise in mercury pollution, and up to a doubling of nitrogen oxides. EPA officials downplayed the whole affair and called it a mistake. Washington State has since joined other states in suing EPA over its failures under the Clean Air Act.

An equally egregious deception that could have had an enormous impact on the health of Americans and their environment came to light in the summer of 2003. Leaked documents revealed that the Administration had held back for months key information that it should have given to Senator Carper. A *Washington Post* story reported that, although EPA acknowledged that the Carper bill would produce greater emission reductions and produce them sooner than would Clear Skies, the agency did not give Carper and the public a key analysis. This hidden research showed that Carper's plan would not cost industry significantly more to implement than would Clear Skies. It also concluded that Carper's inclusion of carbon dioxide reductions could be achieved with only a "negligible" cost to industry. Such information surely could have influenced senators' votes and the public's evaluation of the competing bills. EPA Associate Administrator Edward D. Krenik told the *Post* that Carper "has all the information," but a Power-Point presentation prepared for Jeffrey Holmstead, EPA's chief air pollution administrator, showed otherwise. Leaked to the *Post*, this presentation contained information that EPA withheld from Carper, including some of the vital economic analysis, such as the conclusion that Carper's Clean Air Planning Act would save about $50 billion a year more in health benefits than Clear Skies would. The presentation also contained the striking estimation that, compared to Carper's bill, by 2020 Clear Skies would lead to 17,800 more premature deaths.

Ironically, during that eventful summer of 2003, the Clear Skies Initiative also caught flak from power companies and manufacturers, many of which weren't enamored of the initiative in the first place. Their concerns stemmed from a Department of Energy challenge of EPA's estimate regarding the cost to industry of Clear Skies' mercury reductions. EPA's analysis found that the same pollution controls needed for sulfur dioxide and nitrogen oxides would lead to the 46 percent drop in mercury by 2010 that Bush promises in Clear Skies. But in later research the Energy Department figured that the drop would be only about 4 percent. If accurate, this would mean that coal-burning power plants, which account for about one-third of mercury emissions, would have to spend hundreds of millions of dollars to attain that promised 46 percent reduction and comply with Clear Skies. That possibility prompted some power plant owners and their allies in the Senate to demand that the Administration drastically lower the mercury targets in Clear Skies. Ever obliging, at a Senate subcommittee hearing Randall Kroszner, of the President's Council of Economic Advisors, figuratively winked at the pro-coal senators and invited them to alter the mercury standards in Clear Skies, according to *The Washington Post*. "Occasionally, Congress does change things that the president proposes, and that could be a possibility," said Kroszner. Subcommittee Chairman George Voinovich (R-OH) accepted the invitation and said that he would rewrite the offending standards. In November 2003 Voinovich and Senator James Inhofe (R-OK) introduced a revised version of Clear Skies that would weaken the mercury standards.

The Clear Skies legislation didn't make it into law, but in December 2003 the Administration proposed a rule that essentially would seek to institute Clear Skies via regulation. Called the Interstate Air Quality Rule, it would apply to 29 states in the eastern half of the nation and the District of Columbia. Like the original Clear Skies initiative, this rule would do less about air pollution and do it later. On January 30, 2004, the Administration proposed a separate rule regarding mercury emissions that also followed the Clear Skies pattern of lowering the standards and delaying the onset of compliance. It turns out that at least a dozen paragraphs appearing in the proposed rule came from memos submitted by a law firm representing the utility industry. The Children's Health Protection Advisory Committee formally protested the proposed mercury rule. An EPA panel consisting of pediatricians, scientists, and business representatives, the committee sent a letter to EPA Administrator Mike Leavitt stating that the rule would "not sufficently protect our nation's children." The letter also noted that "while cost effectiveness is important, the priority should be to protect children's health in a timely manner."

Whatever the fate of the Clear Skies Initiative and its offspring, broader concerns about enforcement of our nation's environmental laws will continue under the Bush Administration. Robust implementation of New Source Review, though it may not be a perfect law, should have been a no-brainer. Just think of the tribulations visited upon Mary Lewis, Charlotte O'Rourke, Ruth Enci, and Lisa Marcucci, the women from southwest Pennsylvania, and on their families and friends. Think of their counterparts throughout the country. Think of the elderly and the children, who are disproportionately victimized by air pollution. The federal government should be rushing to help these people, particularly in light of the authoritative health research that has emerged in the last decade. Those studies estimate that 4 percent of deaths in the U.S. can be attributed to air pollution. That's 100 times more fatalities than all the deaths caused by all other pollutants put together. Not to mention the illnesses, the economic impacts, and the damage to natural areas and wildlife.

With the statute and the technology in place and enforcement actions from the previous administration surging forward, to merely allow that momentum to continue would have been easy. Instead, the White House has put considerable effort into unenforcement. And if the Administration seeks to avoid enforcement of a law that produces such enormous health and conservation benefits without causing undue economic burdens, which environmental laws will it enforce? To elaborate on the opinion of Bob Danko, the Masontown resident quoted at the beginning of the chapter, there ought to be a law enforcer.

CHAPTER 5

Inexact Science

The caribou were getting in the way, so Gale Norton moved them. That is to say, Bush's Secretary of the Interior moved them on paper and in her statements to Congress. In reality, the caribou still are using the same places in the Arctic National Wildlife Refuge (ANWR) that they've been using since time immemorial, including some places in which oil companies want to drill.

The caribou scandal began with a May 15, 2001, letter from Senator Frank Murkowski (R-AK) to Norton, freshly installed at Interior. Chair of the Senate Committee on Energy and Natural Resources, Murkowski asked four questions about the impact that drilling in the Arctic National Wildlife Refuge might have on the refuge's caribou. In particular, he wanted to know about the potential impacts in the "1002 Area"—the 1.5-million-acre coastal plain that forms the northern part of ANWR and that the oil companies most covet. An outspoken advocate for drilling, Murkowski clearly hoped that the scientific evidence would indicate that oil and gas development wouldn't unduly harm the caribou; concerns about the welfare of the tens of thousands of caribou that migrate to the refuge constituted a major obstacle to Congressional authorization for drilling. As the senator wrote in his letter, "Much of the concern about development in the 1002 area centers on the impact such activities would or would not have on caribou."

Norton, herself an energetic cheerleader for drilling, did not disappoint. In her reply to Murkowski, sent on July 11, 2001, she wrote, "As the information provided below demonstrates, I believe that we can ensure that any exploration and development of the oil and natural gas reserves in the 1002 Area of ANWR can be conducted in a manner that is protective of the environment and minimizes impacts on wildlife in the area." Indeed, "the information provided below" does demonstrate to Murkowski and, by extension, to Congress and the public, that the caribou and the environment in general would not be degraded significantly by drilling in the 1002 Area of ANWR. The problem is, much of "the information provided below" was inaccurate and incomplete.

Before elaborating on Norton's misrepresentations of the data, I'd like to note that I'm not trying to determine whether we should drill for oil and gas in ANWR. I'm not even trying to determine whether caribou would be seriously harmed by drilling in the 1002 Area. I'm talking about the methods Norton and others in the Interior Department employed in trying to make their case. As the federal government's most important provider of scientific information concerning natural resource issues, the Department of the Interior has a special obligation to provide the rest of the government and the public with full and accurate data, but it did not meet this obligation. Unfortunately, the Department's manipulation of information is not unique to this case nor is this behavior unique to Interior. The White House and the resource agencies it oversees often treat the science informing environmental issues as if it's just another element of public relations to be massaged and spun to suit political ends. Other administrations have played similar games, but not nearly as often nor so blatantly.

In the case of the caribou, Norton's and Interior's mendacity centered around the way they handled a U.S. Fish and Wildlife Service report on caribou and the 1002 Area. After receiving Murkowski's questions Norton naturally turned to Fish and Wildlife for answers. The agency is part of Interior; it is the federal government's premier research institution regarding wildlife issues; and it manages the nation's wildlife refuges, including ANWR. Fish and Wildlife scientists had been studying caribou in ANWR for many years and they readily supplied Norton with answers. The report they gave Norton had been approved every step of the way up the Fish and Wildlife chain of command, though it was so early in the Administration that the chain didn't yet include any Bush appointees. The report was in the form of a draft letter to Murkowski, written concisely and in nontechnical terms. One would have expected Norton simply to look it over, maybe give it to an aide for a few nips and tucks, and then pass it on to the senator. Instead, Norton and her staff substantially rewrote the draft letter. Tellingly, every revision made the report more favorable to the interests of the oil industry. The credit for breaking this story goes to Public Employees for Environmental Responsibility (PEER), a small nonprofit that watchdogs the natural resource agencies and helps agency staffers convey suppressed information to the public, and to the agency employees who through PEER brought these documents out into the sunshine.

Consider Murkowski's first question: "What is the Porcupine caribou herd's historic calving range?" The 130,000 Porcupine caribou, one of the largest herds of wild animals left in North America, migrate between the northwestern corner of Canada and ANWR, in the northeastern corner of Alaska. The prosperity of the Porcupine herd is important in and of itself as well as to several indigenous peoples who depend on it for food and other staples. The health of the herd depends in large part on the survival rate of each year's calves, and, as the Fish and Wildlife draft letter states, "Calf survival is linked to forage quality and quantity and predator densities associated with selected calving habitats." The report also notes that "calving and the early summer seasons (late May to early July) are the periods of greatest sensitivity of caribou." It turns out that the Porcupine herd finds the 1002 Area appealing habitat during this sensitive time. "Caribou arrive on the coastal plain in late May, have their calves, and remain on the calving ground through late June to early July," says the draft letter.

Norton's letter to Murkowski, on the other hand, downplays the importance of the 1002 Area as calving habitat. The Secretary writes that "Concentrated calving occurred primarily *outside* [my emphasis] of the 1002 Area in 11 of the last 18 years." This claim fails in several ways. First, it is flat-out wrong. There was a Fish and Wildlife Web page that stated, "concentrated calving occurred primarily *on* [my emphasis] the 1002 Area in 11 out of 18 years." "On" obviously means inside the area, not outside. When confronted with this discrepancy, Norton admitted the error but she denied intent. According to Norton's spokesman, Mark Pfeifle, she simply made a mistake and accidentally wrote "outside" when she meant "inside." That's a whopper of a mistake given that her wording flip-flopped the science pertaining to a key part of an enormously important issue in a communication to a powerful member of Congress.

What's more, right on the front page of the Fish and Wildlife draft letter, which Interior quotes when the quotes convey information that supports drilling, it states, "There have been PCH [Porcupine Caribou Herd] calving concentrations within the 1002 Area for 27 of 30 years." One also can't help but wonder why Norton and Co. omitted this pertinent information. Actually, Norton's letter to Murkowski often leaves out data contrary to the case for drilling. For example, in his letter the senator asks, "What has been the impact of development in Prudhoe Bay on the Central Arctic caribou herd?" Reasonably, Murkowski is wondering if the effects of oil field development on caribou to the west of ANWR can help inform the debate over drilling in the refuge. Norton's letter cites some of the answer provided by Fish and Wildlife—the part that, on balance, supports energy development—but she omits an entire paragraph that indicates potential harm from such development. "By the mid-1980s," says the Fish and Wildlife draft letter, "caribou use of the Kuparuk and Milne fields during calving declined and the concentrated calving area shifted to the southwest, away from the industrial zone . . ." [Here and elsewhere in the quoted passage are scholarly citations, which I will skip.]

"This shift has continued through 2000. Only sparse calving activity continues within less disturbed pockets of the oilfield areas. The relatively undisturbed eastern calving grounds of the Central Arctic Herd did not show any directional shift during the same time period. The amount of forage available for cows at the time of peak lactation in the area of shifted calving concentration is lower than that for the area where caribou formerly calved." Interior chose not to provide this data, which indicates that oil development may have a significant negative impact on the welfare of caribou. Nor did they send Fish and Wildlife's concluding remarks about lactating Central Arctic caribou: "Caribou on the developed side shifted concentrated calving to an area of less food for lactating cows. There is no compelling biological reason to have expected this shift to poorer quality habitat. More likely, the shift was the result of calving cows avoiding oil development infrastructures."

According to Pfeifle, many of the differences between Norton's letter and Fish and Wildlife's draft letter occurred because Interior sought information from other sources, notably a caribou study published in the winter 2000 issue of *Wildlife Society Bulletin*. Seeking diverse information from sources outside government makes sense, but consistently elevating external information above that of Fish and Wildlife when the two sources conflict, and always in ways that support industry's case, seems dubious. And why did Interior rely so heavily on just one external study, going so far as to include many near-verbatim passages in Norton's letter? One can't help but think Interior found this research compelling because it supports the argument that oil drilling won't significantly harm caribou. Interior didn't even include data from the many outside studies that indicate that drilling would harm caribou, let alone lean excessively on any one such study.

The particular study Norton and her colleagues chose to use so extensively raises questions, too. Interior emphasized the importance of using peer-reviewed science and the fact that the *Wildlife Society Bulletin* article was peer-reviewed. But it wasn't. This scholarly journal has different levels of scrutiny for articles that appear in its pages. The most thorough process, and the one that most closely resembles what the scientific community means by peer review, is what the journal calls "peer-refereed." These articles have been subjected to rigorous review by two to four independent referees who are experts in their fields, an associate editor, and the editor. The article informing Norton's letter was not "peer-refereed." It was "peer-edited." A former editor of the *Bulletin* says the "peer-edited" papers undergo a much less robust process that, importantly, doesn't involve review by authorities in the article's subject area—i.e., no peer review. Now, acceptance by the Wildlife Society, a reputable nonprofit organization of thousands of wildlife professionals, is no small thing and it assures readers that the caribou article is not junk science. But acceptance for publication is a far cry from peer review.

Had Norton et al. truly wanted to consult a wide variety of outside studies, the Wildlife Society would have been a logical place to go. It has thoroughly studied the issues—both the narrow one of caribou welfare in the 1002 Area and the ecological effects of drilling in ANWR more generally—and has even published a Wildlife Policy Statement on these matters. The statement emphasizes that it addresses only the consequences for wildlife and doesn't take on broader issues of national energy policy, but within those bounds the Wildlife Society opposes drilling in ANWR, and especially in the 1002 Area. It lists a dozen primary biological concerns regarding oil and gas development in the refuge; at the top of the list is harm to the Porcupine Caribou Herd. The statement also cites information from studies that undermines a number of key points in Interior's favorite caribou study, some of them the very points that Norton used in her letter to Murkowski. In her letter Norton could have included material from some of the peer-reviewed studies that went into forming the Wildlife Society's position on caribou in the 1002 Area.

Norton also could have consulted with the Ecological Society of America, a venerable organization of nearly 8,000 ecological scientists. It, too, has a position paper, supported by extensive research, on the effects that drilling for oil in the 1002 Area might have on caribou, other wildlife, and the area's overall ecology. The Ecological Society writes, "Development of the coastal plain's petroleum resources could have serious impacts on the ecosystem of the region, in turn affecting numerous plant and animal species." Like the Wildlife Society's statement, the Ecological Society's position paper contains information on drilling and caribou that runs counter to the study trumpeted by Norton.

Another concern regarding Interior's favorite caribou study stems from the affiliations of its authors. In the acknowledgments at the end of the article in *Wildlife Society Bulletin*, the three authors thank several people from BP [British Petroleum] Exploration for having "provided encouragement, funding, and useful comments on our long-term caribou work." The three authors worked for the Alaska office of LGL Research Associates, Inc. LGL's Web site reveals that this consulting outfit has done research for dozens of oil companies and related businesses, including Shell Oil, BP International, Exxon USA, Standard Oil, Chevron Canada, ARCO Alaska, and the American Petroleum Institute. This is hardly conclusive evidence that the caribou study was slanted to favor oil interests. Multinational corporations fund a fair amount of legitimate, independent ecological research (though usually only when the law requires them to do so). But the study's ties to industry put one more question mark at the end of Norton's conclusion about caribou and drilling in the 1002 Area. Considering that the study's authors had connections to oil companies, that lots of other research disagreed with some of the study's main findings, and that the study was not peer-reviewed, perhaps relying so heavily on this one study in providing crucial information to Congress was a mistake on Norton's part.

———

Anyone who came within a mile of the news during the last half of 2003 will remember that at the time the Bush Administration was bleeding credibility. However, the revelations about tampering with information to serve political ends revolved around Iraq and weapons of mass destruction, not around caribou and drilling for oil in ANWR. Partly due to our understandable preoccupation with terrorism and the wars in Afghanistan and Iraq and partly due to the Administration's success at veiling its mistreatment of data, the vast majority of the White House's efforts to shape the science tied to environmental issues has gone largely unnoticed by the media and the general public. For every caribou-type dust-up that rises into view there are dozens of distortions, large and small, that slip by. (That is, there are dozens based on my knowledge; there may well be scores or hundreds—it's hard to know how much you don't know.) Much of this corrupted science influences obscure but significant environmental issues. Some plays a role in major decisions, as in the case of ANWR and the caribou. Cumulatively, the Administration's manipulations of information could have a huge negative impact on the environment and human health.

Despite their actions to the contrary, the White House and Bush's appointees often pay homage to the importance of gathering and using solid information. The Administration recognizes that with environmental issues there is enormous public relations value in appearing to have science on your side. Norton herself, caribou shenanigans notwithstanding, frequently speaks publicly about the need for sound science. Her words at her confirmation hearing are representative: "I am absolutely committed to the idea that the decision-making should be based on the best science, on the best analysis of environmental issues that we can find and, as Secretary of the Interior, would anticipate, if I am confirmed, trying to be sure that our decisions are really made in a fully informed way with full public participation."

Many critics roll their eyes when they hear Administration officials make such pronouncements. These critics, including academics, analysts at conservation groups, representatives of scientific organizations, and resource agency staffers, accuse the Administration of repeatedly acting in ways contrary to its words. "We're hearing from increasing numbers of scientists and engineers who are frustrated and angry at the way this Administration is undercutting the integrity of science in public policy making," said Kevin Knobloch, president of the Union of Concerned Scientists, a nonprofit whose 60,000 members include scientists, engineers, and citizens interested in the role of science in public policy. "We have never seen the science, engineering, and medical communities as upset about this issue as we see today. The world of science, out of necessity, has a rigorous culture and protocol that is aimed at revealing the truth. The whole peer-review culture is part of that. It really is the pursuit of truth. So, nothing upsets that culture more than the sense that public officials don't care to know the truth, or that the political agenda is driving what science gets considered, rather than the best science driving what the policy agenda is." Knobloch went on to remind Americans where the buck stops. "I would pin the responsibility on the President and the Vice President, who set the tenor on these kinds of things. When the Vice President sits down to write a national energy policy in secret, in closed-door meetings with lobbyists from the extractive and polluting industries—coal, oil, gas, nuclear—and zero other input, that really sends a message that they don't care what the environmental science says and they don't care to consider an array of perspectives."

The unprecedented level of dismay within the scientific community prompted the Union of Concerned Scientists to organize a campaign that takes the Administration to task. In February 2004 they announced the campaign and issued a statement signed by some 50 eminent scientists. The signers include such luminaries as E. O. Wilson, the famed Harvard biologist, author, and winner of countless scientific awards; David Baltimore, president of Cal Tech and winner of the Nobel Prize for physiology; and Harold Varmus, CEO of Memorial Sloan-Kettering Cancer Center, former director of the National Institutes for Health, and Nobel Prize winner for medicine. The organizers of the campaign hope to recruit thousands of scientists to their cause.

In this statement the scientists note, "When scientific knowledge has been found to be in conflict with its political goals, the Administration has often manipulated the process through which science enters into its decisions." The statement goes on to say, "Other administrations have, on occasion, engaged in such practices, but not so systematically nor on so wide a front. Furthermore, in advocating policies that are not scientifically sound, the

Administration has sometimes misrepresented scientific knowledge and misled the public about the implications of its policies." The statement concludes with recommendations for improving the government's use of science, saying, "The distortion of scientific knowledge for partisan political ends must cease if the public is to be properly informed about issues central to its well-being . . ."

Members of Congress also have questioned the Administration's handling of science related to environmental issues. Late in 2002, the Democratic staff of the House Committee on Resources, under the direction of Representative Nick Rahall (D-WV), put out a report called "Weird Science." It detailed ten examples of actions taken by the Interior Department that the report's authors consider to be manipulations of science for political purposes. In its executive summary, the authors write, "Time and time again the Administration has put politics and corporate interests above the 'best science.'" In August 2003, a longer report along the same lines but including some non-environmental cases came from the Democratic staff of the House Committee on Government Reform, requested by Representative Henry Waxman (D-CA). In its executive summary, the authors write, "The Administration's political interference with science has led to misleading statements by the President, inaccurate responses to Congress, altered Web sites, suppressed agency reports, erroneous international communications, and the gagging of scientists. The subjects involved span a broad range, but they share a common attribute: the beneficiaries of the scientific distortions are important supporters of the President, including social conservatives and powerful industry groups."

Reacting to the Waxman report in an interview with *The New York Times,* White House Press Secretary Scott McClellan said, "This Administration looks at the facts, and reviews the best available science based on what's right for the American people. The only one who is playing politics about science is Congressman Waxman. His report is riddled with distortion, inaccuracies, and omissions." Waxman indeed may enjoy the political points scored by his report, but its many examples and details can't be dismissed so easily. I repeatedly contacted McClellan's office, as well as two other White House offices, to ask for more information about the "distortion, inaccuracies, and omissions" and to find out what sources McClellan used. After talking to a number of baffled staffers, I finally was told that McClellan got his information from the EPA. So I called over there and asked the same questions. "Huh?" was the gist of its response. It seems that McClellan offered a knee-jerk denial with no data to back it up. Not very scientific of him. In developing its campaign, the Union of Concerned Scientists evaluated many of the Waxman Report's claims and found every one that they examined to be solid.

One tactic the White House employs to get science that supports its desired course of action is to simply ignore the science that doesn't support its positions, even when that contradictory science represents the thinking of a large majority of the scientific community or when it comes from highly regarded sources. For example, on January 18, 2002, the Administration averted its gaze from a National Academy of Sciences report that recommended higher fuel-efficiency standards for light trucks, a category that includes SUVs, minivans, and pickups. Amid all the post–September 11 talk about weaning the country from imported oil, Bush decided to allow vehicles classified as light trucks to continue to go far fewer miles on a gallon of gas than do cars. Though the Administration had the Academy report for six months, it said it hadn't had enough time to properly study it and the Administration went ahead and made its contrary decision.

The Administration again shuns science when it touts the restoration of the Everglades as one of its environmental successes. This claim suffers from a couple of flaws. First, the restoration effort started well before Bush entered the Oval Office. Also, as the details of the plan have emerged many scientists have begun to doubt that the restoration will succeed. Back in 1999, a group of prominent scientists expressed their concern to Interior about the plan; their doubts were shared by some government researchers, according to internal documents. Since then, many others have voiced their lack of faith in parts of the plan. Nonetheless, in 2002 the Administration floated the idea of reducing protections for five endangered species that live in the Everglades, based on expectations that the restoration plan will enable them to recover. Biologists have argued against this optimism, which they consider unfounded, but Administration officials have ignored them and proceeded toward what may be a premature retreat from the protections afforded by the Endangered Species Act. Referring to the Everglades restoration effort, Charles Groat, Director of the U.S. Geological Survey, told *The Washington Post*, "There's a lot of talk about sound science, but it doesn't seem to affect the high-level decision-making."

Bush officials ignored even more scientists when the Administration drastically weakened the species viability provisions of the National Forest Management Act (NFMA). In recent years these provisions had provided considerable protection to a broad array of plant and animal species in America's national forests. This was especially important because the national forests harbor considerably more rare species than any other category of public land. Many of these organisms are listed as "sensitive species"—they're not yet distressed enough to be candidates for the Endangered Species Act but they could be on their way to that emergency status unless they're protected. Given that the Administration and many of its friends in industry desperately want to prevent the listing of more species as endangered, it seems contrary to rescind a provision that is one of the more effective tools in keeping plants and animals off the endangered species list. However, timber companies and other users of national forests complained that it cost them too much to conduct the many surveys required by the species viability provisions and that the surveys too often found sensitive species on sites the companies wanted to log.

Countering industry's protests, scientists continually have affirmed the need to pay particular attention to this array of sensitive species for the health of the forests. Often that affirmation has come from the Committee of Scientists, a prestigious group formed with the passage of NFMA, in 1976, that would periodically be convened to guide the development of the regulations that would implement the act. The influence of the committee ebbed and flowed depending on who occupied the White House. For instance, its data did little to slow the rampant clear-cutting that occurred during the 1980s under Presidents Reagan and George H. W. Bush. But during President Clinton's era science in general and the committee in particular gained more respect. Researchers carried out the species surveys and often the results guided logging and other aspects of the management of the national forests. In 1997, the Committee of Scientists was pulled together to participate in a major revision of NFMA regulations. In 1999, that incarnation of the committee issued the definitive statement on the importance of the species viability provisions, noting the importance of monitoring wildlife populations and not relying only on the existence of habitat as proof of the viability of species.

Taking to heart the information provided by the committee and by other scientists, the Clinton administration, in 2000, finalized its revisions of NFMA regulations. These revised rules emphasized ecological sustainability and noted that biological diversity could not be achieved without special attention to species diversity, à la the species viability provisions. In 2001, just a few months after assuming office, Bush suspended the new NFMA regulations. In 2002, the Administration proposed new regulations that would eviscerate the species viability provisions. In pushing its new regulations, the White House didn't even convene the Committee of Scientists, let alone pay attention to the multitudes of dissenting scientific voices coming from both inside and outside the government.

One of the most notable protests came in the form of a letter from 325 wildlife researchers and conservation biologists, including many prominent figures and some veterans of the Committee of Scientists that produced the 1999 statement on species conservation in our forests. The letter states that the viability provisions are the key to assuring biodiversity in our national forests. The scientists also address what they see as false assertions underlying the Administration's new rules and they urge the President to reinstate the rules finalized in 2000. Finally, they criticize Bush for being the first president in 25 years not to use the Committee of Scientists to help the Forest Service develop such major regulations, especially when the agency managers were asking for more scientific assistance. But Bush did not listen to his resource managers and request more scientific assistance. And he ignored those 325 scientists who wrote the letter just as he ignored other contrary opinions.

Then there's global warming. Bush and his officials have disregarded information and perspectives endorsed by thousands of scientists regarding the human-induced shift in the planet's climate and the far-reaching impacts it likely will have on the world. But the Administration hasn't stopped at neglect. It has also gone to great lengths to bury scientific perspectives on global warming, especially the fact that it is largely caused by human-generated emissions of carbon dioxide and other greenhouse gases—by-products of many of the industries that contributed heavily to Bush's election campaign. The White House denies that it has tried to hide anything.

The overwhelming scientific agreement that global warming is real has forced Bush to make occasional gestures toward addressing the problem, starting with his campaign promise to limit the amount of carbon dioxide spewed by power plants that burn fossil fuels. He soon broke that promise. The Administration also purported to address global warming in 2002 by asking for reductions of 18 percent over the following decade in what it called "emissions intensity"—the amount of greenhouse gas pollution relative to national economic output. Not too big a burden on industry, considering that carbon dioxide emissions relative to economic output have been falling for years—but just to be sure there was no burden the Administration made the reductions voluntary. Even if all polluters adhered religiously to those non-binding goals, Administration projections show that while the "intensity" would decline, the actual tonnage of greenhouse gas pollution produced in the U.S. would rise by 14 percent over the next ten years, just as it did in the previous ten years. Undeterred by this information, the White House produced a fact sheet claiming that even though Bush had shunned the Kyoto agreement, the President's "emissions intensity" plan would achieve much the same result, reducing America's greenhouse gas pollution to 7 percent below 1990 levels by 2012—the Kyoto target accepted by other industrialized nations that signed the treaty. But in reality the Administration's plan would lead to emissions 30 percent higher than 1990 amounts. In December of 2002, after launching all this "emissions intensity" business, the White House pulled out another favorite tool for those who want to bury inconvenient science: delay by study. Despite many years and hundreds of peer-reviewed studies showing ample agreement about the essentials of global warming, the Administration insisted that it must study the matter for another ten years before taking significant action.

As if trying to hide an elephant in the living room by throwing a slipcover over it, the Administration repeatedly has attempted to conceal the reality of global warming in environmental reports. This game started when an EPA-led task force published a report, in May 2002, that laid out a scientifically accurate view of global warming. The Administration stuck the report into the nether regions of EPA's Web site, but it soon slipped out. Industry and its allies howled. Bush sprinted away from the report, dismissing it as some blather "put out by the bureaucracy." Christie Whitman, then EPA Administrator, claimed that she hadn't known about the report until she read about it in a newspaper. All this disowning of the report looked disingenuous when the Natural Resources Defense Council (NRDC), an environmental group, released documents that told a different story—Bush officials had been closely following the report for months prior to slipping it deep into EPA's Web site. A few days after NRDC's revelations, Bush reversed field again and said, through spokesman Ari Fleischer, that now he stood behind the report. But Fleischer added that, somehow, the report didn't contradict the Administration's basic position downplaying global warming.

Perhaps because they'd been burned by the May 2002 EPA report, the Administration didn't take half measures with the next report on global warming. In September 2002, EPA released its annual report on air pollution, which for the previous six years had included a section on global warming. This time, rather than tuck this incendiary information into an obscure corner of the annual report as in the handling of the May document, Bush's EPA appointees completely cut it out.

The Administration's habit of shunning the science of global warming cropped up again the next year. In June 2003, the EPA released an elaborate, book-sized document called the "Draft Report on the Environment." Two years in the making, the goal of the publication was to provide an overview of the state of America's environment. Whitman said that the report used "the most sophisticated science ever" and that it was "comprehensive." How odd then to turn to the section on global warming and find that there is no section on global warming. Instead, the reader looking for information on one of the towering issues of our time found these two sentences: "The issue of global climate change involves changes in the radiative balance of the Earth—the balance between energy received from the sun and emitted from Earth. This report does not attempt to address the complexities of this issue." That's it, except for two references that proved to be thick, almost unreadable technical documents.

The hole in the "Draft Report on the Environment," however gaping, might have gone largely unnoticed except that a former EPA official leaked early versions of the report to *The New York Times*. Originally the EPA scientists and staffers preparing the flagship document intended to include more than two sentences on global warming—a lot more. Judging from the early, pre-White-House-involvement drafts, the report would have presented a reasonably accurate and complete summary of global warming. But early in 2003, the White House inserted itself into the writing of the "Draft Report" and began revising the section on global warming. According to *The New York Times* article that broke the story, the White House deleted references to extensive research showing that global warming could harm health and ecosystems and that increasing emissions from vehicles and industrial plants are at least partly responsible. The White House even cut out information from a National Research Council study that the White House itself had commissioned and that the President had endorsed in 2001. *The New York Times* article also reports that Bush officials removed the reference to a study demonstrating that, compared with the last 1,000 years, global temperatures had climbed rapidly during the previous decade. The White House substituted a reference to a study, partly bankrolled by the American Petroleum Institute, that challenged the idea of this recent spike in global temperatures.

In an interview with National Public Radio, Andrew Revkin, one of the authors of *The New York Times* article, cited a verbatim example of the kind of revisions the White House made. The original sentence read, "Climate change has global consequences for human health and the environment." The White House cut that and substituted a paragraph of masterful obfuscation that started with this sentence: "The complexity of the Earth's system and the interconnections among its components make it a scientific challenge to document change, diagnose its causes and develop useful projections of how natural variability and human actions may affect the global environment in the future."

An internal EPA memo protesting the White House editing job circulated through the agency. It stated that the White House alterations had turned the section on global warming into something that "no longer accurately represents scientific consensus on climate change." If the agency published the "Draft Report on the Environment" including the White House rewrite, noted another memo, then the "EPA will take responsibility and severe criticism from the science and environmental communities for poorly representing the science." Apparently unable to restore the scientific integrity of the global warming summary but loath to publish the White House's dubious version, the EPA decided to remove the whole section. Hence, the two sentences.

When all these manipulations went public, outrage rained down on Bush and his officials. They denied wrongdoing and characterized their changes to the report as ordinary editing. Few observers bought this explanation and the storm of censure continued. I could fill pages with scathing denunciations from critics of the Administration, but instead I've chosen to quote from a letter to the editor written by someone who hardly could be portrayed as a knee-jerk opponent of the President. Entitled "When Politics Trumps Science," the letter came from Russell Train, who served as EPA Administrator under Presidents Nixon and Ford. Here's what Train had to say: "I can state categorically that there never was such White House intrusion into the business of the EPA during my tenure. The EPA was established as an independent agency in the executive branch, and so it should remain. There appears today to be a steady erosion in its independent status. I can appreciate the president's interest in not having discordant voices within his Administration. But the interest of the American people lies in having full disclosure of the facts, particularly when the issue is one with such potentially enormous damage to the long-term health and economic well-being of all of us."

———————

Is the Administration's concerted effort to bury science about global warming an anomaly? Not remotely. While promoting the Administration's plan to greatly reduce wetland protections, Secretary of the Interior Norton quashed a Fish and Wildlife Service document declaring that the plan would "result in tremendous destruction of aquatic and terrestrial habitats" and that the plan "has no scientific basis," according to *The Washington Post*. Fearing restrictions on mountaintop removal mining, the Administration cut off a study examining the possibility that this destructive practice exacerbates flooding. Fish and Wildlife biologists warned the BLM that reopening 49,000 temporarily closed acres of California's Algodones sand dunes to off-road vehicles could lead to the extinction of a plant on the endangered species list, but the BLM director pressured the biologists and pushed their information aside in favor of research funded by an off-road-vehicle group. The 49,000 acres got reopened. An EPA draft study found that a process called hydraulic fracturing, used to extract oil and gas, could pollute drinking water with excessive amounts of benzene. A week after discussing this problem with Congressional staffers, EPA changed its tune and said there would not be excessive amounts of benzene, but it offered no scientific explanation, saying merely that the change was "based on feedback" from an industry source. The Department of Energy produced a draft of the White House National Energy Policy that included concerns about the environmental threats posed by hydraulic fracturing, but the White House did some editing and those concerns didn't appear in the final document. Halliburton, the huge energy company headed by Dick Cheney before he became Vice President, is the leading provider of hydraulic fracturing services.

The Administration's suppression of information extends beyond America's borders, too. Due to a variety of environmental problems, Yellowstone National Park had been listed by the United Nations' World Heritage Committee as an imperiled site that needed international attention. Paul Hoffman, Deputy Interior Secretary for Fish and Wildlife and Parks, asked the committee to take Yellowstone off the list, citing a Park Service report that showed, according to Hoffman, that "Yellowstone is no longer in danger." In a familiar pattern, the draft of the report, written by park staff, mentioned numerous problems, but Interior deleted discussion of those concerns in the version it sent to the U.N. News of Interior's tampering got out and the U.N. hesitated to remove Yellowstone from the list. Finally, it did take the park off the at-risk list, but only after requiring that the U.S. keep the U.N. abreast of those ongoing environmental threats in Yellowstone and requesting that independent scientists and organizations participate in those periodic assessments. Apparently the U.N. didn't trust the Administration to provide unvarnished data.

Perhaps the most notorious example of the Administration burying vital scientific information occurred in the aftermath of the September 11 attack on the World Trade Center. The collapse of the twin towers created an air quality nightmare at and around Ground Zero. The debris clouds that tidal-waved through the streets of lower Manhattan and the fires that kept burning for months filled the air with a frightening assortment of toxic particles. Yet on September 18, just a week after the tragedy, EPA issued a statement telling New Yorkers that "their air is safe to breathe and their water is safe." Even at the time this rapid assurance struck some people as premature and unfounded. But many citizens believed EPA's announcements and went back to homes and workplaces located close enough to Ground Zero to still have dangerously polluted air. Even some people who didn't think the air was safe to breathe had to return or risk the wrath of their employers, who used EPA's statements as proof that there was nothing to fear and insisted that their employees return to work.

A study by scientists at the University of California, Davis, released in September 2003 showed that, in fact, there had been plenty to fear. Speaking to Reuters, Thomas Cahill, a professor of physics and engineering and the lead author of the study, said, "The debris pile acted like a chemical factory. It cooked together the components of the buildings and their contents, including enormous numbers of computers, and gave off gases of toxic metals, acids, and organics for at least six weeks." The paper further noted that some of the most toxic elements in the air had burned or chemically decomposed into particles so fine that they could easily work their way deep into people's lungs.

In August 2003, EPA Inspector General Nikki Tinsley issued a 155-page report on this matter. In it, she writes that the White House had leaned on EPA to "add reassuring statements and delete cautionary ones." For example, according to Tinsley, EPA had wanted to warn people about the hazards of asbestos, pulverized glass, concrete, and lead, but the Council on Environmental Quality (CEQ), a White House office, told EPA to omit that information. Another change engineered by CEQ substantially altered the September 13 draft of a press release that EPA wanted to hand out. One sentence in the original release reads, "Even at low levels, EPA considers asbestos hazardous in this situation," a statement that fit with the agency's long-held position that asbestos in any amount is dangerous. But after meeting with CEQ, EPA altered the wording to "Short-term, low-level exposure (to asbestos) of the type that might have been produced by the collapse of the World Trade Center buildings is unlikely to cause significant health effects." According to the EPA Inspector General, the Administration and EPA didn't have enough data to make such claims. And, as the University of California, Davis, study shows, if the Administration had gathered sufficient data, it would have shown that the air was indeed hazardous.

As of this writing, the Administration still denies that it suppressed information or in any way behaved inappropriately. CEQ Chairman James Connaughton gave the following bob-and-weave explanation to *The Washington Post:* "In the back and forth during that very intense period of time, we were making decisions about where the information should be released, what the best way to communicate the information was, so that people could respond responsibly and so that people had a good relative sense of potential risk." However, after resigning as the head of EPA, Christie Whitman confirmed in a *Newsweek* interview that the White House and EPA had made such changes. In that interview Whitman adds that they made the changes because "we didn't want to scare people." Some in the Administration may also have seen political advantage in whitewashing the health dangers, but Whitman's rationale largely rings true and brings up an important difference between the Administration's hiding of facts in the World Trade Center case and in the cases mentioned previously. Though their post-9/11 actions reveal the same disregard for full and accurate science, their motivations probably were public-spirited. But in the previous examples the Administration apparently played fast and loose with the truth merely to serve the interests of favored industries and loyal constituents.

————

Federal agencies employ many fine scientists, but in order to benefit from an even wider range of knowledge and perspectives the government also maintains a number of scientific advisory committees. As ten scientists writing in *Science* magazine put it, these committees are "the primary mechanism for government agencies to harness the wisdom and expertise of the scientific community in shaping the national agenda for both research and regulation." Recognizing the importance of these often influential panels, the Federal Advisory Committee Act (FACA) mandates that scientific committees be "fairly balanced in terms of the points of view represented" and that they are not "inappropriately influenced by the appointing authority or by any special interest."

The Bush Administration has not respected these FACA requirements and once again has pushed political agendas at the expense of scientific integrity. The key to influencing advisory committees is to influence who sits on them, and the White House has been maneuvering to mold the composition of important committees to the Administration's liking. Kevin Knobloch of the Union of Concerned Scientists reports that his organization has been hearing many complaints about the Administration's meddling. "One behavior that seems very distressing to people is the way this Administration reportedly in some instances has subjected scientists to a litmus test before appointing them to federal advisory panels. Asking them how they voted in the last election, what their views are on issues. Every administration is political to some extent, but this one has gone way beyond the bar." In his decades of public involvement, Knobloch never heard of such litmus tests before.

Whether as the result of litmus tests or by some other means, some advisory committees are losing their balance. "There are instances of independent scientists affiliated with research of academic institutions being dropped and scientists on the payroll of industry, often polluting or extractive industries, being appointed," said Knobloch. Many scientists and public interest advocates point to the White House's blatant stacking of the committee that advises the director of the National Center for Environmental Health (NCEH), part of the Centers for Disease Control and Prevention (CDC). In August 2002, the Administration appointed 15 new members to this committee of 18. Bizarrely, no one bothered to consult with Richard J. Jackson, then Director of NCEH—the person whom the panel would be advising. Many of the new members hail from industries and allied institutions that have a vested interest in understating environmental health risks. Typical are Becky Dunlop, vice president of the Heritage Foundation, an antiregulatory think tank, and Roger McClellan, the former director of the Chemical Industry Institute of Toxicology. Of course, having some industry representatives on an environmental health committee is a good thing for balance; having too many of them on the committee is the problem. Those ten scientists writing in *Science* said, "stacking these public committees out of fear that they may offer advice that conflicts with administration policies devalues the entire federal advisory committee structure and the work of dedicated scientists who are willing to participate in these efforts."

Among the other advisory groups that the Administration has attempted to stack is one that influences an issue of visceral importance to millions of children and their families: the CDC's Advisory Committee on Childhood Lead Poisoning Prevention. Lead poisoning can damage the central nervous system, kidneys, and reproductive system of children (and of adults, to a lesser degree), causing such serious problems as kidney failure and anemia. Most insidious, exposure to lead can cause brain damage, significantly lowering a child's IQ or even causing retardation, striking at the very heart of who a child is and how he or she will fare in life. Recent research indicates that lead also may contribute to behavior problems and juvenile delinquency.

Scientists discovered the harm inflicted by lead poisoning decades ago and in the 1970s the government ordered lead to be removed from most products, notably gasoline and household paint. The number of lead poisoning cases dropped sharply, but experts estimate that 434,000 children under the age of six still have blood-lead levels higher than the federal standard. These kids, and many adults, are being exposed to lead left over from the days before the government crackdown. For example, oil, smelting, and mining companies dumped lead-laced waste into many landfills. But for children the most common source of exposure by far is lead paint, which still is present in some 40 million older houses and apartments in the U.S. In poorly maintained buildings, which are common in low-income neighborhoods, the paint flakes off and the young children eat the sweet-tasting chips.

You may wonder why the Administration would try to stack this committee. What stake do their friends in industry have in this issue, given that they long ago gave up using lead in their products (though not without a big fight)? As reported in a 2002 article in *The New Republic,* it seems that the past has come back to haunt the lead industry in the form of liability suits. Big ones. Reminiscent of the case against the tobacco industry, the Attorney General of Rhode Island, for example, accuses the paint industry of having hidden the dangers of lead for decades and he asserts that the industry should pay to get the lead out of the state's older homes. If industry loses such lawsuits, it could cost millions, even billions of dollars. And the cost of a court-ordered cleanup could rise higher depending on what standard CDC uses to determine what level of lead in the blood is considered "lead poisoning."

Enter the advisory committee. In the summer and fall of 2002 the committee members were preparing for an October meeting at which they would start discussing whether to recommend a tougher "lead poisoning" standard than ten micrograms per deciliter of blood, set in 1991. Research published since 1991 indicates that lower concentrations of lead, perhaps much lower concentrations, can harm children. But it's not an open-and-shut case and the lead industry wanted to make sure it had plenty of people on the advisory committee who would be likely to argue industry's perspective. The companies at risk didn't settle for the usual process of lobbying via the access they had purchased through huge campaign contributions. (Corporations neck-deep in lead poisoning issues, such as Dupont, Dow Chemical, and ExxonMobil, all had contributed generously and disproportionately to Republicans in 2000 and 2002.) In addition to lobbying, the lead industry actively recruited candidates for the committee, including at least two of the three whom Health and Human Services Secretary Tommy Thompson appointed to the panel, just weeks before the October meeting.

Before we discuss who got onto the advisory committee, let's talk about who got left off the committee. Michael Wetzman, pediatrician in chief at Rochester General Hospital and the author of many publications on lead poisoning, expected to be reappointed to the committee, on which he had been serving, but the Department of Health and Human Services (HHS) did not ask him to stay on board. HHS rejected the nomination of Susan Klitzman of the Program in Urban Public Health at Hunter College, another frequent author on lead poisoning. HHS also turned down the nomination of Bruce Lanphear, professor of children's environmental health at Cincinnati Children's Hospital Medical Center and one of the most prominent authorities in the field. Lanphear also happens to be one of the authors of some of the latest and most influential studies indicating that very low concentrations of lead can seriously harm children. These three candidates had risen through the Committee's elaborate nominating process and had been forwarded to HHS for what was traditionally pro forma approval.

Members of the committee were taken aback when Secretary Thompson abruptly rejected their choices, overrode the Committee's nominating process, and chose three other people, despite the lack of endorsement from the existing committee and CDC staff and the protests from many public interest, conservation, and health organizations. Two of Thompson's picks have excellent professional credentials, but they also have ties to industry or espouse industry-friendly positions on lead poisoning. Sergio Piomelli is one of the two who has admitted being contacted by industry. Piomelli enjoys considerable credibility, given that his research in the 1970s helped create the ban on lead in gasoline, but recently he has argued against lowering the lead poisoning standard below the current ten micrograms per deciliter of blood—hence the recruiting call from the lead industry. Skepticism about the second appointee, Kimberly Thompson, stems from her affiliation with the Harvard Center for Risk Analysis, a hotbed of antiregulatory thought that largely is funded by dozens of major corporations, including FMC Corp., Ciba-Geigy Corp., and others with lead-contaminated Superfund sites. Last, we come to a truly unconscionable appointment: William Banner, a professor of pediatrics at the University of Oklahoma. He also got recruited by the lead industry. Banner has not published any research on lead or lead poisoning in humans—only in rats. He has been paid to testify in court on behalf of paint companies in lead poisoning cases. Most telling, he maintains that even a lead level of 60 micrograms per deciliter of blood won't harm children's brains; the mainstream scientific debate is about whether *ten* micrograms is too high. As far as I can tell, this extreme belief is not shared by any authority who is not connected to the lead industry. In fact, evidence undercutting Banner's position emerged some 30 or 40 years ago and solidified into a scientific consensus more than a decade ago.

A key study published in the *New England Journal of Medicine* in 2003, after Thompson had appointed the new members to the advisory committee, found that an increase from one to ten micrograms per deciliter of blood was associated with a decline in IQ of 7.4 points. This means that, if the study stands up under replication, children with even very small amounts of lead in their blood will suffer a significant loss of thinking ability. I wonder how that study will play among the three new members of the advisory committee?

"You need to be even more active in recruiting experts who are sympathetic to your view, and much more active in making them part of your message." Does this sound like advice that guided HHS Secretary Thompson in making his appointments to the Advisory Committee on Childhood Lead Poisoning Prevention? Well, it just may be, at least indirectly. The quote comes from Frank Luntz and the Luntz Research Companies, whom we met in the introduction. He's the Republican pollster and "message developer" (his term) who helped craft the Contract with America and who, more recently, wrote a memo laying out a public relations strategy that Republicans could use to spruce up their image on environmental issues. (The memo appeals mainly to antiregulatory, economically conservative Republicans, not to all Republicans and certainly not to the moderate Republicans who place a high value on federal environmental protections.) As noted in the first chapter, the Luntz memo has been very influential. These days you can't swing a stick without hitting a Bush official or the President himself giving a speech on the environment that bristles with "balance," "common sense," "accountable," and other market-tested words and ideas recommended by Luntz.

It's not surprising that the role of science in environmental issues gets the Luntz treatment. Luntz's marketing research revealed what any observer of environmental debates already knew: the perception of what the science says about an issue exerts enormous influence on citizens' attitudes toward that issue. As the Luntz memo puts it, "People are willing to trust scientists, engineers, and other leading research professionals." Toward the end of the memo, Luntz includes a model speech on the environment to serve as a template for antiregulatory rhetoric. In it he includes four key statements that he urges GOP politicians to use while speechifying, one of which is, "New regulations should be based on the most advanced and credible scientific knowledge available."

This is of course a fine sentiment with which no one would disagree publicly, but it is also a principle from which the President and many of his appointees routinely stray. When introducing his global warming plans in 2002, Bush said, "When we make decisions, we want to make sure we do so on sound science; not what sounds good, but what is real." But earlier in this chapter we saw some of the many ways in which the Administration has mistreated science in the global warming debate. Thousands of scientists have reached a consensus regarding some basic aspects of climate change, yet the Administration instead emphasizes the findings of a handful of dissenting researchers and information provided by corporations that stand to lose money if greenhouse gases are regulated. Clearly, the President is not basing decisions on the "most advanced and credible scientific knowledge available" nor using "sound science." The Bush Administration subscribes— perhaps literally—to Luntz's propaganda approach to science, in which image triumphs over "what is real." Perhaps I should put this in Luntz parlance: When Bush and Administration officials alter or suppress information or present only one side of a scientific discussion, they are behaving in a manner that runs counter to the goal of "balance." When confronted with such deceptive practices, "common sense" tells citizens that they should hold the President and his appointees "accountable." If this mistreatment of science continues and environmental policy drifts away from its scientific moorings, the natural world and human health also will be set adrift.

CHAPTER 6

Bean Counters Rule

t costs $99 billion to save one year of life for one person by reg-
ulating chloroform exposures at pulp mills. Environmental Protection Agency standards for soot and smog do so much damage
to the economy that they lead to the deaths of 27,000 people a
year. Under the Occupational Safety and Health Administration's
1985 regulation governing formaldehyde, it costs $72 billion to
save a single life. An examination of 187 federal regulations found
that together they—especially the 90 environmental rules—suck
so much money away from more cost-effective safety measures
that they prevent us from saving the lives of 60,200 people a year.

I could cite many other examples. For years such revelations
about the excesses of government oversight of business have been
making the rounds on TV talk shows, in Congressional hearings,
in newspaper op-ed pieces, and in think-tank reports. The loud-
and-clear message: regulation has run amok. Federal agencies are

pumping out hundreds of burdensome dictates that provide very little bang for a whole lot of bucks. And some regulations, as noted above, even result in lost lives. Politicians, the private sector, and the public alike find this regulatory excess outrageous.

And it would be outrageous, if it were true.

———————

The Office of Management and Budget (OMB) occupies a nondescript building in downtown Washington, D.C. Acting as appendages of the President, the economists and other staff in this small agency assist the White House in developing and implementing the federal budget, in developing the Administration's position regarding legislation in Congress, and in managing the Executive Branch.

If the federal bureaucracy is the realm of bean counters, then OMB personnel are among the knights of the realm. They churn out long, chart-clogged, small-print reports thick with passages such as "It is important that you utilize revealed preference models that adhere to economic criteria that are consistent with utility maximizing behavior"—prose seemingly intended to compete with Sleep-Eze for the insomniac market. But tucked away within such language, within such reports, within the OMB, lies a way of applying economics to environmental regulation that could decimate coastal ecosystems, sicken agricultural workers, pollute drinking water, deny habitat protection to endangered species, and raise toxin levels in children. Federal agencies produce dozens of "significant" rules (those with impacts of $100 million or more) every year and OMB will scrutinize them all, as well as any less expensive rules that catch OMB's eye. The agency will undertake extensive analysis of the major proposed regulations and delay, send back for revision, or kill those that don't meet its standards. And it will do this quietly, below the radar of most of the media and the public. Under President Bush, OMB already has begun instituting ambitious changes that, if fully executed, will profoundly weaken the implementation of many of America's environmental laws. Citizens who care about the environment and their allies in government had better read the fine print coming out of OMB.

It's fitting that the office of the Director of OMB is located right next to the White House, in the Old Executive Office Building. The agency plays a key role in unobtrusively pushing the President's environmental agenda, serving as a link between the President and the agencies that deal with the environment. In particular, President Reagan used OMB as a vehicle for his vigorous efforts to loosen environmental regulation. This use ebbed during the 1990s, but under President George W. Bush the agency's power over regulatory matters is rapidly climbing to unprecedented levels.

With Bush appointees running OMB, the agency is getting extra attention from "regulatory reform" advocates—a broad network of government officials, think-tank scholars, and industry lobbyists that is forever working to thwart, dilute, or repeal environmental regulation that business finds burdensome. Though much of this network's lobbying muscle goes into twisting Congressional arms, the corporate community knows that the executive branch agencies are responsible for implementing the laws that Congress passes—and, with a little prodding, there can be many a slip twixt the cup and the lip. If business loses the debate over an environmental law at the Capitol, it or its allies can turn up the heat on the EPA, the Forest Service, the Bureau of Land Management, or some other resource agency to try to delay or shape the rules that transform the legislation's intent into on-the-ground action. This strategy requires a tedious, issue-by-issue effort.

On the other hand, because OMB policy can affect all the agencies, it provides one-stop shopping. "If you fix [OMB], you rein in all the agencies," said Bruce Josten, the U.S. Chamber of Commerce's Executive Vice President for Government Affairs, to

The Washington Post. It's no surprise that OMB has earned a place on the speed dials of corporate lobbyists.

Those phone calls are likely to be taken at OMB with the Bush team in charge. The first Bush appointee to sit behind the desk in the OMB Director's office was Mitchell E. Daniels, Jr., a veteran of the Reagan White House and a darling of the laissez-faire faithful. "Mitch's appointment is a total home run," said Stephen Moore, head of the free-market advocacy outfit Club for Growth, in remarks reported in the *National Review* at the time of Daniels's confirmation. Prior to being appointed by President Bush to lead OMB, Daniels had served as a Senior Vice President at pharmaceutical giant Eli Lilly. Daniels stepped down in June 2003, at which point the President appointed Joshua Bolten to be the new Director. Bolten was White House Deputy Chief of Staff and a man that Bush called one of his "closest and most trusted advisors." Bolten has sought to remain in the background and as of this writing little is known about what he'll do at OMB.

But Bolten (nor Daniels before him) is not the Bush appointee at OMB who most heartens industry and worries environmentalists. That would be John D. Graham, a bright, balding, middle-aged man who has been challenging health and environmental regulation almost since he started to shave; at 23, according to a profile of Graham that appeared in the magazine of the Natural Resources Defense Council, Graham coauthored a heated criticism of regulation in which he asserted that many restrictions on such things as PCBs and nuclear power resulted from the "flustered hypochondria" of consumer and environmental groups. Over the years Graham's rhetoric and manner have softened, but his resolve to root out what he considers inefficient regulation remains hard as ever.

On July 19, 2001, the Senate confirmed Graham as Administrator of the Office of Information and Regulatory Affairs (OIRA), an obscure but powerful arm of OMB. Lisa Heinzerling, a law professor at Georgetown University and an authority on regulatory matters, called him "perhaps the most powerful policy analyst in America today." OMB Watch, a public interest group that looks over the shoulder of the budget office, says of Graham: "No health, safety, or environmental standard is beyond his reach." In written testimony to Congress opposing Graham's nomination, Gene Karpinski, Executive Director of U.S. Public Interest Research Group, elaborates on the clout of OIRA and its Director: "This office is the gatekeeper of OMB's regulatory review process, and dictates the creation and use of analytical methodologies that other agencies must employ when developing protections for public health, consumers, and the environment. In his role as gatekeeper, Dr. Graham will have the ability to stop much-needed protections before they ever see the light of day. In his role as director of analysis, he will be able to manipulate agency rule-makings—without Congressional approval or adequate public discussion—by issuing new OMB policies that force other agencies to conform to his narrow and highly controversial philosophy. This could result in a weakening of current protections, and a failure to create adequate future safeguards."

Graham has assured people concerned about the environment that they have nothing to fear from him and OIRA. Speaking before the Society of Automotive Engineers in May 2002, Graham said, "Despite what some of our critics charge, there is no grandiose plot to roll back safeguards or attempt an across-the-board sunset of existing regulations. What the President seeks is a smarter regulatory process based on sound science and economics: a smarter process adopts new rules when market and local choices fail, modifies existing rules to make them more effective or less costly, and rescinds outmoded rules whose benefits no longer justify their costs." Graham added that the changes he intends to make won't be "headline grabbers" but that they will have a "long-lasting impact on the regulatory state."

Graham came to OIRA from 11 years as the head of the Harvard Center for Risk Analysis (HCRA), which he founded. Embedded at one of the nation's leading universities, HCRA sounds like some ivory-tower research group, but it is active in public affairs. The vast majority of its financial backers are Fortune 500 corporations. Though that proves nothing, critics find HCRA's strong corporate ties suggestive. As Senator Richard Durbin (D-IL) said at Graham's confirmation hearing, "These corporate clients came to Professor Graham not to find ways to increase regulation on their businesses but just for the opposite, so that he can provide through his center a scientific basis for resisting Government regulation in the areas of public health and the environment." Critics would add that what Graham provides often is pseudoscience.

Among the hundred-plus corporations and industry associations that fund the center are Alcoa, the American Automobile Manufacturers Association, the American Petroleum Institute, Amoco, ARCO, Boise Cascade, BP America, the Business Roundtable, the Chemical Manufacturers Association, ChevronTexaco, Dow Chemical, DuPont Agricultural Products, Exxon, Ford Motors, General Electric, General Motors, Georgia-Pacific, International Paper, Monsanto, Shell, Texaco, Union Carbide, and Unocal. Several public entities, such as the U.S. Department of Energy, the National Science Foundation, and the Environmental Protection Agency also support the center, but their contributions are restricted grants, unlike those from most of the corporations, and are dwarfed by the corporate dollars.

Graham denies that the corporate contributors exerted any undue influence on his and the center's research, and that certainly could be true, assuming one doesn't consider special access alone to be "undue" influence. As with contributions to political campaigns, it's hard to know whether those who funded Graham and the center simply supported someone whose thinking mirrored their own or if their money directly influenced the research—and perhaps it doesn't much matter in terms of what Graham is doing at OIRA.

Whether the corporate contributions only magnified his voice or actually put words in his mouth, the relationship between Graham and his corporate backers during his HCRA tenure sometimes grew cozy. For example, Graham personally approached tobacco behemoth Philip Morris, now Altria, for money for HCRA. In an October 21, 1991, letter to Philip Morris Vice President for Government Affairs David Greenberg, Graham asked for a $25,000 donation to the center. He closed the letter by stating, "It is important for me to learn more about the risk-related challenges that you face." Eight days later Robert Pages, who worked in the Scientific Affairs Division of Philip Morris, referred to Graham's October 21 letter in an internal memo. He recommended that someone from Philip Morris meet with Graham because "he is a key player in all this risk analysis stuff that's currently going on in government. (Depending on the 'vibes' you guys get when you meet Graham, I would also be in favor of PM [Philip Morris] becoming a contributor to the Center.)"

Philip Morris issued a $25,000 check to HCRA on January 22, 1992. A few days later Graham returned the check. HCRA is tied to the Harvard School of Public Health and, not surprisingly, the dean of the school thought it inappropriate for an institution concerned with health to accept an unrestricted grant from a tobacco company. But in August 1992, Graham and HCRA received—and kept—$20,000 from Kraft General Foods, a subsidiary of Philip Morris. A letter from Kraft's Vice President of Scientific Relations, Enrique Guardia, stated that the money was intended "to support the work of the Center, in general, and your contributions to the food safety debate (Pesticides). I would like to meet from time to time to discuss topics of mutual interest." Over the next few years

Kraft gave tens of thousands of additional dollars to HCRA. Graham also approached Guardia for help in trying to get the food industry to put together a $25 million donation to HCRA.

Philip Morris hardly was the only corporation that found a willing ally in Graham. In their testimony opposing Graham's nomination to head OIRA, 32 faculty members at schools of medicine and public health cited Graham's expansive ties to industry as a serious conflict of interest. They wrote:

> *Time and again, Professor Graham has accepted money from industries while conducting research and policy studies on public health regulations in which those same industries had substantial vested interests. Not surprisingly, he has consistently produced reports, submitted testimony to the Congress, and made statements to the media that have supported industry positions, frequently without disclosing the sources of his funding.*

> *For example:*

> - *He has solicited money from Philip Morris while criticizing the EPA's risk assessment on the dangers of secondhand smoke,*
> - *He has greatly overestimated the costs of preventing leukemia caused by exposure to benzene in gasoline while accepting funds from the American Petroleum Institute,*
> - *He has downplayed EPA's warnings about cancer risk from dioxin exposure while being supported by several major dioxin producers, including incinerator, pulp, and paper companies,*
> - *He has advocated against regulating driving while simultaneously talking on cellular phones in research*

> *underwritten by a $300,000 grant from AT&T Wireless Communication,*
> - *And he has been a major spokesperson before the Congress on behalf of industries' "regulatory reform" agenda, while being supported by large grants of unrestricted funds from chemical, petroleum, timber, tobacco, automobile, electric power, mining, pharmaceutical, and manufacturing industries.*

Numerous opponents of Graham's nomination likewise expressed concern about Graham's corporate sympathies, but their criticisms also ranged beyond his ties to industry. Opponents questioned everything from his general attitude toward government regulation to the details of his methodology in determining the net benefits of agency rules. At Graham's nomination hearing, which was exceptionally contentious for such a low-profile position, many academics, environmental organizations, public health and safety groups, and former cabinet secretaries and deputy secretaries testified against his nomination. The late Senator Paul Wellstone (D-MN) said that the Senate shouldn't confirm as head of OIRA "someone whose entire professional history seems aimed at frustrating efforts to regulate in the public interest."

On the other hand, many people supported Graham's nomination, including 95 academic colleagues, former EPA Administrator William Reilly, and the last five heads of OIRA. They lauded him as someone who simply was trying to bring commonsense reform to regulation, someone who wanted to use science to ensure that the nation gets its regulatory priorities straight. This portrayal of Graham as a nonideological, good government advocate was summed up in a letter of support from Cass Sunstein, an eminent law professor at the University of Chicago and a prominent expert on government regulation. Sunstein wrote, "John [Graham] has emphasized that we could save many more lives if we used our resources on big problems rather than little ones. This should not be a controversial position. And in emphasizing that environmental protection sometimes involves large expenditures for small gains, John is seeking to pave the way toward more sensible regulation, not to eliminate regulation altogether. In fact John is an advocate of environmental protection, not an opponent of it. When he criticizes some regulations, it is because they deliver too little and cost too much."

In his testimony in favor of Graham's nomination, Senator Phil Gramm (R-TX), now retired, voiced the impatience that many of Graham's supporters feel when confronted with what they perceive as an illogical desire to overregulate. "In reality," said Gramm, "what Dr. Graham's opponents object to is rationality. That is what they object to. If there is a garbage dump in the middle of the desert that no one has been close to in 50 years, they object to the fact that someone will stand up and say, 'We could probably do more for child safety by improving traffic safety, by buying helmets for people who ride bicycles than by going out in the desert and digging up this garbage dump.' They object to that statement because it is rational. And they are not rational."

In the end Graham received the most important vote of confidence: the support of the 61 senators who voted to confirm him, as opposed to the 37 senators who voted against him. It is notable, however, that 37 senators voted thumbs-down. Usually senators would perfunctorily approve a nominee to this obscure office, yet Graham attracted the most "no" votes of any Bush nominee, with the exception of Attorney General John Ashcroft.

Shortly after becoming Administrator, Graham began working to expand OIRA's power over the agencies. Bear in mind that agencies, like the Bureau of Land Management and the U.S. Fish and Wildlife Service, operate under statutory authority delegated by Congress to implement laws passed by Congress. Agencies have extensive resources—notably scientific expertise—and they have relationships with the people they regulate, both of which OIRA lacks. OIRA's traditional role, which is enormously influential even without adding any extra power, is to review and approve (or disapprove) significant agency rule-makings, look at costs and benefits, and make sure that alternative regulatory approaches are considered. In order to make a big splash and push the White House's regulatory agenda, Graham decided to insert OIRA into an earlier stage of the agencies' decision-making processes. OIRA also has been hiring scientists for the first time ever, a sign that it intends to weigh in on scientific affairs. OIRA even is being proactive, sometimes suggesting regulatory actions, which critics think exceeds its expertise and usurps the agencies' jobs. In the end, it might make sense to judge the substance of OIRA's initiatives rather than the process. In the name of high returns on low investments, Graham and his office have championed some worthy projects, such as placing defibrillators in airports. But Graham's OIRA rarely has recommended environmental regulations. It has tended to push programs that cost taxpayers, such as the defibrillators, or that cost individuals, such as bike helmets. Seldom does Graham support, let alone initiate, regulations that would cost big money for big business.

Proposing new regulations is a sideline, however. Under Graham, OIRA's full-time job is rooting out "ill-advised" regulations. To augment his own thoughts as to which rules should be loosened or eliminated, he asked the public and a wide range of interest groups to recommend likely candidates. (In his initial request, which he later changed after receiving considerable criticism, he did not ask for lists of regulations that should be expanded and strengthened nor for ideas for new environmental regulations whose absence was "ill-advised.") OIRA received 71 nominations, the vast majority from industry and its allies. Forty-four came from the Mercatus Center, a conservative think tank funded by corporations and represented by Wendy Gramm, the head of OIRA under President Reagan and the wife of former Senator Phil Gramm, quoted above.

OIRA designated 23 of the 71 ideas as high priority—"high priority" meaning that OIRA was inclined to agree and that OIRA would take a hard look at them. All of the 23 high-priority items had been suggested by business interests and all would have the effect of weakening regulation. Of the 23 targets, 13 were environmental rules, among them some that dealt with landmark laws—the Clean Air Act, the Clean Water Act—as well as a number of high-profile issues, such as forest planning rules, arsenic in drinking water, and snowmobiles in national parks.

When Graham and OIRA see a regulation they consider inefficient, they can't weaken it or make it vanish with a simple wave of a wand. They must justify their decision and they must stay within shouting distance of OIRA's legally designated responsibilities. As it is, OIRA's expansion under Graham has convinced some observers that OIRA has exceeded its authority. And, as always, for political reasons the Bush Administration prefers not to risk alienating voters by openly attacking environmental regulations, which most Americans support.

So, what's a deregulator to do?

Graham's tool of choice is cost-benefit analysis. Basically, it means identifying and adding up the costs and benefits of a proposed or existing regulation to determine if it imposes a net cost or delivers a net benefit, then using that information to help decide whether to institute a new regulation or change an old one. Sounds reasonable. Indeed, Graham and other proponents of cost-benefit analysis portray it as a commonsense tool that's neither anti-regulation nor pro-regulation, but a neutral, scientific method of determining the pros and cons of a regulation. However, the details reveal that cost-benefit analysis à la Graham is neither commonsense, neutral, nor scientific.

In our personal lives we weigh costs versus benefits every day. Say your husband is making fruit salad on a Saturday morning but there aren't any apples and you have to decide whether to accede to his entreaties that you go to the farmers' market to get one. On the one hand there are costs: the apple will cost 50 cents, the venture will take 20 minutes, you'll have to get dressed, and it's hard to park at the market. On the other hand, there are benefits: your family really likes having apple chunks in the fruit salad. You instinctively run a quick cost-benefit analysis and it indicates a net cost. The decision: you leave your slippers on and turn to the comics.

Then again, maybe your cost-benefit analysis was too simple, and perhaps you slanted it a bit because you didn't want to bother going out. Take the costs. To be honest, often the farmers will bargain and you probably can get a fine apple for 30 or 40 cents. You also know that they'll sell you a dozen for two dollars. And you were planning on taking your mastiff for a walk to the park after breakfast anyway, so instead you could take Brutus and stroll the mile to the market, which eliminates the cost of lost time and avoids the parking hassle.

And so it goes with measuring the "cost" side of cost-benefit analysis. It seems easy enough to tote up the money that an industry must spend in order to buy new equipment or hire more people in order to comply with a regulation, but even this seemingly straightforward step poses difficulties. One is a general problem that permeates cost-benefit analysis: so much of it is guesswork that never matures into fact. Richard Parker, a law professor at the University of Connecticut and a former Special Counsel to the Deputy Administrator of EPA, puts it this way in his landmark paper, published in the fall 2003 issue of the *University of Chicago*

Law Review: "Every year football pundits on pregame shows take turns guessing the score of the point spread of the Super Bowl that is soon to follow. But then the game happens, and newspapers report the results of the game. Fortunately, there is no record of any occasion in recent history when a newspaper has committed the blunder of confusing the pregame guesses with the actual score of the game. Yet this sort of blunder is virtually universal in score-cards [tables that list regulations and their supposed costs and benefits], where conclusions are routinely described as if they represent actual measurements of costs and benefits when, in fact, the numbers consist exclusively of analysts' educated guesses about what future costs and benefits might be in a variety of hypothetical scenarios."

In addition, two specific problems confound the accurate measurement of costs. One, agencies generally must rely on the regulated industry to supply information on costs. Given business's incentive to inflate the cost side of cost-benefit analysis, it comes as no surprise that it often puts its finger on the expense side of the scale to make it appear heavier. Consider the example of chlorofluorocarbons (CFCs), as reported by Eban Goodstein, an associate professor of economics at Lewis and Clark College and a research associate at the Economic Policy Institute, who has studied regulatory costs. In the early 1990s regulations limited the use of CFCs (which deplete the ozone layer and contribute to global climate change) in automobile air conditioners. Car manufacturers claimed this edict would raise the price of a new car by $650 to $1,200. A few years later researchers pegged the actual costs at $40 to $400 per car.

More surprisingly, the agencies themselves sometimes overestimate the cost of compliance. Goodstein notes the example of the Occupational Safety and Health Administration's vinyl and polyvinyl chloride exposure limits, which the agency's consultant estimated would cost industry $109 million a year. The consultant further asserted that the exposure levels OSHA was contemplating simply couldn't be attained. (According to Goodstein, the president of Firestone's plastics division agreed, claiming that the proposed standard "puts the vinyl plastics industry on a collision course with economic disaster.") Despite these dire predictions, OSHA adopted the tough standards. Several years later researchers at the Wharton School of Business estimated that the actual compliance costs were about $20 million a year and the assertion that the exposure levels simply couldn't be reached turned out to be inaccurate.

The second factor that consistently leads to gross overestimates of the costs of compliance glistens with irony. Many of the same cheerleaders for free enterprise who promote innovation as the engine that drives the universe habitually overlook innovation's role in lowering regulatory costs. Goodstein cites the case of benzene. Back in the 1970s the chemical industry complained that it would cost $350,000 per plant to limit benzene emissions. But soon after the regulation was implemented the industry found a way to use other chemicals and compliance costs dwindled essentially to zero. This well-documented phenomenon goes by the name of "technology-forcing." In an article in *The American Prospect,* Goodstein notes, too, that "frequently the new technology turns out to have higher productivity benefits." President Bush, too, seems to neglect the proven potential of technology-forcing when he cites the economic costs of regulation as a major reason for some of his Administration's antienvironmental actions, such as backing away from the Kyoto Protocol and breaking his campaign promise to regulate carbon dioxide emissions from power plants.

Coincidentally, two weeks before the Administration's announcement, in 2001, that it wasn't going to regulate carbon dioxide emissions from power plants after all, the U.S. Supreme Court issued a unanimous decision in *American Trucking Association v. Whitman* that in essence upheld the federal agencies' approach of basing ambient air-quality standards on scientific evidence of pollution's health effects and not on estimates of the costs of achieving those standards. In his concurring opinion, Justice Steven Breyer, an outspoken critic of some aspects of regulation, notes that technology-forcing plays a major role and makes predicting the costs of regulations problematic.

Are the cases of CFCs, vinyl and polyvinyl chloride, and benzene anomalies? Not at all. In every one of the dozen examples that Goodstein studied, the predictions of regulatory costs exceeded the actual costs, and in 11 of the 12 cases the predictions were at least double the actual costs. Along the same lines, in 1996, the Government Accounting Office (GAO) examined the compliance costs of 15 businesses that had volunteered for the study because they thought federal regulation was too costly to industry. However, none of the companies could nail down its regulatory costs and the GAO found no evidence of a significant burden.

As you can see, figuring out the costs in cost-benefit analysis isn't so easy, after all. But it's a snap compared with figuring out the benefits.

Let's get back to your family's yearning for an apple in the fruit salad. The obvious benefit of going to the farmers' market to get apples is having apple chunks in your fruit salad. But think a little more, and think about less obvious and less tangible benefits. You do enjoy strolling around the farmers' market on a sunny morning. And you could do all your produce shopping there and skip the trip to Sam's Club you were planning for later that day. And the apples you'd get are an heirloom variety that Sam's Club and other supermarkets have never even heard of, so eating them would be a new experience. And buying from that nice couple would support them and help them prevent those rare heirloom varieties from going extinct in a red-delicious world. And they're organic farmers, so buying their apples instead of the ones at Sam's Club means a little less pesticide sprayed. And they're local folks, so more of the money you pay them would stay in the community instead of flowing to Sam's Club executives and shareholders. And Sam's Club is a division of Wal-Mart, and didn't you just read that Wal-Mart has been accused of buying from overseas sweatshops and busting unions and forcing already-underpaid employees to work overtime without pay? And who knows what you don't know—perhaps it'll turn out that apples contain loads of some vitamin that you'll need later in life to combat cancer.

Measuring the benefits of environmental regulations lies at the heart of a scholarly dispute with far-reaching implications for the environment. Bear in mind that just as industry and its allies have a strong incentive to overestimate costs in cost-benefit analysis, they have an equally strong incentive to underestimate benefits.

John F. Morrall III sowed the seeds of this dispute when he published his seminal paper, "A Review of the Record," in 1986. Now Chief of Health, Transportation, and General Government at OIRA, Morrall was an economist with OMB at the time he wrote the paper. Remember the reference in the first paragraph of this chapter to the OSHA formaldehyde rule that cost $72 billion to save a single life? That figure comes from Morrall's paper. "A Review of the Record" is renowned especially for its table showing the expense of saving one life for each of 44 regulations. Though formaldehyde heads that list, Morrall found that dozens of other environmental rules cost millions or billions of dollars each in order to prevent a single death. The regulations that appear to be cost-effective tend to be safety measures aimed at reducing accidents, such as rules requiring steering column protection in cars and adequate venting for space heaters.

For more than a decade after its publication Morrall's paper didn't rouse any rebuttal. What it did stir up was an outcry against regulations branded as grossly inefficient. Predictably, industry brandished Morrall's table and decried the foolishness of spending such fantastic sums—most of it their money—for such small returns. More notably, some people who were not knee-jerk opponents of regulation, overwhelmed by the unmistakable message delivered by Morrall's numbers, also felt compelled to admit that many environmental regulations clearly weren't worth the price.

Morrall's study created a powerful ripple effect that continues to this day. Soon after its publication Morrall's table and his general conclusions began appearing throughout the regulatory universe: in Congressional testimony, in court opinions, in OMB's annual reports to Congress, and in law school textbooks. Morrall's work also spawned a multitude of scholarly papers and popular articles that used his information to give substance to their denunciations of environmental regulation. Notably, Morrall's paper also helped shape the antiregulatory features of the Newt Gingrich–led Republican Revolution's Contract with America. Eventually the ripples spread so far that their origins often got lost, and Morrall's table and figures were being cited as gospel by people who'd never heard of John F. Morrall III or seen his original study. Given the sprawling edifice depending on the foundation laid by Morrall in 1986, it's surprising that it was 1998 before someone closely inspected that foundation—and discovered an unsettling number of cracks.

Lisa Heinzerling, the aforementioned Georgetown University law professor and regulatory expert, sounded the first iconoclastic note in an article published in the *Yale Law Review* in 1998. It was a sustained note—87 pages of digging into the details of Morrall's work. In the article she underscores the impact of Morrall's paper: "These numbers are ubiquitous in the literature on risk regulation," she writes. "Morrall's calculations . . . have been used to support every one of the most prominent current critiques of the regulatory system." Since the mid-1990s, two prominent figures have written seminal papers and broadcast their results widely, joining Morrall to form a cost-benefit trinity: John Graham, whom we've met, and Robert Hahn, whom we'll meet presently.

Heinzerling begins her critique of Morrall's 1986 paper by noting that he seems to have been unscientifically selective in deciding which regulations to analyze, largely choosing material that supports his thesis, including a couple of regulations that were only proposed, never issued. These two nonexistent rules are among those that badly fail Morrall's cost-benefit test. Heinzerling also notes that Morrall did not select a number of prominent regulations that easily met his stated criterion for choosing rules to examine; had he chosen them, they would have challenged his conclusion that regulations protecting human health are seldom cost-effective. She notes that he could have examined certain provisions of the Clean Air Act, for example, which together produced annual benefits of $37.3 billion while costing only $13.7 billion. Morrall replies that at the time he was not aware of any studies of the Clean Air Act that had the cost-benefit information he was seeking, but he now acknowledges that reductions in particulate matter and ozone do provide life-saving benefits that outweigh costs. Morrall also points out that in his article he identified which regulations were implemented and which merely proposed, but these are the kinds of details that usually got lost when antiregulatory interests later cited his work.

Parker, the University of Connecticut law professor, expands on Heinzerling's suggestion that Morrall's study contains hidden biases. In his 2003 paper, Parker pointed out that Morrall's scorecard, like all scorecards, is based on assessments done by others, usually the agencies. The problem, Parker said, is that Morrall "revises agency cost and benefit estimates whenever he disagrees with them—often by several orders of magnitude, and always in the direction of higher costs and lower benefits." Morrall justifies his revisions on the grounds that regulatory agencies "tend to overstate the effectiveness of their actions. Where such biases were evident . . . I made the corrections . . . relying on published studies."

Parker finds this unconvincing. "This defense faces three rather obvious objections," said Parker. "First, Morrall nowhere proves that agencies regularly overstate the effectiveness of their actions. Indeed, we will see shortly that agencies understate (or at least under-quantify) benefits in many cases. Second, Morrall has no training in any of the disciplines which would qualify him to substitute his own judgment for agency scientists on matters of exposure, risk, or compliance costs. Third, Morrall does not document, much less defend, either the studies he allegedly relied on, or the criteria he applied, in generating his own substitute numbers. His assumptions and calculations are, by his own admission, 'scattered about in [his] filing cabinets' and are not available to outside reviewers." It's worth noting that Parker, Heinzerling, and other critics of cost-benefit analysis have encountered unusual difficulties or even have been stonewalled when they requested a scholarly exchange of information with cost-benefit advocates. Even more troubling, says Parker, is the fact that seldom do the cost-benefit backers make available their raw data—standard operating procedure for most scholars.

Heinzerling, Parker, and other critics of Morrall's paper also find fault with what they see as his misuse of an innocuous-sounding but enormously important practice called "discounting," which can dramatically shrink the apparent benefits of environmental and health regulations. The critics agree that discounting is a standard and proper tool for making many practical financial decisions. The basic idea is that money received today is worth more than the same amount of money received in the future, even allowing for inflation, because you could bank or invest that money received today and immediately start earning interest on it. For example, if you get $100 today and invest it at an interest rate of

10 percent, in a year you'll have $110. Discounting is like the reverse of earning interest. At a discount rate of 10 percent—the rate Morrall uses in his paper—$100 received a year from today has a *present value* of only $90 in today's dollars because if you got $90 today and invested it at a 10 percent interest rate you'd have $100 in a year. Simple, no?

No. And it gets much worse. As I doubt that you want to read 50 pages that burrow into the intricacies of discounting and I know that I don't want to write them, I'll grossly summarize. Morrall and other cost-benefit believers blithely discount future environmental and health benefits as if discounting were not highly contentious. Many scholars think that discounting shouldn't be applied to environmental and health benefits; that, even if one accepts the need for discounting, the discount rate of 10 percent used by Morrall is way too high; and that it is inappropriate to use a uniform discount rate for widely varying regulations. In her *Yale Law Review* article Heinzerling lays out the effect discounting has on long-term benefits. "The choice between a 10 percent discount rate and, say, a 1 percent rate makes an extraordinary difference in the attractiveness of programs producing benefits remote in time. (At a discount rate of 10 percent, a rule predicted to save 10 lives in 25 years would be treated as saving 0.92 lives; at a discount rate of 1 percent, the same rule would be treated as saving 7.97 lives.)"

So citizens whose polluted drinking water will kill 10 of them from cancer in 25 years may figure that $10 million spent by the polluter today to eliminate those toxic discharges is saving 10 lives, and $1 million per life is a bargain. However, due to discounting, Morrall's scorecard would show that the corporation's $10 million is saving less than one life—. 92 of a life, to be exact—and society (especially the polluting company) might conclude that spending $10,870,000 to save a single life is not worth it. Philosopher Derek Parfit reveals an element of absurdity in discounting human lives, observing, "At a discount rate of five percent, one death next year counts for more than a billion deaths in 500 years. On this view, catastrophes in the further future can now be regarded as morally trivial."

Heinzerling also takes Morrall to task for limiting the benefits in his cost-benefit analysis to the prevention of sickness and death. "In practice," writes Heinzerling, "this means that the only regulatory benefit captured by Morrall's table . . . is the prevention of premature human death from cancer. Yet . . . the regulatory programs that fare poorly in Morrall's table do not just prevent cancer. They prevent many human illnesses that cannot be quantified; they prevent ecological harm; and they prevent harms to values that are widely shared, such as autonomy, community, and equity." Heinzerling contends that if the full array of benefits had been considered, most of the regulations that Morrall finds irrationally expensive would in fact be bargains.

Even Morrall's regulatory enemy number one, the formaldehyde rule, looks fundamentally different when viewed through a lens other than the number of fatal illnesses caused. This harsh industrial chemical also causes respiratory, eye, and skin conditions in huge numbers of workers. This information may not have been included in the original regulatory proposal from which Morrall gathered his numbers, but even at the time Morrall created his table there was considerable evidence that formaldehyde was the source of serious nonlethal afflictions. By 1987, when the formaldehyde rule was issued, the diminishing of skin problems was cited as a major benefit. Over time the full benefits of the rule have become well known, yet antiregulatory campaigners have continued to excoriate this rule as a lamebrained attempt to save lives at $72 billion each. In a 2002 article in the *Cornell Law Review,* Heinzerling and Frank Ackerman, an environmental economist and Research Director of the Global Development and Environmental Institute at Tufts University, commented on Morrall's treatment of the formaldehyde rule: "To get to Morrall's $72 billion number [his cost per life saved for formaldehyde], just ignore all the real reasons for formaldehyde regulation, and imagine that someone was foolish enough to propose it solely as a way of reducing deaths from cancer. Sure enough, it is an inefficient way of reducing cancer deaths."

Robert Hahn, who followed in Morrall's footsteps, produced related, blockbuster papers in 1996 and 2000 that turn the cost-benefit spotlight on more than 100 major regulations, including a 1992 EPA rule protecting agricultural workers from some of the dangers of pesticides. As Director of the AEI-Brookings Joint Center for Regulatory Studies (that's the American Enterprise Institute and the Brookings Institution), a prestigious and influential think tank collaboration, Hahn casts a long shadow across the regulatory landscape. He not only concluded that fewer than half of these regulations passed the cost-benefit test, but, according to Richard Parker, Hahn found that the EPA rule on pesticide protections produced no benefits. That would surprise the thousands of farmworkers who suffer from pesticide poisoning.

Discovering that Hahn had given the EPA pesticides rule a zero in the benefits column was no easy matter. In his paper Hahn doesn't disclose the names of the regulations he studied nor some of the calculations he used to arrive at his conclusions. Parker had to ask repeatedly over the course of months before he could obtain Hahn's spreadsheets. When he finally got them, Parker was astonished to find that 41 of the 136 rules in Hahn's database are considered to provide no benefits. Not no net benefits, but no benefits at all. Zero. In his paper, Parker said that these reportedly worthless regulations include, in addition to the EPA pesticide rule, a Clean Water Act rule aimed at protecting sensitive coastal areas from non-point-source water pollution; a rule requiring that owner/operators of tankers develop plans to respond to large oil spills; and three rules establishing national primary drinking water standards to limit public exposure to toxic pollutants in drinking water.

As did Morrall, Hahn arrived at these startling results by limiting the types of benefits he examined. He does not acknowledge any health benefits not related to accidents except "reducing the risk of cancer, heart disease, and lead poisoning" and illnesses caused by a small group of air pollutants.

In addition to drastically limiting the benefits he studied, Hahn, with a few exceptions, included only benefits that the agencies had monetized. What does this fine specimen of economics jargon mean? That's a good question, a crucial question, and one that too few people have asked.

The basic answer is simple: to monetize something is to assign it a dollar value, even if it typically doesn't come with a price tag. Let's try it. What's the dollar value of saving a child from a 7.4-point drop in IQ due to lead poisoning? How about the dollar value of having a full suite of native marine invertebrates in an estuary? Or the dollar value of hiking in the Grand Canyon without having sightseeing planes roar overhead every ten minutes? Or the dollar value of slowing global climate change by 20 percent? Or the dollar value of preventing your mother from suffering for six months and then dying of a cancer induced by exposure to a toxic chemical?

You get the picture. Now, as a layperson, you may be tempted to conclude that accurately monetizing many if not most environmental benefits is impossible. But the more hard-core among the economists who favor cost-benefit analysis disagree. They have to, or cost-benefit analysis as they know it would unravel. Monetizing is vital because it allows them to compare apples with apples: it will cost industry a billion dollars to comply with regulation X and the benefits to society add up to only half a billion, so the regulation fails the cost-benefit test. Without monetizing we'd be comparing apples to oranges: regulation X would cost industry a billion dollars and the benefits would be the prevention of 25 deaths and 1,000 serious illnesses a year, a 40 percent increase in the reproductive success of native fish in nearly 100 rivers, and a doubling of the number of native aquatic plants growing in those rivers. Such apples-to-oranges comparisons are messy, imprecise, and rely on human judgment; cost-benefit advocates prefer the clean precision of math.

In an article they wrote, Heinzerling and Ackerman underscore the essential role of monetizing by making it a part of their strict definition of cost-benefit analysis. Likewise, when I use the term "cost-benefit analysis" I mean it in the strict sense that includes monetizing. Others sometimes use the term loosely, when referring to any weighing of pros and cons, as in the apples and oranges hypothetical example above. This is an important distinction. I think society needs to weigh the pros and cons, even though it's messy, imprecise, and relies on human judgment, before issuing costly regulations. But I think that strict cost-benefit analysis, including monetized calculations, offers only false precision and is not a legitimate way to weigh those pros and cons.

Advocates of cost-benefit analysis employ a number of methods to determine the dollar value of environmental and human health benefits. Alan Krupnick, Senior Fellow and Director of the Quality of the Environment division at a think tank called Resources for the Future, says that it's possible to put a price tag on more things than you'd think. "Sometimes there are clever ways of teasing out people's preferences of reducing their risk of having health effects or risk to the environment," says Krupnick. One common and representative method is called "willingness to pay" or "WTP." Researchers survey citizens to determine just how much they'd pay for a particular environmental good. In one famous example people on average said that they'd spend $257 per household to save bald eagles from extinction.

WTP and its kin generate considerable controversy, however. For example, critics worry that WTP researchers tend to reject responses from people whose comments don't fit neatly into the survey's approach, especially those people—"skeptics"—who question some of the survey's premises. For practical reasons surveys can't allow respondents to think outside the box: "They just have to put up or shut up," says Krupnick. A reputable practitioner like Krupnick will try to accommodate some of the skeptics' objections while developing the survey, but not all WTP surveyors do this. Critics also question the very foundation of WTP.

Because they're surveying citizens about complex and often little-known issues, researchers must provide background information to the respondents. In the hands of someone less scrupulous than Krupnick this briefing could be subtly designed to elicit a desired answer. But beyond simple manipulation, these briefings bring up a more basic problem: how can the respondents know enough to give a valid estimate of what a particular benefit is worth to them? Even if you were given some background information, would you feel confident in deciding how much you'd pay to prevent a rise in global temperature of three degrees centigrade? Would your guess have meaning?

Another complicating factor is that many of the issues addressed in WTP surveys involve benefits that not only prove difficult to summarize but that altogether defy summarizing because science as yet knows little about them. And then there are the environmental benefits that neither scientists nor anyone else will ever enumerate in meaningful terms because they're utterly intangible, like the loss of community caused by urban sprawl or the value of spending a weekend in the wilderness with your kids. You can ask someone how much he would be willing to pay for that weekend, but would that really accurately capture its value? When I asked Krupnick about such intangibles, he agreed that some exist but he questioned whether the government should issue regulations to protect such elusive benefits. But "intangible" is not a synonym for "lesser." Many of our most cherished environmental goods resist translation into dollars, but government still has an irreplaceable role to play in preserving them.

WTP also reveals a fundamental inconsistency in the attitudes of the promoters of cost-benefit analysis. On the one hand, WTP calls on ordinary citizens to make dauntingly sophisticated calculations, calculations that become keystones in the cost-benefit edifice. On the other hand, much of the impetus for the development of cost-benefit analysis stems from the expert analysts' deep mistrust of ordinary citizens. Many cost-benefit proponents believe that the public approaches environmental regulation in an uninformed, overly emotional way. (A favorite adjective is "hysterical.") This ignorant fear, according to the analysts, then gets incorporated into regulatory policy via Congress, a political body that bends to the will of the mob instead of following the scientific path the experts lay out. So which is it? Are you and I analytical geniuses or "paranoid" (a word Graham has applied to the public) ignoramuses? That sounds like a rhetorical question, but it's not. Except in the cases of WTP studies and their ilk, many cost-benefit practitioners consider regular folks "irrational."

Then there's WTA. Before I explain the acronym, let me pose two hypotheticals that Thomas McGarity, a law professor at the University of Texas, uses on his students every year. One: You get a glass of water. There's a one in a thousand chance that it contains a poison that will rapidly and painlessly kill you. McGarity has an antidote that he's willing to sell you. How much will you pay to allay that one in a thousand chance of death? That's WTP, willingness to pay. Two: You get a glass of water. There's a one in a thousand chance that it contains a poison that will rapidly and painlessly kill you. How much would McGarity have to pay you to drink that water and take that one in a thousand chance of dying? That's WTA, willingness to accept. "I promise you," says McGarity, "the amount is always much, much higher when it's a question of how much it would cost to get my students to accept the risk rather than how much they'd pay to get rid of the risk."

McGarity has another question, not hypothetical: "Why do economists always use [in cost-benefit calculations] willingness to pay instead of willingness to accept, even though they all acknowledge that either can be seen as valid?" Answering his own question, he says, "Because they want the number to be low," thus holding down the benefit side of the equation. McGarity says that cost-benefit practitioners don't like WTA because it tends to elicit what they see as unreal responses, such as someone asserting that it'd take $10,000 to convince him to accept the death of a bald eagle, as opposed to the $257 an average person theoretically is willing to pay to prevent that bird's death. In most economists' view a rational person couldn't possibly believe that an eagle's life is worth $10,000, ergo that person is irrational and any valuation technique that allows such irrational input isn't valid. Cynically, I must add that some practitioners likely stick to WTP and its much lower benefit figures simply because it caters to their vested interests.

McGarity believes that the technical issue of WTP versus WTA reveals profoundly different views of environmental protection. "I would argue," he says, "that if you use willingness to pay as the measure, you're saying that the world is such a place that people can destroy our resources willy-nilly as long as we can't pay them enough to stop. Whereas, if you use willingness to accept as the measure of these more or less priceless things, then you're saying that we live in the kind of society in which we have a right to clean air, clean water, etc., unless someone convinces us—pays us, if you want to call it that—but at least convinces us that it ought to be destroyed. Basically, in using willingness to pay, they are subtly forcing upon us a view of the world that says that development can proceed unless you persuade us to stop, which is exactly the opposite of how most people think of the world."

Pondering the many pitfalls of monetizing, Richard Parker says, "It has long been recognized that data limitations, scientific uncertainties and difficulties of valuation often make it infeasible to try to quantify and monetize every important cost and benefit. That is why the Annapolis principles for sound cost-benefit analysis . . . advise: 'not all impacts of a decision can be quantified or expressed in dollar terms. Care should be taken to assure that quantitative factors do not dominate important qualitative factors in decision-making.' No one disputes this principle. Scorecards simply do not practice it." The irony is that Robert Hahn coauthored the Annapolis principles.

Even as Graham moves to expand the role of cost-benefit analysis and monetizing in developing and implementing environmental regulations, he, too, acknowledges that not everything can be quantified or monetized. But he relegates nonquantifiable factors to the minor role of maybe sometimes tipping a close decision, a decision almost entirely based on monetized costs and benefits.

With all the talk of monetizing, Parker wonders why it's applied so narrowly. If environmental goods must be economically efficient, how about other social goods? Does society come out ahead in dollar terms when we spend millions of dollars on a high-profile murder trial and the subsequent lifelong incarceration of the murderer? How about the tremendous expense of making thousands of buildings accessible to the disabled? Should we monetize the right to vote in order to decide if it's worth preserving? Even within the realm of the environment, only regulation is subjected to cost-benefit analysis. Why not analyze the source of hazards, asks Parker? Why not tell Dupont to prove that a chemical it wants to produce will provide more benefits than costs? Perhaps then industry would share the skepticism of critics of cost-benefit analysis.

If monetizing marine invertebrates raises eyebrows, monetizing human lives raises hackles. Many people find this practice repugnant. Yet, as we've seen, it's a common, even essential element of the work of Graham, Hahn, and Morrall, the three most influential champions of strict cost-benefit analysis. And remember, the lower the value of a life, the less money a regulation will require industry or some other entity to pay to protect that life. In 2000, in *The Harvard Environmental Law Review,* Heinzerling reports that at that time a statistical life was worth $5.8 million to the EPA, $2.5 million to the Department of Transportation, and $5 million to the Consumer Product Safety Commission.

A standard method for determining the value of a life comes from what economists call a "wage premium." They examine two similar jobs in which one job carries an additional physical risk and higher wages—say, painting the traffic-level guardrails on the Golden Gate Bridge versus climbing way up above and painting the lofty supports. Assuming workers know about the higher risk and voluntarily assume it, cost-benefit economists figure that the difference in pay between the two jobs measures the price someone puts on an increased risk of death. These wage premiums constitute the foundation for the calculations that eventually result in a dollar figure for the value of a human life.

As in the case of calculating the worth of ecological benefits via willingness to pay, measuring lives in dollars via a wage premium suffers from numerous commonsense drawbacks. Maybe the worker painting 300 feet above the roadway on the Golden Gate *likes it.* Maybe she's doing it for the thrill, not the pay. Perhaps the worker is a 20-year-old guy; his employer has apprised him of the extra risk but the risk means nothing to him because he *knows* he's immortal, as all 20-year-old guys know they are. Then there's the matter of choice. The high-wire painters are volunteering to take a risk, but people who die from lung disease brought on by air pollution didn't volunteer to take that risk—and they didn't receive any extra pay.

What about people in other, non-dangerous jobs whose views on the value of life are left out of the wage premium calculations? Take those bridge painters who choose to keep their feet on the ground. As they are not willing to venture up into the bridge's heights in return for a higher wage they aren't part of the pool of risk-taking workers whose willingness to tempt death feeds the calculations. Yet these earthbound painters may feel that no amount of money—not $10,000 a year, not $10 million a year—would get them to ascend those swaying supports. If their viewpoint were included in the wage premium calculation, the result would be a human life of infinite value, which would render all cost-benefit analysis meaningless. Therefore, a cost-benefit believer might conclude, those earthbound painters must be irrational. This makes sense, as anyone who chooses to remain safely on the ground instead of clambering about hundreds of feet off the ground for a few extra dollars obviously isn't thinking straight.

Senior citizens also have a bone to pick with Graham and OIRA, whose version of cost-benefit analysis places a lower dollar value on people's lives as they age. At the margins, there's a logic, however cold, to this practice. Many observers, though reluctantly, probably would agree that the life of a healthy five-year-old is indeed worth more than the life of a fading 90-year-old in the late stages of Alzheimer's disease. But these same observers would likely find it much harder to accept that in regulating the emissions of non-road engines, the Bush Administration reduced the value of seniors' lives across the board. Instead of the $3.7 million figure used for everyone else, people older than 70 were valued at $2.3 million. Seniors gave Bush Administration officials an earful about this devaluation in hearings conducted in 2003 by EPA.

(Ironically, the hearings were held to talk about ways in which the Administration and EPA could better address environmental health issues related to seniors.) In addition, OIRA strongly supports the use of discounting to calculate the value of lives saved in the future, which tends to diminish the effort required of industry to prevent cancers and other diseases that largely afflict the elderly. Interestingly, soon after seniors and others spoke out against discounting, then–EPA Administrator Christie Whitman announced that her agency would stop using the so-called "senior discount." Around the same time Graham issued a memo to the President's Management Council that also backed off the senior discount to some degree.

———

Long before he became head of OIRA, John Graham made problematic calculations regarding life and death, most famously in a 1996 paper called "The Opportunity Costs of Haphazard Social Investments in Life-Saving," coauthored with Tammy Tengs, at the time a graduate student of his. The 1996 paper stemmed from a 1995 paper called "Five Hundred Life-Saving Interventions and Their Cost-Effectiveness," also written by Tengs and Graham, with contributions from several other researchers. Tengs and Graham employed a number of controversial methods already mentioned in this chapter, but these technical issues didn't get nearly as much attention as the conclusion that such methods produced: inefficient federal regulatory practices in the U.S. were committing the "statistical murder" of 60,200 people a year.

Tengs and Graham arrived at this startling accusation first by analyzing the costs and benefits of 587 health, safety, and environmental measures intended to save lives, which served as the grist for their 1995 paper. Regulations addressing toxins fared extremely poorly, sometimes costing tens of millions of dollars just to save one *year* of life. The hands-down loser was a chloroform private well emission standard at 48 pulp mills, which staggered to the finish line at $99 billion for each life-year saved. In their 1996 study, Tengs and Graham took 187 of those 587 measures and determined how many lives could have been saved if the money frittered away on those 187 life-saving measures, most of which got woefully little bang for the buck, instead had been spent on efficient regulations, such as bike helmets and other perennial favorites of Graham's. Tengs and Graham found that by shifting spending to high-return regulations, society could either save the same number of lives while spending $31.1 billion less or spend the same amount of money and save an additional 60,200 people a year from dying.

Not surprisingly, the murder of more than 60,000 people a year drew a lot of attention. As in the case of Morrall's seminal paper on cost-benefit analysis, the results of the Tengs/Graham study fanned out through government, the media, think tanks, and academia. Also as in the case of Morrall's paper, no one challenged the research behind the sensational headlines until a few years ago, when scholars like Heinzerling, Ackerman, and Parker included Tengs and Graham in their debunking of cost-benefit analysis.

In addition to employing some of the disputed techniques addressed earlier in this chapter—discounting future regulatory benefits, neglecting benefits other than saving lives, and down-playing intangible benefits—"Opportunity Costs" is built atop an underlying logic that would profoundly alter the nature of regulation. It would take cost-benefit demands to another level by making all regulations, and even non-regulatory health and safety measures, slug it out over a limited pool of funding. As Graham said in a *Time* magazine article about pesticide residues on fruit: "Phantom risks and real risks compete not only for our resources but for our attention . . . It's a shame when a mother worries about toxic chemicals, and yet her kids are running around unvaccinated and without bicycle helmets."

Let's set aside the fact that Graham is jumbling together voluntary and involuntary risks; bigger flaws compete for our attention. Though the idea of setting priorities according to cost-effectiveness has basic merit, Graham envisions an extreme zero-sum game in which a mother can't be free of worry from toxic chemicals (some of which really do cause health problems) *and* get vaccinations and a bike helmet for her kid. "I think the notion that we're going to trade one life against another life raises enormous problems," says Frank Ackerman. "The notion that we are hard up against the wall, short on money, and we have to ration our money tightly across millions of life-saving investments doesn't correspond to reality. That isn't what's happening."

In his 2003 paper, University of Connecticut law professor Richard Parker, referring to "Opportunity Costs," said, "It turns out that just two interventions—continuous (versus nocturnal) oxygen for hypoxemic obstructive lung disease, and influenza vaccines for all citizens—account for over 42,000 of the more than 60,000 additional lives saved by his hypothetical reallocation.

"Are we to believe that the nation's failure to fully implement influenza vaccinations for all citizens and to provide continuous (vs. nocturnal) oxygen for hypoxemic obstructive lung disease is somehow related to the allegedly excessive regulation of benzene or other interventions at the cost-ineffective bottom of his list? If not, where is the statistical murder?"

If we had to make the choices Graham envisions (and if dubious cost-benefit analysis weren't the tool used to weigh all federal actions against one another), why limit the contestants in the zero-sum game to regulations? Restricting the amount of arsenic in our drinking water may save fewer lives per dollar than vaccinating all Americans, but what about other federal government actions that could be changed to pay for life-saving measures? I suggest that instead of halting the regulation of toxic chemicals to save the money to pay for those vaccinations, the government should eliminate pork-barrel highway projects, fraud by defense contractors, and loopholes that allow corporations to avoid tens of billions in taxes by setting up phony offices in the Cayman Islands. Think of all the bike helmets and vaccinations that money could buy.

Despite its serious flaws, Graham and Tengs's research, like that of Morrall, became poster material for the antiregulatory crowd. Graham himself often told audiences that regulations, especially environmental rules, accounted for some 60,000 statistical murders a year. For example, he made this assertion to Congressional committees at least three times in the mid-1990s alone. Typical was his testimony of September 12, 1997, before the Senate Governmental Affairs Committee: "Based on a sample of 200 programs, by shifting resources from wasteful programs to cost-effective programs, we could save 60,000 more lives per year in this country at no additional cost to the public sector or the private sector."

Laura MacCleery, counsel for Auto Safety and Regulatory Affairs at Public Citizen, a progressive, nonprofit public interest group, suggests that Graham and others make strategic use of regulatory comparisons. "Graham often argues that risks should be compared, for policy making purposes, *with other risks*," writes MacCleery in a report on Graham's activities. "Graham promoted this approach as a media strategy at a Heritage Foundation meeting in 1996, arguing that conservatives would appear more environmentally friendly if they couched regulatory rollback arguments in efficiency terms."

Most of the talk from cost-benefit boosters about setting sound regulatory priorities so we get the most for our money tends to be vague as to just who "we" is. If anything, there's an underlying sense that it is the public purse that needs to be protected. But follow the money. If federal regulations require a coastal power plant to install new cooling systems that will kill fewer fish, it's not taxpayers but the company that owns the power plant that pays the compliance costs. (Some people say that the full expense of compliance simply gets passed on to consumers, but if corporations didn't have to foot a significant portion of the bill then they wouldn't fight tooth and nail to avoid regulation.) If regulators think Monsanto should spend $20 million to detoxify one of its properties but they let Monsanto off the hook because that money would save more lives if it were spent on continuous oxygen for hypoxemic obstructive lung disease, that doesn't get the $20 million to the people with lung disease. Most of that $20 million will just end up in the pockets of Dow's shareholders and corporate officers.

———————

Will cost-benefit analysis à la Graham help Bush succeed in reshaping the federal regulatory landscape? To a large degree that depends on Congress. As it stands, the regulatory agencies are charged with carrying out laws passed by legislators, and those laws give primacy to health and environmental concerns and do not allow cost-benefit analysis to take the driver's seat. The cost-benefit backers would change this. As Robert Hahn and his fellow AEI-Brookings Joint Center scholar, Scott Wallsten, wrote in the June 1, 2003, *Washington Post,* "Congress should insist that all regulations pass a broadly defined benefit-cost test."

One fact that critics of the current regulatory system often overlook is that laws do give agencies the ability to take costs into account, which they do all the time, usually in the implementation phase. That's when the give-and-take between regulators and the regulated occurs, and it's a time when business can plead its case to keep compliance costs manageable. Companies often get their way, or at least secure a compromise. That's one reason that so many companies have been able to remain out of compliance with the health standards of the Clean Air Act, even 30 years after its passage. And consider the fact that while industry complains that the agencies are overregulating business, many citizens and public interest groups complain that the agencies are underregulating business.

Commonly Congress addresses cost issues by employing what is called "technology-based" regulation, in which the agencies decide what kinds of controls are financially and technologically feasible for a particular industry and then the agencies set regulatory standards accordingly. In many cases, it's fine if a company can figure out a way to achieve the technology-based standards without using the technology on which the standard is based, an opportunity that provides some of the flexibility that business famously seeks. In any case, even in the absence of cost-benefit analysis, the regulatory process almost always has taken the costs of compliance into consideration—it's just that the agencies and business don't always come to the same conclusions about how much cost is justified.

Inevitably, this approach is subject to uncertainties, conflicting values, diverse opinions, and personal judgment—the weaknesses and the strengths of democratic deliberation. Cost-benefit promoters instead promise precision: a neat, clean, scientific method by which to make complex regulatory decisions. It's a false promise, but if decision makers and the public aren't aware of the assumptions, uncertainties, and dubious methods upon which cost-benefit analysis precariously teeters, that seeming precision can prove seductive. And the only thing worse than not knowing something is not knowing something but thinking that you do.

Whether from a genuine thirst for precision or from an opportunistic attempt to weaken environmental regulations by any means possible, some members of Congress have responded to the siren call of cost-benefit analysis. This was particularly evident during 1994 and 1995, when cost-benefit analysis became an integral part of the regulatory rollbacks included in the Contract with America. As part of this effort, the American Enterprise Institute

commissioned Graham to help develop regulatory reform legislation. In the end, however, Congress and the American people
declined to sign the Contract with America and for the most part
the "contract"—and its cost-benefit provisions—faded away.

Now, after failing for nearly a decade to convince enough law-
makers that cost-benefit analysis should be a decisive factor in regulatory decisions, some of those who would monetize the world
are trying a quieter approach, using administrative rules and
guidelines. Led by Graham and OIRA, they are positioning cost-
benefit analysis to reign supreme, even when it usurps Congressional prerogatives. Graham has been espousing the primacy of
cost-benefit analysis for years, as when, in 1997, he told Congress
that the agencies' "enabling statutes should be superseded by the
general requirement that each rule's identified benefits must justify
its identified costs."

Reece Rushing of OMB Watch takes a dim view of the notion
that cost-benefit analysis should supersede the law. "The statute
obviously should prevail," says Rushing. "It is the law, and the
executive order [that directs agencies to conduct cost-benefit analy-
ses] is not the law. It's not enforceable in the courts. Regulations
must be made according to these statutory directives. Now, in practice that's often ignored and we've seen that increasingly during this
Administration, where they really see cost-benefit analysis as the
determinative tool in making decisions, frequently contrary to underlying statutes." Rushing notes that some environmental groups
have sued over this matter and likely will win in court—eventually.
But, says Rushing, "Those lawsuits take years and the Administration is making decisions according to cost-benefit analysis right
now." He adds, "And once [the lawsuits] are settled the Administration sometimes has years to . . . institute a more protective regulation
based on the directive from the court. So they [the Administration]
will have succeeded in postponing actions for years, and I think
they'd consider that a win."

Representative Henry Waxman (D-CA), seconds the motion. "As OIRA increasingly dictates regulatory decisions," writes Waxman in the July-August 2002 issue of *The Environmental Forum,* "it is seizing authority that Congress delegated to regulatory agencies, not the White House." Waxman worries that OIRA's aggressive invasion of agency territory will disrupt the balance of power between Congress and the Executive Branch. "In the modern administrative state," writes Waxman, "Congress legislates in part by delegating rule-making authority to executive agencies. By expanding presidential control over agency rule-making activities, the White House is in effect assuming powers that Congress bestowed on agency heads.

"Setting precedent here is important," Waxman continues, "as this area of constitutional law and policy is still evolving. There is general agreement on the big picture. Agencies' authority to regulate is derived from Congress and is subject to the criteria that Congress specifies in statute. At the same time, as the head of the Executive Branch, the President may pursue broad policy goals through the agencies. Most also agree that reconciling these constitutional authorities requires striking a balance." However, concludes Waxman, "The Bush Administration is pushing an expansionist approach that will weight the balance of power in rule-making heavily in favor of the President." In a later statement Waxman added, "It's important to recognize that OMB's fervent insistence on quantified cost-benefit analyses in regulation is not the action of a neutral entity, neutral process, or neutral analytical tool. Rather, the intent and the effect is to make it more difficult for regulatory agencies to carry out the authorities that Congress has delegated to them. Congress should be concerned about this intrusion on its institutional authority. However, because OMB's intervention in the rule-making process acts as a one-way deregulatory ratchet, it is generally supported by those who call for less regulation, regardless of the broader institutional concerns this intervention raises."

Other members of Congress don't see cost-benefit analysis as an intrusion on Congressional authority; in fact, they want to give it a more prominent role. For example, Representative Doug Ose (R-CA), who chairs the House subcommittee on Energy Policy, Natural Resources, and Regulatory Affairs, is pushing the idea of a regulatory appropriations process. In Ose's plan Congress would establish a committee and subcommittees that would examine the costs and benefits of federal regulations. Ose further recommends that the Administration create a regulatory budget, just as it creates a spending budget, that would detail the agency-by-agency regulatory costs it proposes to impose on business for the fiscal year. Then Congress, leaning heavily on cost-benefit analysis, would consider the merits of that proposed regulatory budget.

Perhaps the convincing criticisms of cost-benefit analysis over the last several years will rouse Congress to resist the allure of a simplistic, scorecard answer to the tough questions that come with regulation. These critics aren't saying that all rule-makings are flawless and that the regulatory approaches currently used by the agencies are above improvement. On the contrary, all of the detractors of cost-benefit analysis with whom I spoke readily acknowledged that some problems exist, that some regulations cost too much for the benefits received. These critics just want Congress and the public to understand, as Parker put it in his paper, "that we simply do not know how 'efficient' or 'rational' government regulation is overall, from a cost-benefit perspective, because the principal tests that have been used to reach such judgments are invalid. Until valid tests are adduced, we should withhold judgment on such matters."

In conclusion Parker wrote: "Meanwhile, instead of pointing the finger at government for the poor quality of its data and analysis, some of the leading critics of regulation should look to the quality of their own studies. For they are shockingly bad."

In addition to its doubtful methods and antiregulatory bias, cost-benefit analysis suffers from tunnel vision. With their implicit repudiation of so many intangibles, these analyses offer a narrow and superficial view of what matters on this earth. It is the perspective of the stereotypical accountant, the guy who can only see the numbers in the ledger before him, whose green eyeshade blocks his view of the people and the trees and the river outside his window. This push to monetize beauty, health, wildness, and life itself bespeaks an impoverishing materialism.

CHAPTER 7

What's Next?

S ome observers think that the political planets are aligned in a configuration that will lead to the triumph of the President's antiregulatory agenda, some of which already has been implemented. They point to the presence of George W. Bush in the Oval Office and his appointees throughout the agencies; to the GOP's takeover of Congress in 2002; to the ongoing stocking of the federal judiciary with antiregulatory jurists; and to the fact that with the nation focused on Iraq, terrorism, and the economy, the Administration's stealth attack most likely will slip in under the radar and roll back many environmental protections before enough of the public notices.

Other observers think that if pro-environment forces mount a strong defense they can retain a fair number of protections for human health and the natural world. These observers cite the small but often pivotal group of environmentally friendly Republicans in the Senate, who have already thwarted or diluted some Bush efforts; the frequent success of court challenges to the White House's initiatives; the exceptional unity among environmental organizations as they rally to resist the Administration; and the large majority of Americans who, according to poll after poll, value a strong federal role in protecting the environment.

Both sets of observers think that the public occupies a crucial position. If the Administration succeeds in disguising its intentions and public interest remains dormant, the antiregulatory juggernaut will roll on. If the public realizes what is going on and supports the efforts of pro-environment members of Congress and environmental groups and protests the Administration's actions, the juggernaut will be slowed. However, the public may have to show up in overwhelming force and break through some barriers, because the Administration has been making a concerted effort to diminish the influence of citizens, whether working on their own or together through conservation organizations.

Earlier in the book I discussed some of the ways in which the Administration restricts public participation, such as eliminating administrative appeals of government actions and not inviting the public to sit at the negotiating table. The Administration also has issued regulations without giving any public notice, even on major issues, such as the new policy on mitigation for destroyed wetlands. Citizens are denied information, even when they request it under the Freedom of Information Act (FOIA). When the Natural Resources Defense Council (NRDC) sued the Department of Energy for dragging its feet on a FOIA request regarding the agency's participation in Vice President Cheney's closed-door Energy Task Force meetings, the court agreed with NRDC and found that the Energy Department had been "woefully tardy" and that the agency had "no legal or practical excuse for its excessive delay in responding." The Administration has tried to alter the public comment process to discount communications from individuals who make their feelings known by sending form letters and e-mails organized by environmental groups. Bush and his officials have taken some steps to empower citizens—but typically when those citizens are likely to support the President's policies. For example, the Administration is trying to set up a "charter forest" program that would give greater influence in managing nearby national forests to handpicked locals—think timber interests and Wise Use advocates. The Office of Information and Regulatory Affairs has implemented one genuinely positive example of opening up to citizens by posting its communications with regulatory agencies on the OIRA Web site, but such inclusion of the public is the exception under Bush.

While fighting day-to-day battles with the Administration, many pro-environment people have one eye on a bigger prize: the 2004 presidential election. They figure that the easiest way to win those battles is to not have to fight them. Of course, electing the Democratic candidate (at press time the winner of the Democratic nomination was yet to be determined) wouldn't necessarily mean that the next administration would be a stalwart champion of the environment, but most environmentalists feel certain that any of the Democratic presidential candidates would be an improvement over Bush—most likely a huge improvement. To this end, conservation organizations are getting more involved in the presidential campaign than ever before. For example, the League of Conservation Voters already was running anti-Bush ads in August 2003, while the President was taking his West Coast tour to tout his environmental record—that would be the record for which the League gave him an F. Such attacks, and the Bush campaign's responses to them, will undoubtedly multiply dramatically as we get closer to election day.

Did I say "undoubtedly"? One should never use that word when talking about elections, because circumstances can change so quickly. But as I wrote these words, in early 2004, the President's approval ratings had tumbled and his reelection seemed far from certain. If the election turns out to be tight, many strategists think the environment could be an issue to sway swing voters and tip a close election. Remember the quote in the introduction from the GOP pollsters and marketing experts at the Luntz Research Companies: "The environment is probably the single issue on which Republicans in general—and President Bush in particular—are most vulnerable." That's why Democratic candidates for president have begun blasting Bush's environmental record and why Bush has been defending it.

Some observers warn that the issue of the environment also will crop up in a different way during the 2004 presidential campaign. They expect Bush to use, perhaps even commit, specific acts of deregulation to appeal to voters in swing states. John B. Judis, for example, a senior editor at *The New Republic,* wrote in *The American Prospect* that "Bush's opposition to regulation is part of an electoral strategy designed to win the votes of coal, timber, and oil-producing states." Judis notes that prior to the 2002 Congressional elections—and this wasn't even his own election campaign—Bush made five visits to a single Congressional District in West Virginia. In West Virginia, Kentucky, and Pennsylvania, all swing states and all coal states, Bush played up his Administration's many antiregulatory actions that have helped the coal industry, such as weakening clean air standards and easing mountaintop mining restrictions.

As the campaign heats up, the debate about the environment likely will swirl around these and other specific issues, such as water pollution, wetlands, pesticide regulations, and endangered species. These discussions are necessary and important, especially considering that so much of the environmental harm inflicted by the Administration has been done quietly and needs to be brought up from the depths of detail and out into the light. But at the same time, Bush needs to be held accountable for his broad vision of the environment. Or, more precisely, his lack of one.

For, when it comes to the environment, Bush Junior, like Bush Senior so famously before him, lacks the "vision thing." Our current president sometimes invokes the stew of voluntary compliance, market-based incentives, and localism that Interior Secretary Norton calls the New Environmentalism. Arguably, this could pass muster as something of a vision, but it's mostly about process, about a few new tools—some of which work well in some circumstances and some of which seldom work under any circumstances. Bush has given no sign that he has an inkling that the nation and the planet face enormous environmental challenges and that in some important ways the environment worsens every day. Most notably, he seems unaware of the overarching environmental problem of our time: the fact that we humans can't sustain our present rates of expansion, consumption, exploitation of natural resources, and pollution, and that we're already exceeding some of the Earth's limits. Not that we're headed for a sudden environmental catastrophe, as some environmentalists in the past predicted. But if we don't mend our ways we'll most likely see a steady deterioration of many of our natural assets, which will lead to a corresponding decline in our quality of life.

Bush sounds as if he agrees with two of the tenets one hears often from industry and libertarian think tanks, tenets that restrict one's vision regarding the environment. One is an excessive faith in technology and Yankee ingenuity as the answers to almost every environmental problem. This leads to the idea that industrial civilization can endlessly grow and society can forever increase its appetites, because technology will fix what we break and provide substitutes for what we use up. The other is the belief that for the most part the environment is in good shape and getting better and that people who express serious concern about the environment are alarmists.

This idea that the environment is fine is something that industry, conservative politicians, and libertarian ideologues are determined to believe and to promulgate, despite so much evidence to the contrary. Consider the fact that for several years they have been toasting and giving awards to Bjorn Lomborg, the Danish associate professor of statistics who wrote *The Skeptical Environmentalist,* a book that asserts that the environment is doing well in almost every way. Never mind that piles of books and papers authored by scientists with more relevant expertise have argued otherwise. Never mind that scholars the world over have been lining up to disagree with Lomborg, including a group of 11 eminent scientists who wrote, as reported in *The Washington Post,* "We rarely see this type of careless and manipulative scholarship in the undergraduates we teach." Never mind that *Scientific American* published a long, detailed critique of *The Skeptical Environmentalist* that shredded the book. Never mind that Peter Raven, president of the American Association for the Advancement of Science, one of America's foremost scientific organizations, told *The New York Times* that Lomborg's book should not be portrayed as science and that "this [the criticism from the scientific community] is a just outcome that ought to bring his credibility to a halt except for those who desperately want to believe what he says." It requires blinders to embrace information like Lomborg's, and blinders make it tough to have vision.

Bush's lack of vision constantly shows up in his approach to environmental issues. Take oil, a matter dear to the President's heart. Let's leave aside the fact that the war in Iraq and America's struggle against terrorism involve oil. Its environmental impact alone is reason enough to wean ourselves from oil as rapidly as possible. Consider that the refining of oil and the burning of oil products spew pollutants into the air we breathe; that oil spills from tankers and pipelines harm natural areas and human communities; and that emissions of carbon dioxide from industrial smokestacks and vehicle tailpipes are boosting global warming. And then there's the problem of producing oil. In the U.S. we've already sucked up nearly all of the readily available petroleum, so now the Administration is helping companies go after oil in places where energy development is unwanted and will cause problems. Bush is facilitating drilling in some of our already scarce wilderness areas, such as ANWR; he wants companies to drill off the coast of California, despite the resistance of most of the state's residents; and he is encouraging drilling on both public and private lands in the West against the wishes of many residents.

Given just this short list of the drawbacks associated with oil, one would expect a person with vision to be working hard to move the country away from its dependence on oil and other fossil fuels. But Bush has cut funding for a number of renewable energy programs and is nudging hydrogen-energy development onto a path that would depend on fossil fuels and nuclear power to produce the hydrogen. He won't even take the most obvious of steps, such as pushing for decent fuel economy standards for sport utility vehicles (SUVs). Listen to the incredulous disapproval of Olympia Snowe, a senator from Bush's own political party, talking about the need for such changes: "That's why I teamed with Senator Feinstein on legislation to make CAFE [Corporate Average Fuel Economy] standards for SUVs the same as it is for automobiles. When this move alone would save a million barrels of oil a day, reduce oil imports by 10 percent, and prevent about 200 million tons of carbon dioxide from entering our atmosphere, my question has been, what is there not to get?" The President also has encouraged the purchase of gas-guzzling SUVs by including a provision in his tax-cut package that allows small businesses to write off up to $75,000 spent on SUVs.

Bush's argument that restricting drilling or reducing pollution would harm the economy and cost jobs also reveals a lack of vision. Ten major labor unions are thinking more creatively. They're promoting what they call a new Apollo Project. They say that the Midwest's industrial base could be revitalized by a $300 billion investment in hybrid cars, solar cells, retrofitted buildings, more efficient factories, cleaned-up power plants, wind turbines, and mass transit. Union leaders figure their plan would create about three million new industrial jobs, help the environment, reduce our thirst for imported oil, and turn the Rust Belt into a thriving center of twenty-first-century industry. I don't know the details of this particular plan and I can't judge its specific merits, but it's the kind of fresh vision for the future that's needed. Bush, on the other hand, seems to be looking backward, promoting the same old way of doing business.

Judging from the polls showing widespread support for environmental protections, most Americans have a clearer vision of the future than the President does. I think Bush and his handlers realize this, too, though they no doubt consider it a "different" vision rather than a "clearer" one. It is because they recognize that they're out of step with the majority of citizens that the Administration works so hard to conceal its antienvironmental actions. This is hopeful. Not the Administration's deceit, but the fact that it feels the need to deceive. It wouldn't bother if it didn't fear the public's power. This means that we citizens have an opportunity to force some changes, steer America toward an enlightened vision, and win the case of Bush versus the Environment.

NOTES

INTRODUCTION

6 *Referred to as the "Luntz memo":* Environmental Working Group, *The Environment: A Cleaner, Safer, Healthier America,* Luntz Research Companies memo on the environment, http://www.ewg.org/briefings/luntzmemo/.

7 *In an op-ed that appeared in 2002:* Martha Marks, "A Conservative Conservationist Looks at Roosevelt and Bush," editorial published in The Wilderness Society's spring 2002 newsletter, REP America, http://www.rep.org/opinions/op-eds/20.html.

8 *Michael Leavitt to head the EPA, Train wrote:* Russell Train, "E.P.-Eh?: The Environmental Protection Agency Just Isn't Like It Was in the Good Old (Nixon) Days," *Grist Magazine,* September 22, 2003.

8 *syndicated Knight Ridder newspaper story:* Seth Borenstein, "White House Fulfills Corporate Wish List," *Corvallis (OR) Gazette-Times,* September 8, 2003.

9 *comments from Bill Kovacs:* Ibid.

11 *chief of staff issued a memo:* Andrew H. Card to Heads and Acting Heads of Executive Departments and Agencies, White
House memo, January 20, 2001, copy in author's possession.

12 *"The Bush Administration's Record of Environmental Progress":*
The White House (President George W. Bush), "The Bush Administration's Record of Environmental Progress," October 2002,
http://www.whitehouse.gov.

CHAPTER 1

22 *to which politicians and political parties:* Earthjustice and Public
Campaign, *Paybacks,* September 25, 2002, http://www.earthjus-
tice.org/policy/pdf/payback_report_final.pdf.

25 *"Environmental Crime—The Growth Industry of the '90s":*
Joan Mulhern, Earthjustice, telephone conversation with the
author, November 2003.

26 *old-growth forests in the Pacific Northwest:* Mike Anderson,
The Wilderness Society, telephone conversation with the author,
November 2003.

28 *harmful environmental effects of such drilling:* Steve Griles to
Bill Horn, memo, undated, copy in author's possession.

28 *investigate various aspects of Griles's dealings:* Kristen Sykes,
Friends of the Earth, telephone conversation with the author,
November 2003.

29 *According to* The Washington Post: Christopher Lee, "IG Probes
Interior's Record on Ethics Rule," *The Washington Post,* Section
A, May 13, 2003.

30 *pushing coal-bed methane development in Wyoming and Montana:* Kristen Sykes, Friends of the Earth, e-mail to the author,
November 2003.

33 *two studies of Governor Bush's program:* Environmental
Defense, "Too Little, Too Late," January 1997, http://www.
environmentaldefense.org; Environmental Defense, "Senate

Bill 766, One Year Later," October 2000, http://www.environmentaldefense.org.

36 *trading of invalid credits, and lacked safeguards:* Environmental Protection Agency, Office of Inspector General, "Open Market Trading for Air Emissions Needs Strengthening," report no. 2002-P-00019, September 30, 2002.

CHAPTER 2

40 *forest restoration projects are not tied up in courts:* The White House (President George W. Bush), "The Squires Fire: A Case Study in Fire and Forest Management Obstacles and Effects," http://www.whitehouse.gov/infocus/healthyforests/sect6.html.

48 *turning some trees to ash and leaving others healthy and alive:* Ray Ring, "A Losing Battle," *High Country News,* May 26, 2003.

50 *Republican National Committee during the 2000 and 2002 election cycles:* Earthjustice and Public Campaign, *Paybacks,* September 25, 2002, http://www.earthjustice.org/policy/pdf/payback_report_final.pdf.

56 *Community Protection Zones across the nation:* The Wilderness Society, "Communities at Risk from Wildfire: How Much Is on Federal Land?" March 11, 2003.

59 *larger forest system in which they are embedded:* William Wallace Covington, "Firefighting Funding and Planning," statement to the Committee on Senate Energy and Natural Resources, *FDCH Congressional Testimony,* July 16, 2002.

60 *money will be wisely spent:* Mark Rey, U.S. Department of Agriculture, interview with the author, June 2003.

62 *get around to those lower priorities, too:* Mark Rey, U.S. Department of Agriculture, interview with the author, June 2003.

63 *where most public forestlands are located:* U.S. Forest Service, "A Strategic Assessment of Forest Biomass and Fuel Reduction Treatments in Western States," 2002, http://www.fs.fed.us.

67 *sketches a classic case:* Margaret Kriz, "Bush's Quiet Plan," *National Journal* 34/47–48 (November 23, 2002).

70 *until after the Corps rendered its decision:* Patrick Parenteau, Vermont Law School, telephone conversation with the author, December 2003.

75 *spend one hundred thousand dollars of taxpayers' money:* Mark Rey, U.S. Department of Agriculture, interview with the author, June 2003.

77 *just over 1 percent:* U.S. General Accounting Office, *Appeals and Litigation of Fuels Reduction Projects,* report GAO-01-1114R, August 31, 2001.

77 *in a few days:* Robert Gehrke, "Environmentalists, Forest Service Agree That Fire Report Was Rushed, Figures Were Off," *Las Vegas Sun,* October 2, 2002.

77 *in August 2002:* USDA Forest Service, *Factors Affecting Timely Mechanical Fuel Treatment Decisions,* July 2002.

77 *number of appeals has been declining:* Hanna Cortner, Gretchen Teich, and Jacqueline Vaughn, Ecological Restoration Institute, *Analyzing USDA Forest Service Project Appeals* (Flagstaff: Northern Arizona University, 2003).

78 *within the prescribed 90-day time frame:* U.S. General Accounting Office, "Forest Service: Information on Decisions Involving Fuels Reduction Activities," report GAO-03-689R, Forest Service Fuels Reduction, May 14, 2003.

CHAPTER 3

86 *save them from ecological catastrophe:* Paul Turcke, Boise Cascade, telephone conversation with the author, November 2003.

87 *noting that public comment was voluminous:* Steve Strack, State of Idaho, telephone conversation with the author, November 2003.

88 *pros and cons of the Roadless Rule:* U.S. Senate, Majority Staff of the Committee on Governmental Affairs, "Rewriting the Rules," report, 107th Congress, 2nd session, October 24, 2002.

90 *asked to be included but were refused:* Mike Sherwood, Earth-justice, telephone conversation with the author, November 2003.

92 *included in the discussion, but was rebuffed:* Pete Frost, Western Environmental Law Center, telephone conversation with the author, November 2003.

93 *current generations to experience and enjoy the parks:* A current employee at Yellowstone National Park, telephone conversation with the author, November 2003.

96 *Controversy swirled around the process, especially in Utah:* A former manager at the Bureau of Land Management, e-mail to and telephone conversation with the author, November 2003.

99 *received an inadequate response from Interior:* Leslie Jones, The Wilderness Society, telephone conversation with the author, November 2003.

104 *sickening about one million others:* Gretchen C. Daily and Katherine Ellison, "The New Economy of Nature," *Orion,* Spring 2002.

105 *won only 11 percent of the time:* William Snape and John M. Carter, *Weakening the National Environmental Policy Act: How the Bush Administration Uses the Judicial System to Weaken Environmental Protections,* Report of the Judicial Accountability Project (Washington, D.C.: Defenders of Wildlife, 2003).

107 *jurisdiction over numerous major environmental issues:* Chris Mooney, "Circuit Breaker," *American Prospect* (March 1, 2003).

CHAPTER 4

113 *as reported in* The Washington Post: Guy Gugliotta and Eric Pianin, "EPA: Few Fired for Polluting Water," *The Washington Post,* Section A, June 6, 2003.

114 *transgressions committed by Fortune 500 companies:* Environmental Integrity Project, *Paying Less to Pollute* (Washington, D.C.: Environmental Integrity Project, January 2003).

114 *the rest of that* Bee *article:* Chris Bowman, "EPA Pumps Up Its Record," *Sacramento Bee,* July 6, 2003.

116 *laws that protect wildlife habitat:* Defenders of Wildlife, Earthjustice, Endangered Species Coalition, National Wildlife Federation, *Open Season on America's Wildlife: The Bush Administration's Attacks on Federal Wildlife Protections,* http://www.defenders.org/newsroom/openseason.pdf.

116 *not enforcing the settlement agreement:* Patrick Rose, Save the Manatee Club, telephone conversation with the author, December 2003.

125 *their mothers ingested by eating affected fish:* National Research Council, *Toxicological Effects of Methylmercury* (National Academies Press, 2000), http://www.nap.edu/books/0309071402/html.

126 *killing some 2,400 people:* Conrad Schneider, *Death, Disease & Dirty Power: Mortality and Health Damage Due to Air Pollution from Power Plants* (Boston: Clean Air Task Force, 2000).

126 *increased levels of mortality and cardiopulmonary disease:* Ibid.

127 *their conclusions were accurate:* Ibid.

127 *"harvesting," industry called it:* Ibid.

128 *daily activities restricted in minor ways:* Ibid.

128 *Sudden Infant Death Syndrome:* Clean Air Task Force, "Children at Risk," May 2002, http://www.catf.us/publications/reports/children_at_risk.php.

133 *and of 60 years for others:* U.S. Senate Committee on Environment and Public Works and Committee on the Judiciary, *Hearings on Administration Policy, Regulatory Proposals, and Enforcement Activity Regarding the Clean Air Act's New Source Review Program,* Testimony of John Walke, July 16, 2002.

134 *agency might bring New Source Review to bear:* American Lung Association, Clean Air Task Force, Environmental Defense, Environmental Integrity Project, Mid-Atlantic Environmental Law Center, National Environmental Trust, Natural Resources Defense Council, Southern Environmental Law Center, U.S. Public Interest Research Group, "Comments on the Proposed Rule," EPA Docket Number A-2002–04, May 2, 2003.

134 *you guessed it—routine maintenance:* U.S. Senate Committee on Environment and Public Works and Committee on the Judiciary, *Hearings on Administration Policy, Regulatory Proposals, and Enforcement Activity Regarding the Clean Air Act's New Source Review Program,* Testimony of John Walke, July 16, 2002.

136 *largely rejected by courts:* Jared Snyder, New York Attorney General's Office, telephone conversation, November 2003.

138 *during the 2000–2002 election cycle:* Earthjustice and Public Campaign, *Paybacks,* September 25, 2002, http://www. earthjustice.org/policy/pdf/payback_report_final.pdf.

139 *weaken the pending enforcement cases:* Public Citizen, "EPA's Smoke Screen," October 10, 2003.

140 *gradually being delayed or canceled:* U.S. Senate Committee on Environment and Public Works and Committee on the Judiciary, *Hearings on Administration Policy, Regulatory Proposals, and Enforcement Activity Regarding the Clean Air Act's New Source Review Program,* Testimony of John Walke, July 16, 2002.

141 *Clean Air Act should be enforced in the future:* "Justice Department Affirms Clinton Enforcement of Clean Air Act," *The Boston Globe,* January 16, 2002.

149 *his Clear Skies Initiative:* Environmental Protection Agency, *Clear Skies,* http://www.epa.gov/clearskies.

156 *newspaper published in Tacoma, Washington:* "Papers Show EPA Exaggerated Claims about Washington State Pollution Reductions," *News Tribune,* March 3, 2003.

157 *did not give Carper and the public a key analysis:* Guy Gugliotta and Eric Pianin, "EPA Withholds Air Pollution Analysis: Senate Plan Found More Effective, Slightly More Costly Than Bush Proposal," *The Washington Post,* July 1, 2003.

CHAPTER 5

166　*Wildlife Policy Statement on these matters*: Alaska Chapter of the Wildlife Society, "Position Statement of the Alaska Chapter of the Wildlife Society on the Arctic National Wildlife Refuge," July 3, 2001.

166　*and the area's overall ecology*: The Ecological Society of America, "Position Statement on the Arctic National Wildlife Refuge," March 2002, ESA Resolutions, http://www.esa.org/pao/statements_resolutions/resolutions/anwr.htm.

170　*a report called "Weird Science"*: House Committee on Resources, Prepared by the Democratic Staff, "Weird Science: The Interior Department's Manipulation of Science for Political Purposes," December 17, 2002

170　*Representative Henry Waxman (D-CA)*: House Committee on Government Reform—Minority Staff, Special Investigations Division, "Politics and Science in the Bush Administration," prepared for Rep. Henry A. Waxman, August 2003, http://www.house.gov/reform/min/politicsandscience/pdfs/pdf_politics_and_science_rep.pdf.

176　*"Draft Report on the Environment"*: U.S. Environmental Protection Agency, *EPA's Draft Report on the Environment 2003*, EPA-260-R-02-006 (Washington, D.C.: Office of Environmental Information and the Office of Research and Development, United States Environmental Protection Agency, June 2003).

177　*article that broke the story*: Andrew C. Revkin and Katharine Q. Seelye, "Report by EPA Leaves Out Data on Climate Change," *The New York Times,* June 19, 2003.

184　*whom the panel would be advising*: Richard J. Jackson, Centers for Disease Control and Prevention, telephone conversation with the author, November 2003.

185　*in the form of liability suits*: Jonathan Cohn, "Toxic," *The New Republic*, December 23, 2002.

188 *spruce up their image on environmental issues:* Environmental Working Group, *The Environment: A Cleaner, Safer, Healthier America*, Luntz Research Companies memo on the environment, http://www.ewg.org/briefings/luntzmemo/.

CHAPTER 6

197 *a $25 million donation to HCRA:* All the Philip Morris correspondence can be found on the Web site of Public Citizen, http://www.citizen.org.

200 *usurps the agencies' jobs:* Reece Rushing, OMB Watch, telephone communication, April 2003.

202 University of Chicago Law Review: Richard W. Parker, "Grading the Government," *University of Chicago Law Review* 70 (Fall 2003): 1345.

204 *turns out to have higher productivity benefits:* Eban Goodstein, "Polluted Data," *American Prospect* (November/December 1997).

206 *"A Review of the Record," in 1986:* John F. Morrall, "A Review of the Record," *Regulation* (November/December 1986).

207 Yale Law Review *in 1998:* Lisa Heinzerling, "Regulatory Costs of Mythic Proportions," *Yale Law Journal* 107/7 (May 1998).

211 *article in the* Cornell Law Review: Lisa Heinzerling and Frank Ackerman. "The Humbugs of the Anti-Regulatory Movement," *Cornell Law Review* 87/2 (January 2002).

212 *blockbuster papers in 1996 and 2000:* Robert W. Hahn, "Regulatory Reform: What Do the Government's Numbers Tell Us?" in *Risks, Costs and Lives Saved,* ed. Robert W. Hahn (1996). "Regulatory Reform: Assessing the Government's Numbers," in *Reviving Regulatory Reform: A Global Perspective* (2000).

221 *at the time a graduate student of his:* Tammy O. Tengs and John D. Graham, "The Opportunity Costs of Haphazard Social

Investments in Life-Saving," in *Risks, Costs, and Lives Saved,* ed. Robert W. Hahn (1996).

221   *with contributions from several other researchers:* Tammy O. Tengs, "Five Hundred Life-Saving Interventions and Their Cost-Effectiveness," *Risk Analysis* 369 (1995).

BIBLIOGRAPHY

REPORTS

Community Rights Counsel. *Executive Summary of* Hostile Environment. Web access: http://www.communityrights.org/Combats JudicialActivism/HE/HEexecsumm.asp.

Cortner, Hanna J., Jacqueline Vaughn, and Gretchen M. R. Teich. *Designing a Framework for Evaluating the Impacts and Outcomes of Forest Service Appeals.* Workshop summary of the Ecological Restoration Institute. Flagstaff: Northern Arizona University, 2003.

Defenders of Wildlife, Earthjustice, Endangered Species Coalition, National Wildlife Federation. *Open Season on America's Wildlife: The Bush Administration's Attacks on Federal Wildlife Protections.* Web access: http://www.defenders.org/newsroom/open season.pdf.

Earthjustice. *Policy and Legislation: White House Watch Administration Profiles, Council on Environmental Quality.* Web access: http://www.earthjustice.org/policy/profiles/display.html.

Earthjustice and Public Campaign. *Paybacks*. September 25, 2002. Web access: http://www.earthjustice.org/policy/pdf/payback_report_final.pdf.

Environmental Protection Agency. *Clear Skies*. Web access: http://www.epa.gov/clearskies.

Environmental Working Group. *The Environment: A Cleaner, Safer, Healthier America*. Luntz Research Companies memo on the environment. Web access:http://www.ewg.org/briefings/luntzmemo/.

Heinzerling, Lisa, and Frank Ackerman. *Pricing the Priceless: Cost-Benefit Analysis of Environmental Protection*. Web access: http://www.law.georgetown.edu/gelpi/papers/pricefnl.pdf.

Ingalsbee, Timothy. *Money to Burn: The Economics of Fire and Fuels Management. Part One: Fire Suppression*. June 2000. Web access: http://www.fire-ecology.org/research/money_to_burn.html.

Natural Resources Defense Council. *Rewriting the Rules, Year-End Report 2002*. Web access: http//www.nrdc.org/legislation/rollbacks/rollbacksinx.asp.

Parenteau, Patrick. "Practicing What We Teach: A Critical Review of the Bush Administration's Environmental Record." Paper presented at the Rocky Mountain Mineral Law Institute Twelfth Institute for Natural Resources Law Professors. Grand Junction, Colorado, June 5–8, 2003.

Perks, Robert, and Gregory Wetstone. *Rewriting the Rules, Year-End Report 2003: The Bush Administration's Assault on the Environment*. Web access: http//www.nrdc.org/legislation/rollbacks/rollbacks.pdf.

Schneider, Conrad. *Death, Disease & Dirty Power: Mortality and Health Damage Due to Air Pollution from Power Plants*. Boston: Clean Air Task Force, 2000.

Schneider, Conrad. *Power to Kill: Death and Disease from Power Plants Charged with Violating the Clean Air Act.* Boston: Clean Air Task Force, 2001.

Snape, William, and John M. Carter. *Weakening the National Environmental Policy Act: How the Bush Administration Uses the Judicial System to Weaken Environmental Protections.* Report of the Judicial Accountability Project. Washington, D.C.: Defenders of Wildlife, 2003.

Snape, William, and John M. Carter. *Weakening the National Environmental Policy Act.* Web access: http://www.defenders.org/publications/nepareport.pdf.

White House. *Healthy Forests Initiative.* Web access: http://www.whitehouse.gov/infocus/healthyforests.

BOOKS

Abraham, Rick. *The Dirty Truth: George W. Bush's Oil and Chemical Dependency.* Houston: Mainstream Press, 2000.

Tengs, Tammy O., and John D. Graham. "The Opportunity Costs of Haphazard Social Investments in Life-Saving." In *Risks, Costs, and Lives Saved: Getting Better Results from Regulation,* ed. Robert W. Hahn. 1996.

PUBLIC DOCUMENTS

Covington, William Wallace. "Firefighting Funding and Planning." Statement to the Committee on Senate Energy and Natural Resources. *FDCH Congressional Testimony.* July 16, 2002.

Spitzer, Eliot. "Pollution Control Policy and Enforcement." Statement to the Senate Committee on Environment and Public Works and Committee on the Senate Judiciary. *FDCH Congressional Testimony.* July 16, 2002.

U.S. Environmental Protection Agency. *EPA's Draft Report on the Environment 2003.* Report EPA-260-R-02-006. Washington, D.C.: Office of Environmental Information and the Office of Research and Development, United States Environmental Protection Agency, June 2003.

U.S. Forest Service. *Factors Affecting Timely Mechanical Fuel Treatments Decisions.* Washington, D.C.: July 2002.

U.S. General Accounting Office. *Appeals and Litigation of Fuels Reduction Projects.* Report GAO-01-1114R. Washington, D.C.: August 31, 2001.

U.S. General Accounting Office. *Forest Service: Information on Decisions Involving Fuels Reduction Activities.* Report GAO-03-689R. Washington, D.C.: May 14, 2003.

U.S. House of Representatives Committee on Government Reform—Minority Staff, Special Investigations Division. *Politics and Science in the Bush Administration.* Prepared for Rep. Henry A. Waxman, August 2003. Web access: http://www.house.gov/reform/min/politicsandscience/pdfs/pdf_politics_and_science_rep.pdf.

U.S. Senate Committee on the Environment and Public Works and Committee on the Judiciary. *Hearing on Administration Policy, Regulatory Proposals, and Enforcement Activity Regarding the Clean Air Act's New Source Review Program.* Testimony of John D. Walke, July 16, 2002.

The White House (President George W. Bush). "The Bush Administration's Record of Environmental Progress." October 2002. Web access: http://www.whitehouse.gov.

The White House (President George W. Bush). "The Squires Fire: A Case Study in Fire and Forest Management Obstacles and Effects." Web access: http://www.whitehouse.gov/infocus/healthyforests/ sect6.html.

WEB SITES

Democratic Policy Committee. *Environmental Monitor.* www. democrats.senate.gov/~dpc/pubs/108-1-135.html.

Earthjustice. *The Bush Administration Rollbacks Review.* http://www. earthjustice.org/campaign/display.html?ID=8.

Environmental Protection Agency. http://www.epa.gov.

Natural Resources Defense Council. *The Bush Record.* http://www. nrdc.org/bushrecord.

Office of Management and Budget. http://www.whitehouse.gov/omb.

REP America (Republicans for Environmental Protection). http:// www.rep.org.

Sierra Club. *W Watch.* http://www.sierraclub.org/wwatch.

U.S. Department of the Interior. http://www.doi.gov.

U.S. Forest Service. http://www.fs.fed.us.

White House. *Environmental Speeches and Releases Archive.* http:// www.whitehouse.gov/infocus/environment/archive.html.

ACKNOWLEDGMENTS

This book tackles a sprawling subject that surely would have overwhelmed me if not for the patient help and expertise of a great many people—too many to name them all here. But I want them all to know that I deeply appreciate their taking the time to guide me through the complexities of national environmental policy.

Such policies usually involve the law. Among the many legal experts who provided their knowledge and insight were a number of people with the environmental law firm Earthjustice, including Jim Angell, Marty Hayden, John McManus, and Joan Mulhern. Other attorneys who gave me legal aid were Lisa Heinzerling of Georgetown University Law Center, Pat Parenteau of Vermont Law School, Frank Ackerman of Tufts University, Tom McGarity of the University of Texas, Paul Turcke of Boise Cascade, Steve Strack of the state of Idaho, Doug Kendall of the Community Rights Counsel, and Jared Snyder of the New York Attorney General's office.

I got my taxpayer's dollars' worth from many government employees. Among them were resource agency staffers who asked to remain anonymous because, sadly, they feared reprisals for their criticisms of Administration actions. Other helpful civil servants included Tom Atzet at the U.S. Forest Service, Bruce Buckheit and Hugh Kaufman of the Environmental Protection Agency, John F. Morrall III at the Office of Management and Budget, and Richard Jackson of the Centers for Disease Control and Prevention.

I'm especially grateful to the three high-level Administration officials who agreed to answer my questions. I say "especially" not because they're high-level but because such interaction with Bush's appointees turned out to be rare, as I point out in the Author's Note. This trio consists of James Connaughton, who heads the Council on Environmental Quality; Mark Rey, the Department of Agriculture Undersecretary who oversees the U.S. Forest Service; and John Graham, Administrator of the Office of Information and Regulatory Affairs in the Office of Management and Budget.

Many environmental and public interest groups are teeming with information about Bush's policies, which they freely shared with me. Numerous people from these organizations also spent time with me answering some of my many questions. Among those public watchdogs are Rob Perks and John Walke of the Natural Resources Defense Council, Kevin Knobloch and Jason Mark of the Union of Concerned Scientists, Alan Krupnick of Resources for the Future, Greg Aplet of the Wilderness Society, Tatjana Vujic and Eric Schaeffer of Environmental Integrity Project, Reece Rushing of OMB Watch, Eric Wingerter and Jeff Ruch of Public Employees for Environmental Responsibility, Amy Delach of Defenders of Wildlife, Joseph Vaile and Liz Crosson of the Klamath-Siskiyou Wildlands Center, Cynthia Sykes of Friends of the Earth, and Laura McCleery of Public Citizen.

I'm also indebted to the individuals who told me their personal stories, allowing me to understand and convey to readers the human face and on-the-ground ecological consequences of environmental policies. These folks included Al Burchianti, David Calahan, Bob Danko, Marsha Danko, Ruth Enci, Christine Gardner, Mary Lewis, Lisa Marcucci, Charlotte O'Rourke, Helene Orr, Deb Sanchez, Cathy Sandy, and Farley Toothman. Other individuals with years of experience and knowledge in environmental matters who plied me with their expertise were Martha Hahn and Norm Christensen.

As always, I owe a special thanks to my agent, Robin Straus. She knew exactly the right person to approach with my idea for a book. Without Robin, all I would have ended up with is an idea for a book. I'm also grateful to the person she approached, Marty Asher, the publisher at Anchor, for his passion for the health of our environment, which led him to support this book. I can't begin to list all the reasons I have to thank my editor, Andrew Miller. He guided the course of the book with a light but sure touch, at times saving me from myself and often smoothing out the rough edges. As I write these words I'm particularly appreciative of Andrew's patience, given that I'm several weeks past deadline and he has yet to curse me—at least, when I'm within earshot. Likewise, Marla Jea has shown extraordinary forbearance as I've inflicted one production headache after another on her; thank you, Marla. My thanks to all the other Anchor staff, too, for helping make this book, and to Roberta Sobotka, my friend who stepped up during the book's final moments to help me get the last odds and ends out the door.

Speaking of indispensable, thank you Hal Harvey and all the rest of you at the New-Land Foundation for the financial support. My thanks to Mary Stake Hawker at the Deer Creek Foundation, as well, for helping me locate another much-needed grant. Burt Glass and the Center for Investigative Reporting also have my gratitude for serving as my fiscal sponsor.

Finally, my thanks to my daughter, Sarah, for bearing with me during the sometimes intense writing of this book, and the biggest thank you of all to my wife, Mary, who had to hold our home and family together while I disappeared into these pages.

Abt Associates, 127, 129
acid rain:
  ecological harm by, 125
acid rain program, 34–37, 111
  Black Forest and, 37
  Moore, Curtis, and, 37
  University of Karlsruhe study of,
    37
Ackerman, Frank, 211–12
  monetizing, 214
  reallocation of resources, 223
AEI-Brookings Joint Center for Reg-
    ulatory Studies, 212
Agriculture, Department of, 23
air pollution:
  Bush, G. W., while Texas governor,
    and 33–34
  carbon dioxide, 125
  enforcement of laws, 159
  Environmental Protection Agency,
    annual report on, 176
  fly ash, 118

Hatfield's Ferry power plant and,
    110–12
  emissions, 112
health effects, 119–129
  asthma, 119, 122–23
  deaths from, 159
  death rates map, 128–29
history, 126
Interstate Air Quality Rule and,
    158–59
mercury, 125
particulate matter, 123
  and asthma, 128
  children, effects on, 128
  health effects, 124–28
  heart attacks and, 127
  major studies, 126–28
policy, 123–24
voluntary programs and, 33–34
See also New Source Review
Alexander, Anthony, 153
Algodones sand dunes, 179

Allegheny Energy, 111–12, 118, 138
Alliance for Constructive Air Policy, 138
American Electric Power, 134, 139
American Enterprise Institute, 226
American Forest & Pulp Association, 72
American Petroleum Institute, 197
American Prospect, 107, 204
  deregulation as politics, 234
appeals:
  and logging, 71
  and thinning, 75–79
Angell, Jim, 98
Annapolis principles, 218
Apollo Project, 238
Arch Coal, 151–52
Arctic National Wildlife Refuge, 3
  caribou, 160–67
  Fish and Wildlife Service, U.S., 162
  Norton, Gale, and, 26, 160–67
  Wildlife Society Bulletin article, 165
  Wildlife Society policy statement, 166
Army Corps of Engineers, 70
Arno, Steve, 48
Arnold, Ron, 26
Ashcroft, John, 199
Ashland Watershed Protection Project, 80–83
Aspen Fire, 60
AT&T Wireless Communication, 198
Atzet, Tom, 45–47
  categorical exclusions, 75
automobiles, fuel economy standards, 237
  sport utility vehicles and, 237

Babbitt, Bruce, 96
Baltimore, David, 169
Banner, William, 187
Barbour, Haley, 28, 151
Berg, H. Peter, 153
Biscuit Fire, 45–48
  Bush, G. W., speech on, 47

Black Forest:
  acid rain and, 37
Boise Cascade:
  Roadless Rule appeal and, 84–88
Bolten, Joshua, 193
Boston Globe, 141
Bradley, Michael J., 150
Breyer, Steven, 205
Brownell, Bill, 138
Buckheit, Bruce, 147
Bureau of Land Management, 23
  Algodones sand dunes and, 179
  wilderness and, 16, 94–99, 100–1
  Squires Fire and, 50, 52, 53
"Bush Administration's Record of Environmental Progress," 12, 14–16
Bush, G. H. W., 109, 173
Business and Legal Reports, 143

Cahill, Thomas, 181
Calahan, David, 50–54
California red-legged frog, 89–90
Callahan, Deb, 9
campaign contributions, 21–23
  Bush-Cheney 2000 campaign and, 22, 50
  Republican National Committee and, 22
  timber industry and, 22, 50
  utility industry and, 22, 138
carbon dioxide, 125, 150–51
caribou in Arctic National Wildlife Refuge, 160–67
  calving, 163–64
  Fish and Wildlife Service, U.S., report, 162–65
  Porcupine caribou herd, 162–64, 166
  Wildlife Society Bulletin article, 165
Carmichaels, 119
Carper bill, 152, 155, 157
Carper, Thomas R., 152, 157
Cato Institute, 140
Center for International Environmental Law, 16

Center for Responsive Politics, 21, 153

Centers for Disease Control and Prevention, 183–84

Central Arctic caribou, 164

Chafee, Lincoln, 152

Chamber of Commerce, U.S., 9, 192

Cheney, Dick:
  Barbour, Haley, lobbying of, 151
  energy task force and, 23, 137–38, 139, 169
  Halliburton and, 180

Children's Health Protection Advisory Committee, 158–59

chloroform exposure, 190

Christensen, Norman, 54–55

Chugach National Forest, 15

civil service employees:
  tension with political appointees, 24

Clean Air Act, 14, 35, 130, 201
  Clear Skies Initiative and, 151–52, 155
  cost-benefit analysis and, 208, 225
  New Source Review and, 130–49, 155

Clean Air Planning Act, 152, 157

Clean Energy Group, 150

Clean Power Act, 152

Clean Water Act, 105, 109, 201
  wetlands and, 15
  enforcement of, 113

Clear Skies Initiative, 38, 149–53
  exaggerating benefits of, 156–57
  mercury reductions cost, 157–58
  states, restricted by, 151
  withholding data about Carper bill, 157

Clinton, Bill, 10
  Clinton administration, 134, 173

Club for Growth, 193

coal-bed methane:
  Griles, J. Steven and, 30

coal mining, 15, 30, 93, 108

Collins, Sally, 72

Commerce Clause:
  environmental regulation and, 108, 109

Committee of Scientists, 173–74

Committee on Childhood Lead Poisoning Prevention, 184–88

Community Protection Zone. *See* Wildland-Urban Interface

Connaughton, James, 24, 182

Contract with America, 5, 226–27

Cornell Law Review, 211

cost-benefit analysis, 201–30
  Congress, power usurped by, 226–29
  costs, measuring of, 202–5
  discounting, 209–11
  monetizing, 213–21
    false precision, 214, 226
    human lives, 219–21
    wage premiums, 219
    willingness to accept, 216–18
    willingness to pay, 214–18
  technology-based regulation, 226
  technology-forcing and, 204–5
  See also Graham, John D.; Hahn, Robert; Heinzerling, Lisa; Morrall III, John F.; Parker, Richard; Waxman, Henry

Council on Environmental Quality, 24, 69, 73
  New Source Review, proposed rules and, 146
  September 11, press release rewrite by, 181–82

Covington, Wallace, 59, 60

Crosson, Liz, 81, 82

Daily Environment Report, 142

Daily, Gretchen C., 103–4

Daniels, Jr., Mitchell E., 193

Danko, Bob, 110–11, 112, 159

Danko, Marsha, 111, 112, 118

DeFazio, Peter, 57

Defense, Department of:
  exempting from environmental rules, 17

DeLay, Tom, 109

Desolation Canyon, 98

District of Columbia District Court, 107–8

Dombeck, Mike, 88–89
Donora,
    pollution deaths, 126
Douglas Timber Operators, 92
"Draft Report on the
    Environment," 176–79
Duffy, Linda, 82
Dunlop, Becky, 184
Durbin, Richard, 195

Earthjustice, 99, 101
    campaign contributions and, 22
    Roadless Rule appeal and, 85
Ecological Society of America:
    Arctic National Wildlife Refuge
        position paper, 166
Edison Electric Institute:
    Griles, J. Steven, and, 29
elections, 233
Ellison, Katherine, 104
Enci, Ruth, 120, 122, 123
Endangered Species Act:
    adding species to list, 16–17
    Algodones sand dunes and, 179
    California red-legged frog and,
        90
    critical habitat designation, 116
    economic costs of, 90
    enforcement of, 115–16
    Everglades, 172
    Norton, Gale, and, 27, 115
    species viability provisions,
        172–74
    streamlining and, 66
    underfunding of, 116
Energy, Department of, 23, 140
    energy efficiency and, 17
    hydraulic fracturing, 179–80
    mercury reductions cost, 157
    New Source Review, proposed
        rules, 146
    transition team, 138
energy task force, 23, 137–38, 139,
    169, 232
Environmental Defense:
    Texas voluntary air pollution
        program, study by, 33–34

environmental enforcement:
    budget cuts, 114
    decreasing fines for polluters, 114
    padding administration's enforce-
        ment record, 114–15
    states and, 113
Environmental Forum, 228
Environment Integrity Project, 36,
    114
Environmental Protection Agency, 23
    air pollution, annual report by,
        176
    Clean Water Act enforcement
        study, 113
    "Draft Report on the Environ-
        ment," 176–79
    exaggerating Clear Skies Initia-
        tive benefits, 156–57
    exaggerating enforcement record,
        114–15
    global warming reports, 175–78
    New Source Review enforcement,
        134–46
    New Source Review, proposed
        rules, 146
    September 11 and, 180–82
    soot and smog standards, 190
    Waxman report and, 171
    withholding data about Carper
        bill, 157
Esty, Dan, 8
Everglades, 171–72

farmland conservation programs, 16
Federal Advisory Committee Act,
    183
Federal Land Policy and Manage-
    ment Act, 95
FirstEnergy Corporation, 153
Fish and Wildlife Service, U.S.:
    Arctic National Wildlife Refuge
        and, 162–65
    California red-legged frog and,
        89–91
    elk vaccinations and, 93–94
    quashed wetlands report, 179
    wetlands rules, comments on, 70

Fisher, Mike, 115
Fitzsimmons, Allan, 19
Fleischer, Ari, 176
Ford, Gerald, 10
forest fire policy:
  appeals, 40, 41
    limiting of logging, 79
  fire suppression, 43, 45
  Healthy Forests Initiative, 39–41,
    50, 55–56, 61, 65, 73
    lawsuits and, 79
    Roadless Rule and, 86–87
  Healthy Forests Restoration Act,
    55–56, 58–59
  history, 42–43, 48
  lawsuits, 40, 41
  McInnis/Walden bill and, 73
  National Environmental Policy
    Act and, 73–76
  Norton, Gale, and, 56
  Squires Fire and, 39–41,
    50–54
  streamlining and, 40
  streamlining synergy and, 70
  thinning, 40, 41, 49–65
    acres in need of, 61–64
    appeals and, 75–79
    Ashland Watershed Protection
      Project and, 80–83
    Bush, G. W., speech on, 49
    Calahan, David, on, 50–54
    categorical exclusions and,
      74–75
    Christensen, Norman, on,
      54–55, 64–65
    cost, 58–60, 64–65
    Forest Service study and, 77
    Government Accounting Office
      studies and, 76–78
    lawsuits and, 79
    nonfederal lands and, 56–57
    Northern Arizona University
      study of, 77
    scientists' letter on, 54, 63
    Squires Fire and, 50–54
    timber industry and, 55
    Wildland-Urban Interface and,
      56–61

forest fires:
  Aspen Fire, 60
  Biscuit Fire, 45–48
  development and, 42, 43–45
  factors determining severity, 51
  forest ecology and, 42, 46–47
  Forest Service, U.S., study on
    forest conditions, 63–64
  large, high-intensity, 45–48
  livestock grazing effect on, 44
  logging effect on, 44
  road-building effect on, 44
  Southern California, 2003 fires,
    49
  Squires Fire, 50–54
  Yellowstone National Park, 1988
    fires, 48
forest policy:
  letter from Democratic Represen-
    tatives, 72
  letter from Republican Represen-
    tatives, 72
  species surveys, 92
Forest Service, U.S., 23
  fire policy history, 42–43
  Roadless Rule and, 87–88
  study on forest conditions, 63–64
Foulk, Pat, 91
Fourth Circuit Court of Appeals,
  108–9
FreedomCAR, 13
Freedom of Information Act, 99
Friends of the Earth:
  Griles, J. Stevens and, 30
fuel-efficiency standards, 171

Gingrich, Newt, 5
global warming, 3
  Clear Skies Initiative and, 150–51
  emissions intensity, 175
  Environmental Protection Agency
    reports on, 175–78
  hydrogen energy and, 14
  science of G. W. Bush administra-
    tion and, 174–78
  Watson, Robert, and, 17
Goodstein, Eban, 203–4

Graham, John D., 193–201, 208
benzene research, corporate
funding, 197
cellular phone research, corporate
funding, 197–98
dioxin research, corporate funding, 197
human lives, 221
expanding role of cost-benefit
analysis, 218
"Five Hundred Life-Saving
Interventions and Their
Cost-Effectiveness," 221–22
nomination hearings, 193–99
"The Opportunity Costs of
Haphazard Social Invest-
ments in Life-Saving,"
221–25
secondhand smoke research,
corporate funding, 197
statistical murder, 221–25
Gramm, Phil, 199, 201
Gramm, Wendy, 201
Grand Teton National Park, 92, 99
Grasser, John, 28
Greenberg, David, 196
Greene County, 119
Gregg, Judd, 152
Griles, J. Steven, 27–30
Inspector General's investigation
of, 28–29
recusals and, 29
grizzly bears:
reintroduction, 17
Groat, Charles, 172
Guardia, Enrique, 196

Hahn, Robert:
cost-benefit analysis, 208, 212–13,
218, 225
Halliburton:
hydraulic fracturing and, 180
hard-rock mining:
weakening rules for, 17
Harvard Center for Risk Analysis,
187, 195–97
funders, 195–97

Philip Morris (Altria) funding of,
196–97
*Harvard Environmental Law
Review,* 219
Harvard School of Public Health,
196
Hatfield's Ferry power plant,
110–12, 118–20, 122
Hayden, Marty, 57, 73–74, 76
Haynes II, William, 107
Health Effects Institute, 126–27
Healthy Forests Initiative. *See under*
forest fire policy
Healthy Forests Restoration Act.
See under forest fire policy
Heinzerling, Lisa:
discounting, 210–11, 219
Graham, John D., nomination,
194
Morrall III, John F., critiqued by,
207–12
Heritage Foundation, 224
Hoffman, Paul, 180
Holmstead, Jeffrey, 138–39, 157
Home Builders Association of
Northern California, 90
Horn, William, 92–93
Hudson River, 3, 12
hydrogen energy, 13–14
hydrogen-powered vehicles, G. W.
Bush program, 13–14
hydraulic fracturing, 179–80

Inhofe, James, 109, 158
international environmental issues:
Bush, G. W., and, 16
Interior, Department of the, 23,
160–61
undermining of Endangered
Species Act by, 116
Yellowstone and, 180
Interstate Air Quality Rule, 158–59

Jackson, Richard J., 184
Jeffords, James, 152
Jeffords/Lieberman bill, 152, 155

Josten, Bruce, 192
J. Steven Griles & Associates, 28
judicial appointments, 105–9
  District of Columbia Circuit
    Court, 107–8
  Fourth Circuit Court of Appeals,
    108–9
  Haynes II, William, 107
  Myers III, William G., 106–7
  Reagan, Ronald, appointments,
    107
Judis, John B., 234
Justice, Department of:
  New Source Review enforcement,
    134–37, 141–46, 153
  Roadless Rule appeal and,
    85–86, 89

Kalmiopsis Wilderness, 47
Karpinski, Gene, 194
Klamath-Siskiyou Wildlands Center,
  81
Klitzman, Susan, 186
Knobloch, Kevin, 168–69, 183
Kovacs, Bill, 9
Kraft General Foods, 196
Krenik, Edward D., 157
Kriz, Margaret, 67
Kroszner, Randall, 158
Krupnick, Alan:
  willingness to pay, 214–16
Kyoto Protocol, 3, 175, 204

Lanphear, Bruce, 186
lead poisoning, 184–88
  liability suits, 185
  standards, 185, 187
League of Conservation Voters, 9,
  233
Leavitt, Mike, 146, 158
Leopold, Aldo, 31
Lewis, Mary, 120, 122
LGL Research Associates, 167
Lieberman, Joseph, 152
livestock feeding:
  pollution from, 17

lobbying:
  Connaughton, James, and,
    24–25
  Griles, J. Steven, and, 28–30
  Rey, Mark, and, 25
logging:
  Rey, Mark, and, 25–26
Lomborg, Bjorn, 236
London:
  pollution deaths, 126
Los Angeles Times:
  Roadless Rule poll, 86
Luntz, Frank, 188
Luntz memo, 6, 20, 188–89
Luntz Research Companies, 6, 188,
  234

MacCleery, Laura, 224
manatee, 116
Marcucci, Lisa, 118, 119, 123–24
market-based regulation.
    See pollution trading
Marks, Martha, 7–8, 11
Masontown, 110–11, 112
McCain, John, 8
McClellan, Roger, 184
McClellan, Scott:
  Waxman report and, 170–71
McGarity, Thomas:
  willingness to accept, 216–18
media coverage:
  avoiding, 5
  environment and, 167–68
  forest fires and, 48–49
  shallow, 4
Mercatus Center, 200–1
Miller, George, 57
Molloy, Donald, 76, 78–79
Mooney, Chris, 107–8
Moore, Curtis, 37
Moore, Stephen, 193
Morrall III, John F.:
  formaldehyde regulation and,
    211–12
  "A Review of the Record,"
    206–12
  ripple effect of, 207

Mountain States Legal Foundation, 26
mountaintop removal mining:
  Circuit Court decision, 93
  and flooding, 179
  Griles, J. Steven, and, 30
  judicial nominations and, 108–9
Murkowski, Frank:
  oil drilling in Arctic National Wildlife Refuge, 160–64
Myers III, William G., 106–7

National Academy of Public Administration, 148–49
National Academy of Sciences:
  fuel-efficiency standards, 171
National Center for Environmental Health, 183
National Coal Council, 137, 139
National Elk Refuge:
  court cases, 94
  elk vaccinations, 93–94
National Environmental Policy Act, 68–70
  appeals, administrative, 75–79
  Ashland Watershed Protection Project and, 80–83
  categorical exclusions, 74–75
  industry's views on, 73
  judicial appointments and, 105
  ocean activity and, 69
  oil and gas exploration and, 69
  thinning and, 74–75
  transportation projects and, 69
National Environmental Strategies:
  Griles, J. Steven, and, 28–29, 30
National Forest Management Act:
  species viability provisions, 172–74
National Hydrogen Energy Roadmap Workshop, 14
National Journal, 67
National Mining Association, 28, 29
National Parks:
  snowmobiles in, 92–93, 100
  underfunding of, 12–13

National Parks Conservation Association:
  report card on G. W. Bush, 13
National Park Service:
  Stillwater Bridge and, 67
National Research Council:
  global warming study, 177
National Review, 193
National Wildlife Refuges, 94
natural resource agencies, 23–24
  appointments to, 23–30
Natural Resources Defense Council, 135, 137, 146, 176, 232
  John D. Graham article by, 193
New England Journal of Medicine, 187
New Environmentalism, 30–34, 235
New Republic:
  lead liability suits, 185
New Source Review, 14–15, 130–49
  Clear Skies Initiative and, 149
  Department of Justice enforcement of, 134–37, 141–46, 153
  economic value of old facilities, 131–32
  energy task force and, 137–8, 139, 140–42
  Environmental Protection Agency enforcement of, 134–46
  grandfathering of old, polluting facilities, 130–31
  history, 130–35
  Holmstead, Jeffrey, and, 138–39
  industry lobbying and, 137–38
  life extension strategy, 133–34
  National Academy of Public Administration report, 148–49
  perpetual immunity and, 136, 148
  power capacity and, 140
  proposed new rules, 146–49
  routine maintenance, 132–36, 145, 147–48, 154–55
  Sammis Plant decision, 153–55
  Whitman, Christie, 139
Newsweek, 182
News Tribune, 156

New York Times:
  carbon dioxide emissions, 151
  "Draft Report on the Environ-
      ment," 177–78
  Skeptical Environmentalist, 236
  Waxman report, 170–71
Ninth U.S. Circuit Court of
    Appeals:
  Roadless Rule, 84–85, 89
Nixon, Richard, 10
Non-road diesel rule, 11
Norton, Gale, 15, 26–27
  Endangered Species Act, under-
      mining by, 116
  Fish and Wildlife report, quashed
      by, 179
  forest fire policy, 56, 61
  manatees and, 116
  New Environmentalism and,
      30–34
  oil drilling in Arctic National
      Wildlife Refuge, 160–67
  science and, 168
  snowmobiles in Yellowstone and,
      92
  wetlands rules and, 70

Occupational Safety and Health
    Administration:
  formaldehyde regulation, 190, 206
  vinyl and polyvinyl chloride
      regulations, 203–4
Office of Information and Regula-
    tory Affairs, 193–95, 233
  agencies and, 199–200
  expanding power of, 200
  regulatory hit list, 200–1
Office of Management and Budget,
    191–93, 194, 228
  lobbyists and, 192–93
  New Source Review, proposed
      rules, 146
off-road vehicles, 179
offshore oil drilling, 17
  Griles, J. Steven and, 28
Ohio Edison Company, 153, 154,
    155

OMB Watch, 194, 227
Orion, 103
O'Rourke, Charlotte, 120, 121, 122,
    123–24, 128
Ose, Doug, 228
Outdoor Industry Association, 103

PA Consulting, 140
Pages, Robert, 196
Parenteau, Patrick, 85, 105
Parfit, Derek, 210–11
Parker, Richard, 202, 229
  Hahn, Robert, critiqued by,
      212–13
  monetizing, 218
  Morrall III, John F., critiqued by,
      208–10
  "The Opportunity Costs of
      Haphazard Social Invest-
      ments in Life-Saving," 223
particulate matter. *See under* air
    pollution
peer review, 169
  and Arctic National Wildlife
      Refuge caribou, 165
Piomelli, Sergio, 187
Pfeifle, Mark, 163
Philip Morris (Altria):
  funding Harvard Center for Risk
      Analysis, 196–97
pollution trading, 34–38
  acid rain program, 34–37
  Clear Skies Initiative and, 38
  open-market trading, 35–36
  Schaeffer, Eric, and, 36–38
Porcupine caribou herd, 162–64, 166
Prudhoe Bay, 164
Public Citizen, 138–39, 224
Public Employees for Environmental
    Responsibility, 162
public opinion:
  shaping of, 4–7
Public Research Interest Group,
    U.S., 112, 113, 194

Quarles, Steven P., 72

Rahall, Nick, 170
Raven, Peter:
　Skeptical Environmentalist,
　　critiqued by, 236
Reagan, Ronald, 4, 107, 109, 173,
　190
　and New Source Review enforce-
　　ment, 132
Red Zone. *See* Wildland-Urban
　Interface
Reilly, Ed, 52
Reilly, William, 198
REP America (Republicans for
　Environmental Protection), 7
Republican National Committee,
　22, 50
Republicans:
　historic environmental policies,
　　10
　moderate U.S. Senators, 231–32
　opposed to G. W. Bush policies, 8
Resources for the Future, 214
Revkin, Andrew, 177–78
Rey, Mark, 25–26, 50, 60, 61, 62, 63
　categorical exclusions and, 74–75
Roadless Rule, 15
　active management and, 87
　Dombeck, Mike, comments on,
　　88–89
　Forest Service, U.S., and, 88–89
　Ninth Circuit appeal, 84–89
　public comment, 87–88
Rogue River National Forest, 80
Roosevelt, Teddy, 6–7, 31
Rove, Karl, 6
Rushing, Reece:
　cost-benefit analysis, 227

Sacramento Bee, 114–15
St. Louis Post-Dispatch, 151
Sammis Plant, 153
San Jose Mercury News, 91
Sansonetti, Thomas, 142, 143–44
Sargus Jr., Edmund:
　Sammis Plant decision, 153–55
Schaeffer, Eric, 36–38, 114, 135,
　142, 144–45

Schumer, Charles, 91, 107–8
Science, 182
science and G. W. Bush administra-
　tion, 168–89
　Everglades and, 171–72
　fuel-efficiency standards and, 171
　global warming and, 174–78
　National Forest Management Act
　　and, 172–74
　scientists' campaign, 169–70
　September 11 and, 180–82
　Waxman report, 170–71
　"Weird Science" report, 170
　Yellowstone and, 180
scientific advisory committees,
　183–88
　Committee on Childhood Lead
　　Poisoning Prevention,
　　184–88
Scientific American:
　Skeptical Environmentalist,
　　critiqued by, 236
September 11:
　environmental hazards, 181–82
Sierra Nevada Ecosystem Project,
　44
Siskiyou National Forest, 45, 75
Skeptical Environmentalist, 236
Snowe, Olympia, 237
Southern Company, 134
Southern Indiana Gas and Electric,
　143
Spengler, John, 127
Spitzer, Eliot, 142–43
Squires Fire, 50–54
　Bush, G. W., speech at, 39–41
Stockholm Convention on Persis-
　tent Organic Pollutants, 16
streamlining, 40–41
　appeals and lawsuits, 66, 75–79
　different perspectives of, 66–68
　judicial appointments and,
　　105–9
　National Environmental Policy
　　Act and, 68–70, 80–83
　project delays and, 80
　Stillwater Bridge and, 67–68
Studt, John, 70

Suarez, J. P.:
  and environmental enforcement,
    113, 114
sue and settle, 89
  advantages for administration,
    99–100
  excluding the public and, 99
  handcuffing agencies, 100
  species surveys, 92
  Schumer, Charles, report on, 91
Sunstein, Cass, 198–99
Superfund:
  shifting cost of, 17
Supreme Court, U.S., 107, 108, 115
  American Trucking Association v.
    Whitman, 204–5

Tengs, Tammy:
  "Five Hundred Life-Saving Inter-
    ventions and Their Cost-
    Effectiveness," 221–22
  "The Opportunity Costs of Hap-
    hazard Social Investments in
    Life-Saving," 221–25
  statistical murder, 221–23
Tennessee Valley Authority, 147
Texas:
  voluntary air pollution program,
    33–34
timber industry:
  campaign contributions and, 22
Tinsley, Nikki, 181
Thompson, Kimberly, 187
Thompson, Tommy, 186, 188
Tongass National Forest, 15
Toothman, Farley, 118–19, 122
Train, Russell, 8, 178–79
Transportation, Department of, 67

Union of Concerned Scientists,
    168–70, 171, 183
  scientists' campaign, 169–70
United Nations:
  Yellowstone and, 180
University of California, Davis:
  September 11 study by, 181, 182

University of Chicago Law Review,
    202–3
Utah Wilderness Coalition, 96
utility companies:
  campaign contributions and, 22

Vaile, Joseph, 81, 83
values, environmental, 18
Varmus, Harold, 169
Veneman, Ann, 88
Viet, Dinh, 141
vision thing, 235
Voinovich, George, 158
voluntary programs, 33–34

Walke, John, 135, 137–38
Wallsten, Scott, 225
Washington Department of Ecology:
  Clear Skies Initiative and,
Washington Post:
  carbon dioxide emissions, 150
  Clean Water Act enforcement, 113
  Clear Skies mercury standards,
    158
  Everglades, 172
  Griles, J. Steven, 29
  lobbyists and, 193
  Office of Management and
    Budget, 193
  proposed logging rules, 72
  U.S. Fish and Wildlife report, 179
Watson, Rebecca, 61
Watson, Robert, 17
Watt, James, 4, 26
Waxman, Henry, 170–71
  cost-benefit analysis, 228
"Weird Science" report, 170
Wellstone, Paul, 198
wetlands, 15, 179
  mountaintop removal mining
    and, 15
  California red-legged frog and, 90
Wetzman, Michael, 186
Wharton School of Business, 204
White House National Energy
    Policy, 179–80

Whitman, Christie:
    discounting, retreat from, 221
    global warming reports and,
        176
    September 11, press release
        rewrite, 182
wilderness:
    Bureau of Land Management
        and, 94–99
    Bush, G. W., record on, 15
    development of, 101
    geography of, 101–2
    industry and, 94–95
    inventories of, 96, 97, 98
    New York City drinking water
        and, 104
    Outdoor Industry Association
        and, 103
    right-of-way claims and, 15
    sue and settle and, 94–99
    Utah case, 96–99, 100–1
    value of, 102–4
    Wilderness Study Areas, 96, 97

Wilderness Act, 95
Wilderness Society, 99, 101–2
    Wildland-Urban Interface map,
        56–57
    Wildland-Urban Interface, 44–45,
        56–61, 80
    cost of protecting, 58–60
Wildlife Society Bulletin, 165, 166
Wildlife Society, 165–66
    Arctic National Wildlife Refuge
        policy statement, 166
Wilson, E.O., 19, 169
Wiser, Glenn, 16
Wise Use movement:
    ties to Rey, Mark, 26
World Heritage Committee, 180

Yale Law Review, 207, 210
Yellowstone National Park:
    forest fire, recovery from, 48
    snowmobiles in, 92–93, 100, 106
    United Nations and, 180